FAMILIES LEARNING TOGETHER

BOOK 3: JESUS, HEALER AND HELPER

Karyn Henley

Cover design by Brian Lovell
Inside illustrations by Rusty Fletcher
Design and typography by Liz Howe
Project editor, Ruth Frederick

The Standard Publishing Company, Cincinnati, Ohio
A division of Standex International Corporation

05 04 03 02 01 00 99 98   5 4 3 2 1

ISBN 0-784-70923-8

Contents

Introduction 5

■ ■ ■

Sharing 17

Trusting Jesus 20

Words From the Heart 23

Jesus' Authority 26

Friends 29

Showing and Sharing Faith 32

When We All Pray for the Same Thing 35

Forgiving 38

Marriage 41

Intercessory Prayer 44

The Law and the Heart 47

God Answers Prayer 50

Serving 53

Seeking and Following Jesus 56

Each Person Is Important 59

Introduction

Home groups. Cell groups. Care groups. Family groups. Community groups. These are some of the names for small gatherings of church members meeting together weekly in homes. Many church leaders have found these meetings to be an effective way to provide caring relationships for church members as well as being an effective format for evangelism. Membership in these groups can be quite diverse. One group may include couples, singles, older adults, and families with a variety of ages of children. And often, the question that is foremost in their minds is, "What do we do with the children?"

HOW DO I USE THIS GUIDE?

THE DECISION IS YOURS!
If you want step-by-step structure, you can follow each lesson as written. But remember:

> The structure was created to serve you.
> You were not created to serve the structure.
> That's where your decisions come in.

WHAT DECISIONS?
Decide which Building Blocks to use.

WHY?
Some of them may not fit your group's needs.
You may want to do things in a different order.
You may want to leave out a block or two.
You may want to add a block of your own.

Measure the building blocks by your group's needs.

So, choose the blocks you need, in the order you need.

    * This block requires kids and adults together.
   ** This block requires kids to separate from the adults.
       However, do provide two adults to facilitate.
    + Options:
        1. Do with kids and adults OR
        2. Do with kids only.

Add or delete as needed.

WHAT SHOULD I KNOW ABOUT THIS GUIDEBOOK?

GOAL: to help children and adults develop and exercise faith in God the Father, the Son, and the Holy Spirit.

ADAPTABILITY: This guide is yours, so be flexible.
- Feel free *not* to follow the order of the lessons. Skip around, if you like.
- You may want to stay close to a subject your pastor has emphasized in a large assembly. For example, if your pastor has given a lesson on prayer, you may want to use one of the lessons on prayer, even though you are going out of sequence.

CHOICES: Don't try to do every activity. You'll only have time for one, maybe two. See page 8 for other decisions you may want to consider.

AGE SPAN: It is for multiage groups of kids in an intergenerational setting. There are activities for all ages of children. Older children are encouraged to help the younger children when necessary, in family-style cooperation.

MATERIALS: All items listed are commonly found in most households or are readily available at the nearest grocery or discount store.

IMPORTANT: Again, this is a collection of suggestions. As with any teaching guide, you may change it to suit your particular needs. This guide is quite structured to help those who rely on specific steps spelled out. Feel free to change it in any way you need to.

WHAT DO I DO WITH THE CHILDREN?

One of the first questions to be asked about cells and home groups is, "What do you do with the children?" That is a very good question. Place the emphasis on the word *with*. "What do you do *with* the children?"

If you want to reap the richest rewards from your group, include the children. Be a family. Once you worship *with* children, do an object lesson or activity *with* children, snack and fellowship *with* children, you'll find out that God has planned all along for them to do for you much more than you had ever imagined!

So, *what* do we do with our children? We show them they belong. We value them. We treat them as part of the group, which is an extended family.

WHY INCLUDE THE CHILDREN?
1. To promote family togetherness. The family in our society is broken. Time for developing family relationships is preempted by school, sports, lessons, work, TV. Malachi wrote, "See, I will send you the prophet Elijah before that great and dreadful day of the Lord comes. He will turn the hearts of the fathers to their children, and the hearts of the children to their fathers; or else I will come and strike the land with a curse" (Malachi 4:5, 6). This guide is to help facilitate parent-child interaction.

2. Parents will know what their children are learning and will be able to build on the teaching during the week. This places the responsibility where it should be: parents teaching their children about life in the Lord.

3. Adults will be reached by participating in the children's lessons. We touch their hearts by going in the back door so to speak. Adults often think they are observing or helping out when they watch and listen to someone teaching children. Then they realize that the spiritual truth, presented so simply, has impacted their lives in a memorable way.

4. Children can minister to adults too. They can pray powerful prayers for adults. They can come up with profound insights. God uses them. They are not the future church. They are part of the church today.

5. Single adults often long for "connectedness." They often struggle with loneliness, and for that reason, they enjoy being with families. "God sets the lonely in families" (Psalm 68:6). It is also good for singles and young couples to watch the loving interaction between parents and children. Single adults can sometimes give children special attention that children long for.

HOW DO WE SHOW THEM THEY BELONG?
We develop a meaningful relationship with them. It's the best way to make a difference in their lives.

HOW DO WE DEVELOP A MEANINGFUL RELATIONSHIP WITH THEM?
We listen to them. We *do* things with them. We play with them. Hemfelt and Warren, in their book *Kids Who Carry our Pain*, tell us "play is the single most effective way to communicate with children less than nine years old."

WHEN DO THE ADULTS GET TO TALK AND SHARE TOGETHER WITHOUT THE CHILDREN?
Adults do need time to share concerns with other adults. Children need time away from adults in the group too. So after spending some time gathered as a large group, you will want to separate and allow time for kids and adults to continue separately. Decide when this time will be according to your group's needs. See options on page 5.

WHO TAKES CHARGE OF THE CHILDREN'S TIME?
Take turns. Rotate each week, so each adult can get to know the children, and the children can get to know each adult. Anyone who feels uncomfortable working with the children can be an assistant for awhile to another adult who is perhaps more familiar with children.

It is best to have at least two people working with the children. Older children can help the younger, just as in a real family. This helps both the older and younger child feel valued.

WHAT SHOULD I KNOW ABOUT CHILDREN?
1. The younger the child, the shorter his attention span will be. Most kids have a hard time sitting still for more than ten minutes at a time, less than that for young ones.

2. The more of their five senses you involve, the greater the possibility that they will remember. Some learn best by simply hearing, but most learn best by seeing and doing.

3. Children younger than 8 or 9 do not understand symbolism and do not have a good perspective of time and history.

4. Decide on rules of conduct. Let the children know what those rules are. Link responsibility (to behave properly) with privileges (joining the activity, snack, and so on). Be consistent in enforcing the rules and encourage those who misbehave that you are confident they'll do better next time.

WHAT ABOUT TEENS?

Your group will have to decide. Some groups like to continue to preserve the family togetherness by involving the teens with the family's cell group. Teens can be in charge of the story time. If there are few teens, they can help with the younger children when the kids and adults separate. If there are several teens, they can form a third group to share their concerns and pray for each other.

Other groups encourage teens to have special teen cells entirely separate from the family cells.

HOW DO WE DO THIS? GIVE ME SPECIFICS.

Feel free to
- take lessons out of order.
- do the segments of the lesson in any order.
- leave out any portion of the lesson.
- choose only one or two of the activities.

NOW, LET'S INSPECT EACH BUILDING BLOCK.

I. WORSHIP (songs and praise)

Encourage children to suggest songs and to lead songs sometimes. Children will also enjoy singing energetic songs and songs with hand motions.

II. STORY (optional)

If you have all heard your pastor speak on a certain passage, you may want simply to refer to what everyone has heard and then move on to a memory verse or activity that would be appropriate.

If you need a story, you will find suggestions in each lesson for ways to tell the story. Some are object lessons. You can choose one adult to be in charge of the story time each week, or let adults take turns. You do not have to use the suggestions given. Feel free to tell the story your own way. Children can even tell the story or read the passage. But try not to do the same thing every week. Vary the approach to keep it interesting and fun.

III. MEMORY VERSE (optional)

Most verses are short. Explain any words children may not understand. Each memory verse includes a song or active method to help children remember the Scripture. Give parents an index card and ask them to write the verse on the card so they can take it home with them and continue to review the verse during the week as a family.

There may be children who come without their parents. In that case, another child can get together with this child during the following week, either by phone or in person, and help him review his memory verse.

IV. ACTIVITIES

A variety of activities are suggested. You will only be able to do one or two of them. Vary the type of activity from week to week. Choose activities according to the abilities, interests, and needs of the specific children in your group. Let older children and adults help the younger ones.

You will find suggestions for discussion included with most activities. There is also a list of questions after the activity section. During the activity, while hands are busy, use these questions to guide discussion toward the concepts you want everyone to discover and think about.

V. KIDS' COUNCIL
Try to make this time special by your attitude and the atmosphere you set, so the children feel like the focus is on them and their needs. You can sit together on the floor or ground if that helps make it a special time. Or you may choose a special room or corner that the children can feel is their own. You may even want to have Kids' Council in a clubhouse or tent.

1. **Bring It Home.** Apply the Scripture and activity to their daily lives in the coming week. Questions are suggested for you.
2. **Share and Pray.** Sometimes the previous discussion with the children will expose prayer needs. At other times, children may have very different needs. Share answers to prayers that you've prayed in past weeks. Let children pray for each other.
3. **Extra.** As needed, do another activity (section IV), or allow free play. Play with the children to strengthen your relationship.

VI. ADULT STUDY QUESTIONS
While the children are having a special time together, adults will want to share their needs with each other. The study questions allow adults to go deeper into the theme of the lesson. The questions are meant to be a challenge and lead into thoughtful discussion. But if your group has other needs, you will want to skip the study questions so you can share those needs and pray for each other.

VII. SNACK AND FELLOWSHIP TIME
You may wish to have this time at another point in the meeting. The advantage of having it at the end is that it gives you the option of letting the children prepare and serve the snack.

HOUSE RULES

A home group is like an extended family. Just as a family has practical guidelines for behavior, your group can also have guidelines. It is helpful if everyone in the *group* is aware of the guidelines. If these are group guidelines, then there is an understanding that everyone will remind one another that "this is the way we behave in our group."

Generally, there should be only a few rules, and they should be stated in the positive. See the examples shown.

Remember that children younger than 4 need to be reminded often, and wiggliness and a short attention span are not misbehaviors.

House Rules

1. We speak kind words.
2. We keep our feet off the furniture.
3. We walk indoors (not run).
4. We use quiet, indoor voices inside the house.
5. We help clean up. We put away any toys we get out.

You may find it helpful to write your rules on a poster. Or you may want to use a group meeting time to list the ways everyone agrees to behave. Let all the children sign this list as a contract or agreement to abide by the guidelines.

Rules usually fall into three basic categories:
1. Honoring God
2. Respecting and encouraging others
3. Respecting property

These may be the only guidelines you want to write down. It will be helpful for children if you discuss each one briefly and let them tell you how they can achieve each rule and what behaviors might be considered violations of the rules.

Children can also give suggestions for what the consequences for violating the rules might be. Generally, effective consequences are
■ removing the privilege that the behavior is abusing.
■ removing the child from the group for a period of time.
■ removing material that is being abused or that is being used to hurt others or property.

Sometimes children misbehave when they are in situations in which it is unclear who the authority is. It may be helpful to let everyone know that
1. when you meet as a large group (adults and children together), the parents are in charge of their own child's behavior.

2. when children and adults meet separately, the people who are supervising the children are the ones to be obeyed. They will enforce the rules.

3. the person at whose house you are meeting has the last word on what is or is not out of bounds for their house. It will help if doors are closed to any room that is off limits and if fragile or treasured objects are put in safe places.

For suggestions on dealing with misbehavior, see the eight-page folder *Behavior Management* or the book *Child-Sensitive Teaching* (Standard Publishing).

If you have problems with certain specific behaviors, it is very appropriate to discuss it in a group meeting and help each other decide on the best way to handle it. Remember that you may not immediately arrive at a solution that will work. If what you try doesn't seem to be working, try something else.

INVOLVING CHILDREN WITH ADULTS

THE SITUATION
In the beginning, God created family. Older family members taught the younger family members through example and counsel. Younger family members challenged the thinking of older family members and were often a source of joy as the older members watched them grow stronger and wiser. Older people were comfortable being around the younger ones. Little ones were comfortable interacting with the older generations.

But in our society today, children spend most of their time with peer groups. Adults spend much of their time with adults. So it is not unusual for adults to feel bothered and impatient with children whose needs they do not understand. And it is not unusual for children, especially older children, to feel impatient and bothered with adults.

THE NEEDS

In order to form an intergenerational group, you will need adults who are willing to move out of the traditional peer-oriented comfort zone. They will need to be

- **Patient**

  If this is the first time adults and children have been in an intergenerational group, do not expect everything to flow smoothly at first. The children will have to get used to what is happening and what is expected of them. The adults will have to get used to a group whose members may wiggle more and make more noise.

- **Willing to Learn**

  In the intergenerational group, everyone comes to learn together. Adults don't come in order to pour their knowledge into children. Instead, they establish an atmosphere where everyone learns together. Adults ask and listen and guide. An intergenerational group challenges everyone's thinking.

- **Good Examples**

  Children don't know what it's like to be an adult, so they watch and listen to adults. Adults in the intergenerational group need to be aware that younger eyes are watching them, and younger ears are listening to them. The adults in the group are teaching more by their example. They are modeling life as a follower of Jesus.

- **Willing to Love and Encourage**

  One of the primary benefits of family is the love and encouragement that can be given to each other. Being family is . . .

  > . . . being valued and respected for who you are.
  > . . . being able to contribute to the welfare of the family unit.
  > . . . being accountable to people who care about you.
  > . . . being able to make mistakes and still be loved anyway.
  > . . . being able to talk and be listened to.
  > . . . being encouraged and not discouraged.
  > . . . being prayed for day in and day out.

- **Willing to Sacrifice Self-Interest for the Interests of Others**

  In God's kingdom, those who give up their lives find true life. Those who cling to their lives lose life. It takes work to mature in a family. It takes thinking and praying and giving up self. It means doing the difficult. It means giving up current pleasure in order to receive future rewards.

  So "let us throw off everything that hinders and the sin that so easily entangles, and let us run with perseverance the race marked out for us. Let us fix our eyes on Jesus, the author and perfecter of our faith, who for the joy set before him endured the cross, scorning its shame, and sat down at the right hand of the throne of God" (Hebrews 12:1, 2).

HOW GOD MADE US

INFANTS

- are self-centered
- depend on others to care for them
- learn through their senses
- focus on the present
- do not make conscious choices between right and wrong
- are sensitive to tone of voice

If you have infants in your group,

- they will enjoy listening to your group sing.
- they will enjoy holding and chewing on their toys.
- they may want to be with mom and/or dad.
- or they may be happy being held by someone else.
- they can stay with the adults during Kids' Council, or they can go with the children if an older child will help care for them.
- they may want someone to hold them and walk them around the room during parts of your group time.
- let them feel the atmosphere of love, joy, and peace, so they will know this is a safe, loving place.
- you can introduce infants to God by saying: "God made (whatever they are eating, touching)." "God takes care of you" (when you are taking care of them). "God loves you" (when you are rocking or snuggling with them).

EARLY CHILDHOOD: Ages 2 and 3

- are wanting to be more independent
- may have strong wills
- have short attention spans
- sit still for only a few minutes
- want to know that mom and/or dad are nearby
- are still self-centered and self-focused
- learn by touching and doing
- play *beside* but not cooperatively with other children
- need to know what the rules are
- need patient, consistent training from adults
- need to be able to do some things for themselves
- get fantasy and reality mixed up
- do not understand the flow of time
- do not understand symbolism or figures of speech
- imitate the faith of significant adults around them

If you have toddlers in your group,
- be prepared to let them wiggle.
- try to find ways that they can help.
- let them play a rhythm instrument when you sing.
- let them move into and out of the activities as their attention ebbs and flows.
- give them things to touch and do.
- ask older children to help them as big sisters and brothers help their younger siblings.
- be patient.
- let them hold a small sturdy book for a songbook and a Bible so they can imitate you.
- let them go with the other children to Kids' Council, but be ready to let them go back in with the adults to get the assurance that mom and dad are still nearby.
- have extra toddler toys for them to play with.

EARLY CHILDHOOD: Ages 4 and 5
- enjoy exploring and discovering
- are usually very active
- ask many, many questions
- learn by touching and doing
- still have a short attention span, although it's getting longer
- need to know what the rules are
- are beginning to be more self-controlled because their conscience is now developing
- can begin to be aware that they sin
- get fantasy and reality mixed up
- do not understand the flow of time
- do not understand symbolism and figures of speech
- imitate the faith of the significant adults around them
- realize that they are growing and getting older
- now play *with* and not just beside other children
- want to help and like to surprise people with their good deeds

If you have four and five year olds in your group,
- actively involve them as much as possible.
- explain symbolic concepts and language in simple ways, relating it to something they know.
- let them choose and lead some songs.
- choose touching and doing activities, as well as activities that fit their abilities.
- enjoy their curiosity.
- tell them how proud you are that they are getting so big and growing up.
- acknowledge and compliment their efforts.
- listen to them.
- let them use songbooks and Bibles for preschoolers.
- be patient.
- point out that the Bible stories really happened.
- help them without making them feel incapable.
- provide ways for them to help.

ELEMENTARY: Ages 6 through 10

- want to be busy doing productive things
- enjoy projects
- like to show their skills and abilities
- want to feel like a valued member of a group
- want to hear adults' testimonies about how God is working in their lives
- want to tell about what God is doing in their own lives
- sit still longer but may still wiggle
- learn best by touching and doing and seeing visual aids
- easily feel inferior if they are put down or if they feel incapable
- are seeing their need for a Savior
- can be very sensitive to spiritual issues
- want to see how God is real and how he relates to everyday life
- have a growing understanding of symbolism
- understand the flow of time
- are concerned about what's fair and just
- are more consistent about discerning right from wrong
- memorize more easily

If you have elementary age children in your group,

- treat them as full-fledged members.
- ask them about their schools, sports and other interests, and listen with interest.
- let them take an active part in group discussions, activities, preparations, and cleanup.
- involve them in service projects with your group.
- try to utilize their skills and abilities.
- let the older children help with the younger.
- encourage them to pursue their own relationship with the Lord through Bible reading and prayer.
- ask adults to tell how God is working in their lives.
- let children tell about God working in their lives.
- help them apply the spiritual lessons you discuss in your group to their daily lives.
- compliment their efforts.

LEADING A CHILD TO JESUS

Each child is a unique individual. So the best way to know a particular child's spiritual level is to listen to him and observe him. This requires developing a relationship with him. Developing relationships is one of the blessings of intergenerational groups. The preceding pages have given a foundation of important facts that help us lead children to Jesus. Here is a review.

- **Self and Sin.** Children are born self-focused. Since self is the basis of sin, we can say that children are born sinful. But in their first few years, they're not aware that they sin.
- **Right and Wrong.** As children get close to two years old, they begin exhibiting a strong will. They want some independence in decision making but are not mature enough to make consistent decisions between right and wrong. In fact, they decide what's right and wrong by knowing whether they'll be rewarded or punished for certain behaviors.
- **Awareness of Others.** Around three years old, children reach a major milestone: becoming aware that other people have possessions, opinions, and needs. They begin to see how their choices affect others.
- **The Conscience.** The four-year-old child reaches another major milestone. His conscience begins to develop. This guides more of his choices. Now he can understand that he sometimes makes the wrong choice. This awareness allows him to say, "I am a sinner," and he can begin to see the need for a Savior.
- **Fantasy and Reality.** Everything a young child experiences gets stirred into one big world in his brain, interpreted largely by imagination. Spiritual concepts and Bible stories get mixed in with cartoon stories and super heroes. But around age five, children begin distinguishing fantasy from reality. They can know that the salvation message is real.
- **Death and Life.** Young children have a hard time telling what is alive and what is not. Until they are about five or six, they will not understand what it means when we say that Jesus died.
- **Symbolism.** When children are six or seven, they begin to understand symbolism. In fact, some people call the child's seventh year "the age of reason." This is significant, because many of the methods we use to tell the salvation message are symbolic.
- **Seeing a Need.** Elementary age children begin feeling a need for God's help as they face their everyday lives.

SO AT WHAT AGE CAN A CHILD RECEIVE JESUS AS HIS LORD AND SAVIOR?

He can learn to love Jesus and believe in him very early. Then he must see that he sins and needs a Savior. He must be willing to let Jesus be his Lord, his Boss, his King. How much do children have to understand? That's a good question. But God never asks us to understand. He just asks us to obey. And that's something even a child can do.

THE SALVATION MESSAGE IS REALLY VERY SIMPLE.

- God is perfect. He never does wrong.
- God does not allow anything bad, wrong, or imperfect to be around him.
- We are not perfect. Even if we try to be perfect, we sometimes make the wrong choice. We lie, or say bad words, or throw a fit, or take things that really aren't ours.
- Since we are not perfect, we cannot be around God. We will never be able to live with him where there's no hurting or crying or dying, where there's joy and peace and love forever.
- But God loves us and wants us to be able to live with him. So he sent Jesus, his Son. Jesus was a man, a human like we are, except for one thing: he was perfect.
- So Jesus traded with us. He took our sins, our wrongs. And he was punished for all the bad things we've done or will do. He was killed on a cross.

- So Jesus took our sins and gave us his perfectness. If we say YES to Jesus, if we tell him we will let him be our Savior (to save us from the punishment our sin would bring us), then we get his perfectness. We become perfect in God's kingdom, and we will get to live with joy and peace and love forevermore.
- In fact, there's more good news: God brought Jesus back to life again, and now Jesus is preparing a place for us with him in heaven.
- And there's even more good news: When we let Jesus be our Savior and our Lord (our Boss, our King), he sends his Holy Spirit to live inside us. In that way, Jesus can always be with us. The Holy Spirit puts joy and peace in our hearts. He teaches us and leads us and tells us God's thoughts. He helps us become all that Jesus wants us to be.

Sharing

OBJECTIVE: *To encourage each other to share even the small things we have.*

WORSHIP

Sing praise and worship songs as well as songs about doing good that are familiar and meaningful to your group. Here are some suggestions.

"Freely, Freely"
"Give and It Will Be Given"
"I Have Decided to Follow Jesus"
"Pass It On"
"They'll Know We Are Christians by Our Love"
"This Is My Commandment"
"This Little Light of Mine"

STORY

Jesus Feeds 5,000, John 6:1-13

- Jesus is teaching a crowd of over 5,000 people, and it's supper time.
- One boy shares his food with Jesus.
- Jesus turns the boy's supper into enough food to feed everyone.

In a basket, place a layer of fish-shaped crackers and oyster crackers. Cover them with a napkin or paper towel and put two fish-shaped crackers and five oyster crackers on top. Show the crackers that are on top of the napkin when you tell the story. Lift up the napkin to reveal the rest of the crackers at the right time. Pass them around and snack as you finish the story.

MEMORY VERSE

"Do not forget to do good and to share with others" (Hebrews 13:16).

To help the children remember this verse, sing it to the tune of "Are You Sleeping?" When everyone has learned this song, you can sing it as a round.

ACTIVITIES

Choose one or more of the following activities to support the story and to provide a springboard for discussion.

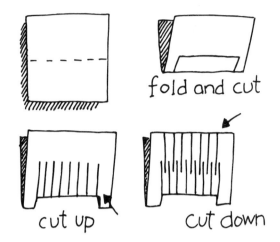

fold and cut

cut up

cut down

STEPPING THROUGH PAPER. Practice this before showing it to everyone. Turn a piece of plain white paper so that the 11-inch length points north and south. Fold it in half horizontally. Save a 1-inch space on the east and west sides of the fold and do not cut these. Cut off the rest of the fold: cut into the paper 1 inch north, 6½ inches east-west, then 1 inch south, through both thicknesses (making a window in the middle of the unfolded paper). Then, with paper folded, make eight evenly spaced north-south cuts from the edges of the window to within 1 inch of the edge of the paper. Then from the edge of the paper, make seven evenly spaced north-south cuts that go between the previous cuts to within 1 inch of the window. Point out how small the folded paper is. Then unfold, shake out, and let everyone take turns stepping through the hole. Say: "Something small turned out to be big. How can God make the small things you share turn into big blessings for others?" Let everyone try making a paper window.

BUILDING BLOCKS. Ask everyone to build a tower of blocks or boxes. Then ask one person to pull out one of the blocks or boxes from the bottom. Ask: "What happens? Each block may be small by itself, but it has an important part. Together they make something big. We may be small by ourselves, like the little boy who shared his small supper, but the part we have in God's family is important."

PLAY BALL. Play a game of volleyball (stretch out a string or sheet, use a soft ball, balloon or beach ball), basketball, softball, or kickball. Talk about the important part each person plays. Read the memory verse. Ask: "What part do you have in God's kingdom? What skill or ability can you share?"

CANDLES. This activity requires adult supervision. It's best if you do this as a large group, with each family helping their children with the candles. Give each child a small paper plate and a candle. Punch a small hole in the center of the plate. Stick the candle through it, narrow end first. Force the plate to slide three-fourths of the way down the candle. Hold onto candles beneath the plate. Darken the room. Light one candle for yourself. Show how much light it gives. Leave the room with your candle. Ask: "Is the room darker now?" Then, with your candle, light the other candles. Ask: "Is the room lighter?" Discuss how sharing what God has given us results in more for everyone. **Option:** To do this in conjunction with your snack, bake cupcakes. Put birthday candles on them. Then follow the lighting of candles and discussion as above.

QUESTIONS

1. When we get together as a group, what can each of us do to encourage the others?
2. Did you ever feel small or unimportant? Why is each person important?
3. How can God take something small that you share and turn it into a big blessing for many people?

KIDS' COUNCIL

BRING IT HOME

- What has God given you that you can share this week?
- Do you know someone who needs to be encouraged? What can you share that might encourage them? (Encourage the children to name things that are not material: a smile, a listening ear, and so on.)
- Do you ever forget "to do good and share with others"? What can you do if you realize that you forgot?

SHARE AND PRAY

- Ask the children to share their concerns and pray for each other.
- Pray that God will show them what to share, when to share, and who to share with.
- Thank God for giving us more than enough to share, and for sharing his blessings with us.

ADULT STUDY QUESTIONS

- Tell about a time when you did something small and it turned out to be very important.
- Read and discuss Ezekiel 16:49. These people had plenty but didn't share. What happened to them? Can you think of a people who are arrogant and overfed today?
- Read and discuss 2 Corinthians 9:11. Why are we made rich?
- Sharing does not have to be confined to material possessions. What might be even more important to share?

SNACKS AND FELLOWSHIP

Giant Cookie. Make this ahead of time, or use this as an activity. Let the children help mix your favorite cookie dough, or use the following recipe. Beat ¾ cup softened margarine, ½ cup granulated sugar, and 1½ cups brown sugar. Add 2 eggs and 1 teaspoon vanilla. In a separate bowl, mix 2½ cups flour, 1 teaspoon soda, ¾ teaspoon salt, and 1 teaspoon cinnamon. Add the flour mixture to the sugar and eggs. Beat it. Stir in 12 ounces of chocolate chips. Let the children help spread the cookie dough onto a greased pizza pan. Bake about 10 minutes at 350 degrees. Talk about how one person could keep the giant cookie for himself and make himself happy for awhile, or he could share it, and everyone could be satisfied.

Trusting Jesus

OBJECTIVE: *To encourage each other to keep our eyes on Jesus and trust him.*

WORSHIP

Sing praise and worship songs as well as songs about doing good that are familiar and meaningful to your group. Here are some suggestions.

"Be Still and Know"
"Great Is Thy Faithfulness"
"He's Got the Whole World in His Hands"
"Jesus, Jesus"
"Leaning on the Everlasting Arms"
"My God Is So Great"
"O How I Love Jesus"
"O Lord, You Have Been Good"
"O Most High"
"The Steadfast Love of the Lord"
"'Tis So Sweet to Trust in Jesus"

STORY

Jesus Walks on Water, Matthew 14:22-33
- Jesus' friends are unable to cross the lake because of high winds.
- Jesus walks across the water to help his friends.
- Jesus allows Peter to walk across the water to him and ends up rescuing Peter from the water.

Place a blue sheet on the floor. Ask one person to get at each end of the sheet and shake the sheet gently to make waves. They can shake it harder to make stormy waves. Act out the story with one person representing Jesus and one being Peter. The rest can be disciples in the boat.

MEMORY VERSE

"Let us fix our eyes on Jesus" (Hebrews 12:2).

Help the children remember this verse by asking them to point to their eyes when they say *eyes* and point upward when they say *Jesus*.

ACTIVITIES

Choose one or more of the following activities to support the story and to provide a springboard for discussion.

FOOTPRINTS (for younger children). Let children stand barefooted on paper. Draw around their feet. Discuss Jesus and Peter walking on water, Matthew 14:22-33.

MAKE A STORY. Let everyone help record the story as an audio drama. Use a narrator and let others be voices and sound effects.

SOAP FLAKE SEA. Pour Ivory clothes detergent into a large bowl. Add water a little at a time, whipping it with the electric mixer until it's thick and creamy. Add blue food coloring. Each person uses the mixture as finger paint, painting it onto cardboard or a paper plate, making peaks as if they were waves. You may cut out a small half-circle to represent a boat and stick it onto one of the waves. Let it dry. Caution: Since this mixture is soap, do not let the children get it into their eyes or mouths. Discuss Matthew 14:22-33.

WALK THIS WAY. Pantomime walking on different surfaces: mud, deep snow, rocks, ice, hot sand, puddles, deep grass, a swinging bridge, a row of tires, a crowded sidewalk, deep soft carpet, and so on. If you want, whisper one of these into each person's ear. The person then mimes it, and the others guess what he's pretending to walk on. Discuss Matthew 14:22-33.

FEEL THE PATH. Lay out a path made of a variety of materials: cotton balls, linoleum tiles, carpet samples, plush bath mat, masking tape (sticky side up), leaves, piece of plywood, cardboard, sandpaper, and so on. Let everyone walk barefooted over the material. Talk about how it might have felt to Peter when he walked on water.

QUESTIONS

1. What does this story tell you about Jesus?
2. What does this story tell you about Peter?
3. When Peter was sinking, how did he call for help?
4. When Peter failed, who picked him up? When we fail, who picks us up?

KIDS' COUNCIL

BRING IT HOME

- Why did Peter begin to sink? Read Hebrews 12:2. What does it mean to fix (or keep) our eyes on Jesus?
- What are some fears (wind and waves) in your life? What did Jesus say in Matthew 14:27?
- How will you keep your eyes on Jesus this week? In other words, how will you keep thinking about Jesus and trusting him?

SHARE AND PRAY

- Ask the children to share their concerns and pray for each other.
- Ask God to help us not to be afraid, because Jesus will help us.
- Thank God that Jesus helps us and we can trust him.

ADULT STUDY QUESTIONS

- Are there any situations right now in your life in which you need to fix your eyes on Jesus?
- What are some things that draw our eyes away from Jesus?
- What are some specific, practical things you can do to help yourself keep your eyes on Jesus?
- In the story of Jesus walking on the water, we often focus on Peter's failure. What was Peter's success? Have you ever focused so much on your failure in a situation that you forgot about the successful aspects of it?

SNACK AND FELLOWSHIP

Pizzas With Eyes. Make small pizzas out of English muffins. Spread pizza sauce on top of English muffins. Place sliced black olives on top to make two eyes. A crescent-shaped slice of onion, green pepper, or avocado can be a mouth. Shredded mozzarella cheese can be hair. Broil until bubbly and serve. Talk about fixing our eyes on Jesus.

Words From the Heart

OBJECTIVE: *To learn how and why to guard our hearts.*

WORSHIP

Sing praise and worship songs as well as songs about the heart that are familiar and meaningful to your group. Here are some suggestions.

"All Consuming Fire"
"As the Deer"
"Oh, Be Careful, Little Eyes"
"Change My Heart, O God"
"Come Bless the Lord"

"Down in My Heart"
"God the Lord Is the Strength of My Heart"
"In My Life, Lord, Be Glorified"
"Into My Heart"
"Pure and Holy I Would Be"

STORY

Jesus Teaches About the Heart, Matthew 12:33-37
- Jesus says that good trees produce good fruit, bad trees produce bad fruit.
- Jesus compares people's hearts to the trees: people who store good in their hearts say good things.
- Jesus says that we will have to give an account for the careless words we've spoken.

Set up a paper grocery sack. Draw a face on it as shown and cut out a mouth large enough for a child to stick his hand in. On slips of paper write different types of things that might be said by people (lies, curses, dirty jokes, kind words, *please*, *thank-you*, encouraging words). Put these slips of paper in the sack. Read the passage. Then let each person reach in and bring out one of the slips of paper and read it. Ask them to tell what was in the heart of the person who said that.

Cut out mouth →

MEMORY VERSE

"Out of the overflow of the heart the mouth speaks"
(Matthew 12:34).

Help the children learn the verse by writing each word of the verse on a Styrofoam cup turned upside down. Mix the cups up so the words are not in order. Let everyone line up. When you say, "Go," the first person runs to the cups and selects the first word of the verse to put to the left of the other cups, starting the sentence. He then runs back and taps the next person's hand. The next person runs to the cups, finds the second word and places it to the right of the first word. Continue in this way until all the cups are arranged in the right order. If someone places a word out of order, the next runner replaces it with the correct word. Time the group and see how fast they can get at arranging the verse correctly.

ACTIVITIES

Choose one or more of the following activities to support the story and to provide a springboard for discussion.

SOFT AND HARD HEARTS. Cut a hard, dry sponge into a heart shape. Let everyone feel it. Talk about Ezekiel 36:26, 27 (ICB), "I will take out the stubborn heart like stone from your bodies. And I will give you an obedient heart of flesh. I will put my Spirit inside you. And I will help you live by my rules." Let someone drop the sponge into a bowl of water. Squeeze out the excess water and let everyone feel it. Discuss living water (John 7:38, 39).

TREASURE HUNT. Let the children prepare a treasure hunt for the adults by hiding clues in different places, each clue leading to another clue until the last clue finally leads to the treasure. The treasure is a Bible. On top of the Bible is a heart on which is written, "Where your treasure is, there your heart will be also" (Matthew 6:21). **Option:** Prepare a treasure hunt for the children like the one described above. Along with the Bible, another prize (stickers or a snack) can be included.

WORKING HEARTS. Let each child lead an exercise. (Or play a game of basketball.) After working out, feel the heart pumping. Ask: "Why do we exercise our physical hearts? Is this the heart God talks about? (See Scriptures in previous activities.) How can we exercise our spiritual hearts?"

FILL 'EM UP RELAY. With a red permanent marker, draw a heart on each of two white garbage bags. Blow up enough balloons to fill up the two garbage bags, plus some extra in case some of the balloons pop. Divide the group into two teams. Give each team a garbage bag. When you say, "Go," the teams fill their bags with balloons. The team that fills their bag first wins. Give everyone a balloon as a prize. Discuss the importance of what we fill our hearts with.

QUESTIONS

1. Is it possible for a person to obey, yet have a hard heart (or a bad attitude)?
2. Can we make our hearts soft (kind, loving) all by ourselves? Who can help?
3. How can we tell what is in a person's heart?

KIDS' COUNCIL

BRING IT HOME
- Read Proverbs 4:23. What does this mean? How can we guard our hearts?
- What are some things that children might fill their hearts with?
- Have you heard people say things on TV or on videos that show their hearts are not filled with good things?
- How will you guard your heart this week?

SHARE AND PRAY
- Ask the children to share their concerns and pray for each other.
- Confess and repent of any bad things that we have let into our hearts.
- Ask God to put his Spirit in our hearts and fill us with his goodness.
- Thank God for helping us guard our hearts.

ADULT STUDY QUESTIONS
- Read Proverbs 4:23. How can you as an adult guard your heart?
- As you were growing up, were there some bad things that crept into your heart? Have any of those things overflowed at times when you least needed them? Explain.
- How can you help your children guard their hearts?
- Read and discuss Matthew 12:35-37. These words are very strong. Why do you think Jesus spoke out so strongly about our words?

SNACK AND FELLOWSHIP

Heart Biscuits. Mix biscuit dough or use ready-made dough. Shape the biscuits like hearts, or, if you use this as an activity, let the children shape them like hearts. Bake them. Cut them open as if to butter them. Ask: "What would you put in them: rocks? sand? glue? paper? Why not? What do we *not* want to put in our spiritual hearts?"

Jesus' Authority

OBJECTIVE: *To learn about Jesus' authority and what it means to make him Lord.*

WORSHIP

Sing praise and worship songs as well as songs about Jesus that are familiar and meaningful to your group. Here are some suggestions.

"All Hail the Power of Jesus' Name"
"Father, I Adore You"
"God With Us"
"Greater Is He That Is in Me"
"His Name Is Wonderful"

"Jesus, Mighty God"
"Jesus, Name Above All Names"
"Praise the Name of Jesus"
"We Believe"
"We Bow Down"

STORY

Peter Confesses That Jesus Is God's Son, Matthew 16:13-20
- Jesus asks his disciples who people say he is.
- His disciples tell Jesus that many people say he's one of the prophets.
- Peter says that Jesus is the Son of God, and Jesus is pleased.

As you tell the story, ask three children or adults to stand together in the middle of the room. Let the other children bind this group together with streamers or toilet paper. Talk about why you would bind someone physically. Talk about spiritual binding. (See an explanation at the end of this session.) Why would you do it? How? Now unbind the people. Talk about what it means to loose something physically and spiritually (Matthew 16:13-20).

Note: Children do not usually begin to understand symbolism until they are around seven years old. If you talk with younger children about *keys to the kingdom*, remind them that a kingdom is where the king lives, where he's boss. Try to link the symbolic to something concrete.

MEMORY VERSE

"The one who is in you is greater than the one who is in the world" (1 John 4:4).

To help the children remember the verse, sing it to the tune of "The Farmer in the Dell."

ACTIVITIES

Choose one or more of the following activities to support the story and to provide a springboard for discussion.

DOOR POSTERS. Ask the children to make door posters for their rooms out of paper or poster board. Help them write *Jesus Is the Boss Here* or *Jesus Is in Charge Here* (explain *being in charge*). The children can color their posters. Discuss authority, the authority Jesus has, and the authority we have when Jesus is our Lord.

KEYS. Place keys under plain white paper and rub over the paper with the side of a crayon to reveal the keys. Discuss what a key does, what the *keys of the kingdom* are (Matthew 16:13-20), and who can use the keys.

Jesus is the key!

WHO HAS THE KEY? Everyone sits in a circle, hands cupped and held in front of them. Two players stand in the middle. One is IT. The other holds a key and passes by each player, pretending to drop the key into each person's hands. Everyone closes their hands as if receiving a key, but the key is dropped into only one person's hands. Then everyone chants, "Key, key, who has the key?" IT has three guesses to find the key. Then the player with the key becomes IT, and IT becomes the key giver. Talk about the *keys of the kingdom*.

FREEZE TAG. Play this outdoors. When a person is tagged by IT, he must stand still and remain frozen until another person who has not been tagged touches him and releases him. Discuss *binding* and *loosing* (Matthew 16:13-20).

BADGES. Make a badge like that used to identify FBI or police agents. Ask each person to fold an index card in half. On the inside, each person draws a badge shape or a heart. In the badge or heart, he writes *Jesus*. Practice flipping it open and saying, "I'm with Jesus, ma'am." Discuss the authority that Jesus gives his followers.

QUESTIONS

1. What is authority? Who do you know who has authority? How does he show authority?
2. What are you in charge of?
3. Who did Peter say Jesus was? Who do you say Jesus is?

KIDS' COUNCIL

BRING IT HOME
- When you follow Jesus, what kind of authority does that give you? Read 1 John 4:4. What do you have authority over?
- How does someone become a follower of Jesus? How does Jesus become your Lord?
- Have you asked Jesus to be your Lord? If not, do you want to ask him now?

SHARE AND PRAY
- Ask the children to share their concerns and pray for each other.
- Give the children an opportunity to ask Jesus to be their Lord if they want to.
- Thank God for sending Jesus and for being the strongest and wisest of all.

ADULT STUDY QUESTIONS
- Read Matthew 16:13. Why do you think Jesus referred to himself as the Son of Man?
- Who do you say Jesus is?
- Read Matthew 16:18. Notice that Jesus, in turn, told Peter who Peter was. Is there a sense in which when we confess Jesus as Lord, he then lets us know who we really are and who we are meant to become in his kingdom? Read and discuss Psalm 138:8.
- What did Jesus mean when he said *keys of the kingdom*? What does he mean by *what you bind* and *what you loose*?

SNACK AND FELLOWSHIP

Following a Recipe. Measure out these ingredients, keep them separate, and set them aside: 1 cup shortening, 1½ cups sugar, 2 eggs, 2¾ cups flour, 2 teaspoons cream of tartar, 1 teaspoon soda, ½ teaspoon salt, 2 tablespoons sugar, and 2 teaspoons cinnamon. Now set out an unmeasured amount of the above ingredients. Tell the children to mix these ingredients any way they want to make cookies. Bake at 400 degrees 8 to 10 minutes. Set out the measured ingredients and recipe. Ask the children to follow the recipe: mix the shortening, sugar, and eggs. In another bowl, mix the flour, cream of tartar, soda, and salt. Stir the flour mixture into the egg mixture. Spoon it onto a cookie sheet. Mix 2 tablespoons sugar and 2 teaspoons cinnamon. Sprinkle it on the cookies. Bake them at 400 degrees 8 to 10 minutes. Try both batches of cookies. Ask: "Which is best—the one made however you wanted, or the one made following the recipe? Life is best if we follow God's plan and not our own."

SPIRITUAL BINDING: The literal translation of Matthew 16:19b is "whatever you bind on earth shall be, having been bound in the heavens, and whatever you loose on earth shall be, having been loosed in the heavens." The Greek word for *bind*, used in this context, means *forbid*. The Greek word for *loose* means *permit*. Forbidding and permitting are the privilege of whoever is in authority. Peter has just confirmed his belief in Jesus' position of authority as God's Son. Jesus then confers authority on those who believe he is God's Son. But Jesus has said that he "can do only what he sees his Father doing, because whatever the Father does the Son also does" (John 5:19). So this privilege of authority comes with the responsibility of seeking God and "being about our Father's business." Simply put, when we are under Jesus' authority, we forbid what God forbids and permit what God permits. Therefore, we *bind* or forbid evil to have authority over us and we *loose*, release, or permit Jesus' authority to be in control. Because of Jesus living in us, we say no to Satan and his plans. The memory verse for this lesson indicates the basis for our authority in Jesus.

Friends

OBJECTIVE: *To encourage each other to be good friends and to have Jesus as our best friend.*

WORSHIP

Sing praise and worship songs as well as songs about fellowship that are familiar and meaningful to your group. Here are some suggestions.

"Father Abraham"
"He's Got the Whole World in His Hands"
"Jesus Loves the Little Children"
"Praise the Lord Together"
"They'll Know We Are Christians by Our Love"
"We Are One in the Spirit"
"You Have Called Us"

John 15:12-17
Luke 5:17-26

STORY

Jesus' Friends See Him Transfigured, Matthew 17:1-8
- Jesus, Peter, James, and John go up onto a mountain.
- Jesus begins to shine brightly, and Moses and Elijah appear and talk with him.
- God says that Jesus is his Son. He loves Jesus, and the disciples should listen to Jesus.

Make six puppet figures by drawing faces on the bowls of six plastic spoons with a permanent marker. Let the children work the puppets as you read the Scripture. At the point in the story when Jesus is transfigured, shine a flashlight onto the puppet that represents Jesus.

MEMORY VERSE

"A friend loves at all times" (Proverbs 17:17).

To help the children remember this verse, ask them to say it several times together, shaking hands with a different person each time.

ACTIVITIES

Choose one or more of the following activities to support the story and to provide a springboard for discussion.

PYRAMID PARTNERS. Each person chooses a partner. Give each pair a large stack of paper cups. When you say, "Go," everyone works with their partners to see how high they can build a pyramid of cups in 2 minutes. Stop at the end of 2 minutes. Talk about Jesus' friends and our friends.

RELAY. Have a relay race or game. Take a break and talk about friends. Ask: "Why do we need friends? Who were the friends Jesus took with him to the mountain?"

SIT AND GET UP. Everyone sits on the floor, knees bent. Tell them to try to get up without using their hands. Then tell them to choose partners. They sit on the floor the same way, except partners sit back to back and link elbows. Then ask them to try to stand up together. Ask: "Can you stand up by yourself? Can you stand up if you have a partner? Do you need a third friend to help? How did Jesus' friends help him? How did he help them?"

TIN CAN PHONE. Punch a hole in the bottom of two cans. Thread one end of a long string through one can and the other end through the other can so that the open ends of the cans are facing away from each other. Tie each end of the string to a paper clip to secure it inside the can. Now stretch the string out. One person talks into one end while someone listens at the other end. Ask: "What did God say about listening?" (See v. 5 of the story.)

QUESTIONS

1. Why do you think Jesus chose Peter, James, and John to go with him?
2. We have a clue about how Peter felt when he saw what happened. How do you think James and John felt? How would you have felt? What would you have done?
3. Why do we need close friends? Can Jesus be your best friend?

KIDS' COUNCIL

BRING IT HOME
- How do you know when someone is your friend? How does Jesus know if you are his friend?
- Could you become a closer friend to Jesus? How? What do you think would happen if you did?
- Can Jesus be a best friend? How will you treat him if he's your friend?
- Why is it important to listen to Jesus? How can we do that?

SHARE AND PRAY
- Ask the children to share their concerns and pray for each other.
- Give the children an opportunity to ask Jesus to be their best friend if they want to.
- Thank God for sending Jesus to be a special friend for us.

ADULT STUDY QUESTIONS
- What is the significance of the transfiguration?
- Peter, James, and John seem to have been closer to Jesus than any of the other disciples. Why do you suppose this was true? Do you have a small group of friends that are closer to you than others? Why or why not?
- Could you become a closer friend to Jesus? If so, how? What do you think would happen if you became a closer friend? Do you want to be closer to Jesus?
- What do friends typically do together? What do you do with Jesus?

SNACK AND FELLOWSHIP

Friendship Cracker-mallows. Give each person a square graham cracker. Let him place a marshmallow on top and place the cracker on a cookie sheet. Broil the marshmallows on the crackers until they puff and start melting. Let each person have their cracker-mallows back. Tell each one to ask a friend to put a graham cracker square on top of their cracker-mallow. Talk about how friends help us.

Showing and Sharing Faith

OBJECTIVE: *To contemplate the significance of faith, growing our faith, and sharing our faith.*

WORSHIP

Sing praise and worship songs as well as songs about faith that are familiar and meaningful to your group. Here are some suggestions.

"All Hail the Power of Jesus' Name"
"Amazing Grace"
"Anywhere With Jesus"
"Behold, Behold"
"Faith Is the Victory"
"Freely, Freely"
"Go, Tell It on the Mountain"

"I Love to Tell the Story"
"My God Is So Great"
"Praise the Lord Together"
"They'll Know We Are Christians by
    Our Love"
"This Is My Story"

STORY

Jesus Heals an Epileptic Boy, Matthew 17:14-21
- A father asks Jesus to heal his son.
- Jesus sends a demon out of the boy.
- Jesus says that nothing is impossible for those who have faith.

Point out a real father and son in your group, and encourage everyone to remember that this story took place with real people, just like those sitting and listening to you now. Read the Scripture. As you read verses 20 and 21, hand each person a small seed.

MEMORY VERSE

"This is the victory that has overcome the world, even our faith" (1 John 5:4).

To help the children remember the verse, ask them to repeat it several times using hand motions.
    This is the victory that overcomes
        (hold hand up with forefinger and middle finger extended in a victory sign)
    the world (arms overhead in a circle to represent the world)
    even our faith (right hand over heart)

ACTIVITIES

Choose one or more of the following activities to support the story and to provide a springboard for discussion.

EGG TOSS. Do this activity on a lawn or surface where you don't mind having broken eggs. Each person chooses a partner. One holds a raw egg; the other stands about 1 yard away. One tosses the egg; the other catches it. After each toss, partners take a step back. See how far apart you can stand and still catch the egg. Discuss faith in your partner, trusting him to catch the fragile egg. Discuss faith in God, trusting him with your needs and the needs of others.

SEED MATCH. Get different kinds of seeds from seed packets or from fruit. Tape each kind of seed onto two different index cards. You should have two matching cards of each seed. Turn the cards over, mix them up, and put them in rows. Then play a memory game. Taking turns, each person turns over two cards, trying to find the two that are alike. When matching cards are turned over, they are removed. Talk about how faith is like a seed. Say: "Our faith can grow. How? How can we share our faith?"

DOUGH MOUNTAINS. Make mountains out of play dough. (You can make play dough by mixing together 3 parts flour, 1 part salt, and 1 part water.) If you want, everyone can connect their mountains to make a mountain chain. Talk about what Jesus said: "If you have faith as small as a mustard seed, you can say to this mountain, 'Move from here to there' and it will move" (Matthew 17:20).

SPROUTING SEEDS. Give each person a disposable bowl and a sponge. Each person dampens the sponge, places it in the bowl, and sprinkles the sponge with grass seed or bird seed. Ask each person to take his bowl home, keep the sponge wet, and watch the seeds sprout. Talk about faith *as small as a mustard seed*. Talk about growing faith, showing faith, and sharing faith.

QUESTIONS

1. What is faith?
2. Everybody has faith in something. What are some things people put their faith in? Will these things really help them or not?
3. Why would someone want to put his faith in Jesus?
4. How can we know someone has faith in Jesus? How does it show?

KIDS' COUNCIL

BRING IT HOME

- What do you think Jesus meant when he said that faith the size of a mustard seed could move mountains? Who has this kind of faith? Did his disciples have it?
- Talk about how we sometimes call big problems in our lives *mountains*. Why would we call a problem a mountain? Can faith help us with this kind of mountain? How?
- Why would we want to share our faith? How can we share our faith?
- How will you show your faith this week?
- Is there someone you can share your faith with this week?

SHARE AND PRAY

- Ask the children to share their concerns and pray for each other.
- Thank God for giving us faith.
- Ask God who he wants us to share our faith with this week. Ask him to give us the courage, the right words, and the right actions to show our faith.

ADULT STUDY QUESTIONS

- Have you ever experienced your faith moving mountains? How did it happen?
- What are some ways a person shows his faith?
- What are some specific ways to share your faith with others?
- How can faith grow? Is it possible that, just as when we exercise our muscles, our muscles grow, when we exercise our faith, our faith grows?
- We sometimes call big problems in our lives *mountains*. Why would we call a problem a mountain? Can faith help us with this kind of mountain? How? What mountains are in your life right now?

SNACK AND FELLOWSHIP

Frosted Mountains. Use cans of ready-made crescent roll or biscuit dough. Form each dough roll or biscuit into a small mountain. Make one for each person. Place these on a cookie sheet. Sprinkle each biscuit mountain with cinnamon. Bake as directed on the package. Make powdered sugar frosting by putting 1 cup of powdered sugar into a small bowl and adding milk 1 teaspoonful at a time, stirring after each addition until the frosting is the right consistency to pour. Then pour a little frosting on top of each mountain so that it looks like there's snow on the mountain.

When We All Pray for the Same Thing

OBJECTIVE: *To encourage each other to agree together in prayer.*

WORSHIP

Sing praise and worship songs as well as songs about prayer that are familiar and meaningful to your group. Here are some suggestions.

"Bind Us Together"
"Kum Ba Yah"
"Praise the Lord Together"
"Sometimes Alleluia"
"We Believe"
"We Gather Together"
"What a Friend We Have in Jesus"
"Whisper a Prayer"

STORY

Jesus' Teaching About Agreeing in Prayer, Matthew 18:19, 20

- Jesus says that when people agree in prayer, it will be done.
- Jesus says where two or three come together, he's there with them.

Before you gather, ask the children who can read to be prepared to read one of these Scriptures: Mark 16:20; Acts 2:1, 2; Acts 2:42-47; Acts 12:1-19 (especially v. 12). As leader, you should begin by reading Matthew 18:19, 20. Ask everyone to hold hands together as you read these verses. Then ask each child to read the verses assigned to him. Tell everyone to listen for the way the people got together and to notice how Jesus and God's power were with them, even though these events took place after his ascension.

MEMORY VERSE

"Where two or three come together in my name, there am I with them" (Matthew 18:20).

Help the children remember this verse by asking them to do hand motions as they say it with you. Everyone should sit in a circle. When they say the word *two*, they hold up two fingers. When they say *three*, they hold up three fingers. As they say *come together in my name*, they hold hands and continue holding hands to finish the verse.

ACTIVITIES

Choose one or more of the following activities to support the story and to provide a springboard for discussion.

weaver

STREAMER WEAVING. Choose one person to be a weaver. Divide the others into two groups, facing each other. Give each person in one group a 5-foot length of streamer. Each person holds one end; the person facing him from the other group holds the other end. Every other person kneels, placing his streamer on the floor. Those left standing raise their streamers. The weaver walks under the raised streamers and over the floor streamers, pulling a streamer after him. Then the kneelers raise their streamers, standing people kneel, and the weaver takes a new streamer back the opposite direction. Continue until the weaver has woven all the streamers together. Discuss the strengths of gathering together.

PUSH A BOX. Fill a big box with heavy objects (books work well). Ask the smallest child to push the box across the room. (It's too heavy.) Ask the next smallest child to help. Keep getting help until the box moves easily. Talk about the benefits of gathering together as Jesus' followers.

HANDSHAKES. Ask everyone to give examples of different kinds of handshakes (including high five). These are signs of agreement. Each person chooses a partner. They meet privately and invent a new handshake. Then each pair shows the group their new handshake. Discuss agreeing in prayer.

PAPER CLIP NECKLACE. Give each person a paper clip and ask him to make a necklace with it. It's impossible. Say: "Sometimes we need more than one to get the job done." Then let each person link enough paper clips together to make a necklace that easily fits over his head. Discuss having more than one person praying (Matthew 18:19).

SHIELDED DODGE BALL. Choose one person to be IT. Let the others roll sheets of newspaper into balls. With these balls, they try to hit the person who is IT. When IT gets hit, he can choose one person to be his shield and try to keep balls from hitting IT. When IT is hit again, he chooses another person to join the first one in helping to shield him. More and more friends become shields until IT can no longer be hit. Discuss the strength that comes with a group.

QUESTIONS

1. What does it mean to agree? What does it mean to agree in prayer? What is a word we say in prayer that is a sign of our agreement with what is being said? (Amen.)
2. What kinds of things do we know we agree on?
3. Why is it important to gather together as Jesus' followers?

KIDS' COUNCIL

BRING IT HOME

- Why is it important to come together as believers?
- If Jesus is with us when two or three gather together, does that mean he's not with us when we are alone? What do you think Jesus meant in Matthew 18:20?
- Whom can you agree with in prayer? Is your family a group of believers with whom you can agree in prayer?
- What can we agree on in prayer right now?

SHARE AND PRAY

- Ask the children to share their concerns and pray for each other.
- Thank God for giving us other believers to pray with.
- Thank Jesus for being with us now as we are gathered together, praying as a group.
- Pray as a group for each other and any concerns the children may want to pray for.

ADULT STUDY QUESTIONS

- If Jesus is with us when two or three gather together, does that mean he's not with us when we are alone? What did Jesus mean in Matthew 18:20?
- What significance does this verse give to family devotionals?
- Read and discuss Matthew 18:19. Does there seem to be some difference between what we read here and what we experience? Are there other factors involved in prayer that might be significant? If so, what are they? You may want to discuss James 4:1-3 and 1 John 5:14, 15.
- Even when we are praying as a group, does that mean that everyone there necessarily agrees with what is being prayed? Does Matthew 18:19, 20 mean that the agreeing people have to be in the same location, meeting as a group?
- Have you ever been in a group praying when your mind wandered and you found yourself not even listening or thinking about the prayer? Are there some practical things we can do to keep our minds and spirits on the prayer?
- What can we agree on in prayer right now?

SNACK AND FELLOWSHIP

Bread Stick Ropes. From a can of refrigerated bread stick dough, make ropes by twisting two or three dough sticks together. Bake according to package instructions. Read and discuss Ecclesiastes 4:12.

Forgiving

OBJECTIVE: *To learn how to forgive and to encourage each other to forgive as Jesus did.*

WORSHIP

Sing praise and worship songs as well as songs about mercy that are familiar and meaningful to your group. Here are some suggestions.

"Down in My Heart"
"I Will Sing of the Mercies of the Lord Forever"
"Into My Heart"
"Jesus Loves Even Me"
"Lord, I Lift Your Name on High"
"O How I Love Jesus"
"Oh Lord, You Have Been Good"
"Only by Grace"
"The Steadfast Love of the Lord"
"This Is My Commandment"

STORY

The Unforgiving Servant, Matthew 18:21-35
- A king forgives a servant's large debt.
- The servant then demands payment from a man who owes him a small amount.
- The king punishes his servant for not extending mercy after he'd been given mercy.

Fill three small bowls with water. Tell the story. Sprinkle pepper over the surface of the water in the first bowl as you tell about the servant who owed lots of money. The pepper will represent all the money he owed. When you tell that the king forgave him, drop one drip of dish washing liquid into the center of the bowl. Talk about how the water represents our hearts. The pepper immediately races off to the sides of the bowl. The servant owes nothing.

Then use the second bowl. Sprinkle a little pepper in the center of the bowl. Tell how the servant demanded payment from the other man, even though the man owed him only a little money. Do not put the washing liquid in this bowl. Finish telling the story.

Then go to the third bowl to make the application. Sprinkle pepper onto the water. Say: "The pepper represents sin. God is like the king who forgave our sins. But other people sin against us. (Give examples.) If we do not forgive, our hearts hold onto those things and get full of bitterness, and we hurt inside. So God wants us to forgive others just like he forgave us. (Drop one drip of dish washing liquid in the center of the bowl.) When we forgive, it takes away all the darkness (bitterness) and our hearts can be clean, full of joy and peace.

MEMORY VERSE

"Forgive as the Lord forgave you" (Colossians 3:13).

To help the children remember the verse, make six beanbag
sock balls. Put about ¼ cup of dried beans or rice in each of six
baby socks or other old socks (without holes). Tie each sock
just above the beans or rice to make a beanbag ball with a
"tail" on it. With permanent marker, write one word of the
verse on each ball. Give one ball to each of six people. Sit in a
circle. The person with the ball that has *Forgive* written on it, tosses
that ball to another person while saying *Forgive*. The person who has *as*
tosses it, saying *as*. The person with *the* tosses it and says *the*. Continue until the
verse has been said. Then start over again with the people who have caught the balls.

ACTIVITIES

Choose one or more of the following activities to support the story and to provide a springboard for discussion.

CLEAN HEART. Cut a heart shape out of paper. Make a circle of tape and stick it onto the back of the
heart. Stick the heart onto another piece of paper. Paint over the heart and the paper it's on. Say: "The
paint represents the bad feelings we have toward someone who has wronged us. When we pull the
paper heart off the page, there is a clean, unpainted heart underneath. That's what forgiving does."

HUNGER. Talk about baking cookies (or biscuits). Make it sound delicious. Talk about how good they
taste and how wonderful they smell. Ask: "But does talking about them fill our stomachs? We just get
hungrier. Which is better: to talk about baking or to bake? Which is better: to talk about doing what
Jesus told us or to do it?" Then bake cookies or biscuits using ready-made dough or making them from
scratch. Use these cookies or biscuits for snack and fellowship time.

HOW MANY WORDS? Use this activity for groups in which everyone can read and spell, or with
nonreaders who are old enough to be interested in watching and "helping" a reader figure out words.
Give each person a piece of paper. Ask each one to write *forgive* at the top of the paper. Then ask him to
write down as many words as he can make out of the letters in the word *forgive*. Let each person read
the words he has found. Ask if *give* is one of the words. Ask if *for* is one of the words. Point out that to
forgive someone is to *give for* them. Say: "We *give* mercy *for* them. We *give* up our anger *for* their benefit.
What else could we *give for* them to show we *forgive*?"

MIRROR IMAGE. Two people stand face-to-face. One person is chosen to be the leader. When he
moves, the other person tries to move exactly as he does, as in a mirror image. Discuss how we try to
do what Jesus did and forgive as God forgave us.

QUESTIONS

1. What are some things Jesus told us to do? What are some things he did?
2. Is it possible to be like Jesus? If so, how?
3. Why is it important to forgive?
4. Is it easy to forgive someone?

KIDS' COUNCIL

BRING IT HOME

- How do you forgive someone? What if they don't say they're sorry? What if they're not sorry?
- Tell about a time you forgave someone.
- Is there someone you need to forgive now? How can you forgive?
- Can you forgive and forget about it too? If so, how?

SHARE AND PRAY

- Ask the children to share their concerns and pray for each other.
- Thank God for forgiving us of our sins.
- Ask God to help us forgive people who have done wrong to us. If a child has decided during this time that there's someone he needs to forgive, encourage him to go ahead and forgive that person in his heart and to tell God that he forgives that person.

ADULT STUDY QUESTIONS

- Do you find it easy or hard to forgive others? If it's hard, why do you think it's so hard?
- Read and discuss Matthew 18:35. Why do you think God is so firm about forgiving others?
- Read and discuss Hebrews 12:14, 15. How could you apply these verses to forgiveness?
- Read and discuss 2 Corinthians 2:10, 11. What does this suggest about forgiveness and unforgiveness?
- Is it realistic to expect to forgive and forget too? Why or why not? Share any practical suggestions you may have to help forgive and to help forget.

SNACK AND FELLOWSHIP

Cookies or Biscuits. If you made cookies or biscuits for the Hunger activity, you may eat them now. If you did not, provide cookies or biscuits for snack time. You may link it to the theme by having discussion as suggested in the Hunger activity.

Marriage

OBJECTIVE: *To recognize God's perfect plan for marriage, while affirming God's continuing love for those who are married, single, or divorced.*

WORSHIP

Sing praise and worship songs as well as songs about love that are familiar and meaningful to your group. Here are some suggestions.

"All Consuming Fire"
"Bind Us Together, Lord"
"Change My Heart, O God"
"Great Is Thy Faithfulness"
"His Banner Over Me Is Love"
"Peace Like a River"

"Praise the Lord Together"
"Pure and Holy I Would Be"
"The Steadfast Love of the Lord"
"They'll Know We Are Christians
    by Our Love"
"Thy Word"

STORY

Jesus' Teaching on Marriage, Matthew 19:1-12
- The Pharisees ask Jesus if it's right to divorce for any reason.
- Jesus says God planned for a man and his wife to become one with each other.
- Jesus says divorce is wrong unless one of the partners has already left the marriage for another person.

Before your group gathers, glue two pieces of paper together. Let them dry. When your group gets together, read the Scripture. As you finish the reading, pull the two pieces of paper apart. If the glue is dry, they will not come apart without tearing each other. Compare the glued paper to marriage and the tearing apart to divorce.

Note: If children in your group have divorced parents, be sensitive. It's important for them to know what is God's best for them when they marry. But right now they may feel confused and hurt. They may even feel that the divorce is their fault. Let them share their feelings and stories if they feel comfortable. End with encouragement and hope, remembering the last lesson about forgiveness. See the Dough Sea activity later in this lesson.

MEMORY VERSE

"What God has joined together, let man not separate" (Matthew 19:6).

Discuss the meaning of the word *separate*. To help the children remember this verse, suggest that everyone say the verse together with hand motions. Each person should fold his hands in front of him on the word *together* and pull them apart on the word *separate*. This will also help younger children remember what the word *separate* means.

ACTIVITIES

Choose one or more of the following activities to support the story and to provide a springboard for discussion.

JOINED HEARTS. Give each person a 12-inch square of waxed paper. Draw a heart on it with permanent marker. Put newspaper on an ironing board and put the square of waxed paper on it. Each person sharpens two colors of crayon, dropping the shavings in the middle of the heart. Put another piece of waxed paper on top. Iron them on a low setting to melt wax and blend colors. Talk about love, two people joining lives like colors blending in the heart. Ask: "What would happen if you pulled the two pieces of waxed paper apart?"

HEART BREAD. For each person, cut two slices of bread into heart shapes. Each person presses one slice flat and bakes it at 350 degrees for 15 minutes. Compare the baked bread and soft bread. Ask: "What happens when you bend the hard bread? What happens when you bend the soft bread?" Discuss hard and soft hearts in people. Review forgiveness. Discuss marriage.

A TOWER. Build a tower with blocks or paper cups. Show how each block holds a place, like a promise that says, "I will hold up the ones depending on me." Pull out one of the bottom blocks. What happens? Discuss marriage and divorce.

DOUGH SEA. Make a play dough sea with waves (3 parts flour, 1 part salt, 1 part water). On small strips of paper, everyone writes problems, including divorce (and perhaps jealousy, anger, cheating). Tape each small paper to a toothpick. Stick it into a wave. Ask: "If you're a swimmer, what can waves do to you? What do you need?" Give everyone candy Lifesavers. Ask: "Who is our Lifesaver?" Each person writes on paper: "Jesus is my . . ." Glue a candy Lifesaver at the end.

QUESTIONS

1. Why did God plan for people to marry?
2. Why is it important for a husband and wife to promise each other they'll never leave each other?
3. Is it important for both husband and wife to be dedicated to God? Why or why not?
4. Does God forgive people who are divorced? Does he love them?
5. Will God ever stop loving you? Will he ever leave you?

KIDS' COUNCIL

BRING IT HOME

- What helps people live together in peace?
- What should a person look for in someone he may marry?
- Is divorce the fault of the children in the family?
- Can you decide now that when you marry, you'll marry someone who loves Jesus?
- Can you decide now that when you marry, you'll stay married?
- If your parents are divorced, have you forgiven them?

SHARE AND PRAY

- Ask the children to share their concerns and pray for each other.
- Thank God that he will never leave us. Thank him that he will never stop loving us.
- If children of divorced parents feel like they need to forgive their parents, they can tell God in prayer.
- Pray that God will lead each child, when the time is right, to decide whether to marry or not. Ask God to show them who he has chosen for them to marry.

ADULT STUDY QUESTIONS

- What is hard about living with someone all the time? Why is it hard? If it's so hard, why did God tell us not to leave each other?
- If you are divorced, and you feel comfortable talking about it, share your viewpoint. If you feel like you shouldn't have gotten a divorce, or didn't want it, do you feel guilty and why? Have you forgiven yourself? Remember last week's lesson on forgiveness.
- How can we teach our children about divorce without making them judgmental and critical toward their friends, their friends' parents, and perhaps even toward their own divorced parents?
- Let the couple in your group who has been married the longest give a testimony about the difficulties and the blessings of being together so long. Let others who have been married a long time add their comments. How can we encourage others to stay married?

SNACK AND FELLOWSHIP

Wedding Cookies. Buy a package of wedding cookies and make punch by mixing fruit juice with lemon-lime carbonated soda. Add a scoop of sherbet if you want. Talk about weddings and marriage.

Intercessory Prayer

OBJECTIVE: *To recognize that Jesus and others intercede for us before God, and we can intercede for others.*

WORSHIP

Sing praise and worship songs as well as songs about prayer that are familiar and meaningful to your group. Here are some suggestions.

"Come Into His Presence"
"I Will Call Upon the Lord"
"Jesus Loves Even Me"
"Jesus Loves Me"
"Jesus Loves the Little Children"

"Only by Grace"
"Standin' in the Need of Prayer"
"What a Friend We Have in Jesus"
"Whisper a Prayer"

STORY

Children Brought to Jesus for Prayer, Matthew 19:13-15

■ People bring their children to Jesus.

■ Jesus' disciples tell the children to go away.

■ Jesus tells the disciples to let the children come, and he blesses them.

Ask the adults to make a circle, and ask the children to sit outside the circle. As you read, ask the children to try to come into the circle but tell the adults not to let them. Then when Jesus tells the disciples in the story to let the children come, the adults let the children into the circle. Finish the story with the children sitting inside the circle.

MEMORY VERSE

"Let the little children come to me, and do not hinder them, for the kingdom of heaven belongs to such as these" (Matthew 19:14).

Talk about the meaning of the word *hinder*. Help the children remember the verse by singing it to the tune of "Jesus Loves Me."

ACTIVITIES

Choose one or more of the following activities to support the story and to provide a springboard for discussion.

Note: When talking to children, it may help to refer to intercessors as people who pray for other people, places, or events. Jesus prayed for the children, so he was an intercessor. Romans 8:34 says that even now, Jesus "is at the right hand of God and is also interceding for us."

OVER/UNDER RELAY. Players line up behind each other in two teams. Give the first player on each team a ball. The object is to get the ball from the first player to the last player. The first player represents a person who needs God's help, the last player represents God, and the ball represents the message. Ask: "How might the message get to God?" On "Go," the first player passes the ball over his head, the second passes it under, through his legs, the third passes it over, so the ball goes over and under to the last person. The last person runs to the front of the line with the ball and the game continues until one team wins by making it back to their original lineup.

COTTON BALL RELAY. Players line up behind each other in two teams. Give each person a cotton ball. In front of each team, place a box far enough away so players can't possibly throw the cotton ball into the box. Each team must choose an intercessor. This person stands between his team and their box. When you say, "Go," the first person tries to throw the cotton ball into the box. The intercessor picks it up wherever it lands, puts it into the box, and then runs to the back of the line. The first thrower becomes the intercessor. The second person throws. Each team tries to be the first to get their cotton balls into their box. Talk about how an intercessor goes between others to help. Talk about what this means in prayer.

LINE DESIGN. Tell each person to put six dots at random on a sheet of paper. Then, using rulers, each person draws a line from each dot to every other dot to make a line design. Use plain or colored pencils or markers. Compare each dot to a person. Say: "Each person prays for the others. If the lines were prayers, how many prayers are being said in this picture?"

CODE BREAKER. Write down a code in which one symbol or shape stands for each letter in the alphabet. Choose one person to be the Code Breaker. Give the Code Breaker a copy of the code. Everyone else chooses a partner to work with. One partner looks at the code and writes something simple, like "Jesus loves me" or "happy birthday" in code. He then gives the message to his partner, without talking. The Code Breaker can show the code to the partners trying to decode the message. The Code Breaker is an intercessor. He goes between the two partners, helping them understand each other. Ask: "How was Jesus an intercessor between the children and God? How is he an intercessor now between you and God?"

QUESTIONS

1. What is prayer?
2. What kinds of prayers are there?
3. When do you pray?
4. What is intercession? Why is it important?

KIDS' COUNCIL

BRING IT HOME

- If you were one of the children who was brought to Jesus, what do you think he would pray for you? What would you want him to pray for you?
- Read Romans 8:26, 27, 34. Who intercedes for us? What does that mean?
- Can you think of a person who intercedes for you?
- Can you think of a person, place, or event that you can intercede for? Who will you intercede for this week?

SHARE AND PRAY

- Ask the children to share their concerns and pray for each other. Explain that when you pray for someone else, you are interceding for them.
- Thank God that Jesus and the Holy Spirit are interceding for them.
- Intercede for other people, places, or events.

ADULT STUDY QUESTIONS

- Why do you need an intercessor? Read and discuss Hebrews 4:14-16; 7:23-25.
- Read and discuss 1 Corinthians 2:9-14. Why do we need the Holy Spirit to intercede for us? Read and discuss Romans 8:26, 27.
- Read and discuss Matthew 5:44; Ephesians 6:18; and 1 Timothy 2:1-4. Who should we intercede for?
- Do you know of someone who interceded for you as you were growing up? Do you think that made a difference in your life? If so, how?
- Share concerns and intercede for each other.

SNACK AND FELLOWSHIP

Bread Sticks. Let each child roll out one stick of dough from a can of refrigerated bread stick dough. Roll it in cinnamon and sugar. The child makes a thumbprint at each end of the stick and one in the center. Put some jelly in each thumbprint. Bake according to package directions. Say: "The thumbprint at one end represents someone who needs prayer, the print on the other end stands for God. You could be the one in the middle praying (interceding)."

The Law and the Heart

OBJECTIVE: *To encourage each other to "store up treasures in heaven" by setting our hearts on things of eternal value.*

WORSHIP

Sing praise and worship songs as well as songs about commitment to the Lord that are familiar and meaningful to your group. Here are some suggestions.

"All Hail the Power of Jesus' Name"
"Change My Heart, O God"
"I Have Decided to Follow Jesus"
"Into My Heart"
"Jesus in the Morning"

"Jesus, Name Above All Names"
"Lord, I Lift Your Name on High"
"More Love, More Power"
"Pure and Holy"
"This Is My Story"

STORY

The Rich Young Ruler, Matthew 19:16-26
■ A rich man asks Jesus what he should do to have eternal life.
■ Jesus tells him to sell his possessions, give to the poor, and follow him.
■ The man goes away sad.

Choose someone to represent the rich man. Let each person give him an object of some kind. Try to fill his arms with lots of stuff. Give another person a piece of paper or poster board on which is written *eternal life*. Read the story and ask the person holding the stuff to face the person holding the poster. When you tell about the young man going away sad, the person holding the stuff should walk away. Point out how the choice he made showed what he really valued most.

MEMORY VERSE

"Where your treasure is, there your heart will be also" (Matthew 6:21).

Help the children learn the verse by singing it to the tune of "Row, Row, Row Your Boat."

ACTIVITIES

Choose one or more of the following activities to support the story and to provide a springboard for discussion.

VOLLEYBALL. Play volleyball. You can use a beach ball or other soft, large ball. For a net, tie a sheet or length of yarn or string between trees or other uprights. Ask: "Does everyone know all the rules? Does everyone agree on all the rules? If you play the game well, does that mean you know the person who first invented it? If you do all the things you know Jesus would want you to do, does that mean you know Jesus? What's the difference?" Talk about the young man keeping all the laws but not giving his heart to Jesus.

COIN RUBBINGS. Give each person a piece of plain white paper. Place a variety of coins under the paper. Have each person rub over the coins with a crayon to reveal the image on the paper. Discuss the story. Talk about people trusting money instead of trusting Jesus. Ask: "Is money something you can trust?"

DESIGN-A-COIN. Give each person a small Styrofoam picnic plate. Let him turn the plate over and cover it with foil. Using pencils, everyone draws a design on the foil as if he is designing a coin. Discuss the story and questions from the previous activity.

IDOLS. Ask everyone to look through magazines and cut out pictures of things that people might make idols (something more important than the Lord to them, something they put their hope and trust in). Glue these on paper to make a montage. Discuss things that people value above the Lord. Talk about why we can't rely on those things.

QUESTIONS

1. What was the rich man's treasure? Where was his heart?
2. Why do you think Jesus asked the rich man to sell what he had?
3. What do you think Jesus meant when he said that it's hard for a rich man to get into God's kingdom?

KIDS' COUNCIL

BRING IT HOME

- What are some things that kids might trust in? Are these things worth trusting? Why or why not?
- If you asked Jesus the same question the rich man asked, what do you think Jesus might tell you? What heart treasure would he ask you to give up for him?
- How can you show that you think God is the most important?
- How will you put God first this week?

SHARE AND PRAY

- Ask the children to share their concerns and pray for each other.
- If there are children who have not put Jesus first in their hearts, but would like to, encourage them to tell that to God in prayer.
- Thank God for giving them eternal life.

ADULT STUDY QUESTIONS

- How did the rich man think he could get eternal life? How can we get eternal life?
- What are some things that could be idols today? Are these things worth trusting in? Why or why not?
- If you were to ask Jesus the same question the rich man asked, what might Jesus ask you to give up for him?
- What do you think Jesus meant when he said that it's hard for a rich man to go into the kingdom of heaven? Are we rich? What could keep us from going into the kingdom of heaven?

SNACK AND FELLOWSHIP

Ask someone to bring cookies or muffins for a snack, but don't let anyone know who baked them. Talk about the rules of good table manners. Ask: "Even though you enjoy these treats and follow all the rules of good table manners, does that mean you know the cook?" Talk about how the rich man knew and followed all the rules but didn't really know Jesus. There were other things that were more important to him than Jesus and eternal life.

God Answers Prayer

OBJECTIVE: *To encourage each other to always pray and not give up.*

WORSHIP

Sing praise and worship songs as well as songs about prayer that are familiar and meaningful to your group. Here are some suggestions.

"God Is So Good"

"He Has Made Me Glad"

"Only by Grace"

"Standin' in the Need of Prayer"

"Sweet Hour of Prayer"

"The Steadfast Love of the Lord"

"What a Friend We Have in Jesus"

"Whisper a Prayer"

STORY

The Persistent Widow, Luke 18:1-8
- A woman keeps asking a judge for justice.
- The judge gives her what she wants just to keep her from bothering him.
- Jesus says God will help us when we ask him.

Before your group meets, ask one person to be the judge and the other to be the widow. Ask the judge to pretend to read a newspaper silently and ignore the widow. Ask the widow to do different things to try to get the judge's attention: tap him on the arm, jump up and down, wave, tug at his sleeve. They should do this the whole time you are reading the passage. When you read the part about the judge finally giving the woman what she wanted, the judge should say, "OK! OK! I'll give you what you want!"

MEMORY VERSE

"Jesus told his disciples a parable to show them that they should always pray and not give up" (Luke 18:1).

Discuss the meaning of the word *parable* and repeat the verse together several times. Then, to remember the point of the verse, sing part of it to the tune of "Jimmy Cracked Corn."

ACTIVITIES

Choose one or more of the following activities to support the story and to provide a springboard for discussion.

WALL HANGINGS. Give each person seven index cards. On each card, the person writes one word of the verse, "Always pray and don't give up." Put the reference, Luke 18:1, on the last card. Punch a hole in the top and bottom of each card. Thread a ribbon or yarn through the holes, tying it at each top hole to keep the card from slipping. Tie a loop in the top of the ribbon or yarn to hang it.

PRAYER BOOKLETS. Fold sheets of paper in half. Staple them on the fold. Each person places one hand, palm down, fingers together on the top sheet of the booklet. He traces around his hand to make praying hands. Inside, he writes prayers and leaves spaces to record the answers. Discuss Luke 18:1-8.

DON'T GIVE UP. Play a game with index cards. There should be three or four players for each game. For each player in the game there should be seven cards, each marked as in the Wall Hanging activity. For example, there should be one card per player that says *Always*, one that says *pray*, and so on. Shuffle cards and deal three to each player. The rest go facedown in the center. The first player asks another for a card that matches one in his own hand. If the other player has that card, he gives it to the first player. If he doesn't have that card, he says, "Don't give up," and the first player has to draw from the cards in the center. When a player gets four cards that match (or three if only three people are playing), he stacks them nearby. The first player to get rid of his cards wins. This is like the game "Go Fish."

SKILLS. Try some physical skills, such as jumping rope, using a hula hoop, throwing a beanbag into a basket or box. You might use milk jugs with the bottoms cut out to throw and catch a ball. Do a crab walk: sit down, support your body with your hands and feet, then walk on hands and feet. Have two people sit back-to-back, link arms, and then try to stand up. Talk about not giving up. Read Luke 18:1-8. Ask: "Why should we not give up praying?"

QUESTIONS

1. How can we pray? When? Where?
2. Do you remember a time when you prayed again and again for something and God finally gave you what you asked for? If so, tell about it.
3. Tell about a time God answered no to a prayer that you or someone else prayed. Why would God answer no?

KIDS' COUNCIL

BRING IT HOME
- Give some reasons why God might not give you what you ask for.
- Read and discuss James 4:1-3.
- Why would God want us to keep on asking after he heard us the first time?
- What can you do to help you remember to pray about something and not to give up?

SHARE AND PRAY
- Ask the children to share their concerns and pray for each other.
- If there are things that some children have kept asking God for, pray again for these things together.
- Thank God for hearing and answering prayers.

ADULT STUDY QUESTIONS
- Why would God want us to keep on asking after he heard us the first time?
- Is there ever a time to stop praying for something before you know God's answer? If so, when?
- Is there something you are praying now that you've been praying for a long time and have not yet seen God's answer? Would you like the group to join you in praying for this?
- Has God ever answered a prayer of yours with a no, and later you were glad he didn't give you what you asked for? Tell about it if you are comfortable sharing that experience.

SNACK AND FELLOWSHIP

Sourdough Bread. Serve hot sourdough bread with butter and jam, jelly, or honey. If someone in your group bakes bread and has sourdough starter, show everyone the starter. If not, tell everyone how sourdough bread is made. (The starter is used over and over again as the leavening agent for the bread.) Use this as a springboard to discuss praying for something over and over again like the widow in the story did.

Serving

OBJECTIVE: *To learn what it means to be a servant and to consider ways to serve others.*

WORSHIP

Sing praise and worship songs as well as songs about serving that are familiar and meaningful to your group. Here are some suggestions.

"Come Bless the Lord"
"Freely, Freely"
"I Have Decided to Follow Jesus"
"They'll Know We Are Christians by Our Love"
"This Little Light of Mine"
"What a Mighty God We Serve"

STORY

Disciples Want to Be Great in the Kingdom, Matthew 20:20-28

■ The mother of James and John asks Jesus to let her sons rule in his kingdom with him.

■ Jesus says it's God's job to decide who rules with him.

■ Jesus says whoever wants to be great must be a servant.

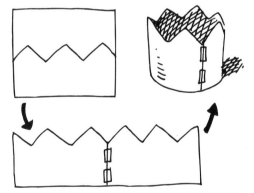

Make two crowns. For each one, cut a piece of plain white paper in half as shown and tape the short ends together. Curve this paper strip around to form a crown and tape or staple it to fit a child. As you tell the story, choose one child to stand on your right wearing a crown and another child to stand on your left wearing a crown. But when Jesus talks about being a servant, give each of them a dustcloth and ask them to dust the furniture.

MEMORY VERSE

"Whoever wants to become great among you must be your servant" (Matthew 20:26).

To help the children remember this verse, ask them to repeat it several times with hand motions. On the word *great*, each child forms a crown shape with their hands and holds it above their heads. On the word *servant*, they kneel.

ACTIVITIES

Choose one or more of the following activities to support the story and to provide a springboard for discussion.

SERVING. Serve someone by washing a car, cleaning a room, weeding a garden, taking out trash. Discuss the Scripture.

APRONS. Ask each child to bring a dish towel. Make aprons out of these by cutting 1-inch vertical slits like button holes, spacing them evenly across one short end of the towel. Let the child weave ribbon or ¾-inch strips of cloth (2 yards long) through the slits. Tie the ends of the ribbon around the waist to put on the apron. If the dish towels are too long, fold them in half. Discuss serving.

SERVANT'S RELAY. Divide into two teams. Mark a starting line and a goal line. The teams line up single file at the starting line. Give the first person on each team a tray with a cup of water on it. When you say, "Go," the first players hurry to the goal line and back without spilling the cup of water. Then each gives his tray to the next person in line, who hurries to the goal and back, and so on. Players must stop to get a refill of water if it spills. Option: carry an egg (plastic or real) in a spoon instead of tray and cup of water. Discuss serving.

SERVANTS' MUSICAL CHAIRS. For eight or more players, divide into two groups. The first group sits in a wide circle on the floor. Provide chairs for every player in the second group except one. Players in the second group walk around the chairs during the music. When the music stops, each tries to touch one chair, calling the name of a player on the floor, who must come and sit in it, while the player who touched the chair sits on the floor. Let the player without a chair control the music for the next round.

QUESTIONS

1. What is serving?
2. Is a servant always a hired person? Who can be a servant?
3. Do you know anyone who is a servant? What does that person do?
4. How was Jesus a servant?

KIDS' COUNCIL

BRING IT HOME
- How do most people in the world try to become great?
- Are you a servant? Tell ways you serve others. Suggest other ways to serve.
- Who will you serve this week?
- How will you serve?

SHARE AND PRAY
- Ask the children to share their concerns and pray for each other.
- Ask God to show them what they can do to serve this week.
- Thank God for giving us people in our lives who serve us, and for sending Jesus to show us how to serve.

ADULT STUDY QUESTIONS

- Tell about someone who has become great in your eyes by becoming a servant.
- What would you list as some character traits of a servant?
- What does the world consider great? How do most people in the world try to become great?
- Read and discuss Philippians 2:5-11. How can you take on this attitude like verse 5 encourages us to?

SNACK AND FELLOWSHIP

Servants and Muffins. Bring boxed muffin mixes and the ingredients required to prepare the muffins. Ask the children to mix, bake, and serve the muffins as part of being servants. Discuss the Scripture.

Seeking and Following Jesus

OBJECTIVE: *To realize what it means to seek Jesus and to encourage each other to seek him.*

WORSHIP

Sing praise and worship songs as well as songs about Jesus that are familiar and meaningful to your group. Here are some suggestions.

"All Consuming Fire"
"As a Deer"
"I Stand, I Stand in Awe of You"
"I Will Call Upon the Lord"
"Into My Heart"

"More Love, More Power"
"My Life Is in You, Lord"
"O Lord, You're Beautiful"
"One Thing I Ask of the Lord"
"Seek Ye First"

STORY

Two Blind Men Seek Jesus, Matthew 20:29-34
- Two blind men call out to Jesus.
- Jesus asks what they want, and they say they want to be able to see.
- Jesus touches their eyes and they are healed.

Ask each person to close his eyes and imagine what it would be like to be blind. Ask him to keep his eyes closed and imagine he is the blind man as you read the story from Scripture. All may open their eyes when you read about Jesus healing the blind men.

MEMORY VERSE

"Those who know your name will trust in you, for you, Lord, have never forsaken those who seek you" (Psalm 9:10).

Talk about the meaning of the word *seek*. Help the children remember the verse by teaching them to sing it to the tune of "Oh, Susanna."

ACTIVITIES

Choose one or more of the following activities to support the story and to provide a springboard for discussion.

FOLLOWING. Play "Follow the Leader." Ask: "Can you follow the leader if you are not watching the leader?" Read and discuss Hebrews 12:2, "Let us fix our eyes on Jesus." Read verse 3 to find out why. Discuss the story. Say: "When the blind men were healed, they followed Jesus."

LISTENING. Everyone sits in a circle with one person in the center, blindfolded. One person in the circle speaks, disguising his voice if he wants, saying: "Maybe I'm tall, maybe I'm small. Try to guess. Who am I?" The person in the center tries to guess who spoke. Then he trades places with that person and chooses a new person to speak. Talk about how the blind man learned things by listening. Discuss the Scripture. Talk about seeking Jesus.

GUESS THE SOUND. Make a recording of common sounds (water dripping, dog barking, phone ringing, hammer, typewriter, piano, door slam). Play these one at a time and let everyone guess what the sound is. Talk about how the blind men heard that Jesus was coming by and began to seek him.

MASKS. Make half-masks by cutting large paper plates in half. The mask fits over the eyes, round side up. Cut an arch along the straight side for the nose. Punch a hole in each side and tie string to the holes and around the person's head to hold the mask on. Mark where the eyes should go. With the mask off, cut *U* shapes for the eyes, leaving the top of the *U* attached. Fold along that line, so the eyes open and close. Everyone may color and decorate his mask, gluing on yarn hair, if he wants. Talk about the blind men seeking Jesus.

QUESTIONS

1. Has anyone ever told you to be quiet? How do you think the blind men felt when people told them to be quiet? Should they have been quiet? Why or why not?
2. What does it mean to *seek* the Lord?
3. What did the blind men do after they were healed? How can you follow Jesus?

KIDS' COUNCIL

BRING IT HOME

- Read Psalm 9:10; 34:10; 105:4; Proverbs 8:17; and Jeremiah 29:13. What do these Scriptures say about seeking the Lord?
- Even though people see with their physical eyes, can they be blind in their spiritual eyes, in their hearts? How can you tell if someone's spiritual eyes are blind?
- Read Hebrews 12:2. What does it mean to *fix our eyes on Jesus?* How can you fix your eyes on Jesus each day?
- How will you seek the Lord this week?
- How can you help other people seek Jesus?

SHARE AND PRAY

- Ask the children to share their concerns and pray for each other.
- Thank God for letting us find him whenever we seek him.
- Ask God to show us how to help others seek and find him.

ADULT STUDY QUESTIONS

- Read and discuss Psalm 9:10. Why would this be true? What are some names of God? Use your own words to describe the God you have found as you have sought him. Explain.
- Read and discuss Psalm 34:10. What is God's promise to you if you seek him?
- Read and discuss Psalm 105:4; Proverbs 8:17; and Jeremiah 29:13. What do these Scriptures have to say about seeking the Lord?
- Even though people see with their physical eyes, can they be blind in their spiritual eyes, in their hearts? How can you tell if someone's spiritual eyes are blind?
- Is there ever a time when a person can or should stop seeking the Lord? Explain.

SNACK AND FELLOWSHIP

Hide and Snack. Bring small individual size bags of chips or pretzels and small boxes of juices. While the adults are meeting together, ask the children to hide one snack (a bag of chips and a box of juice) for each adult. When it's time for their snack, adults must *seek* their snack. Children can give them hints and tell them when they are close (hot) or far away (cold) from their snack. Talk about seeking Jesus.

Each Person Is Important

OBJECTIVE: *To learn what the body of Christ is, and to recognize each person's importance in the body.*

WORSHIP

Sing praise and worship songs as well as songs about unity that are familiar and meaningful to your group. Here are some suggestions.

"Blest Be the Tie That Binds"
"Come Bless the Lord"
"Father Abraham"
"He's Got the Whole World in His Hands"
"I'm in the Lord's Army"
"Let Us Break Bread Together"

"Now Thank We All Our God"
"Praise the Lord Together"
"They'll Know We Are Christians by Our Love"
"Zacchaeus"

STORY

Zacchaeus, Luke 19:1-10

■ Zacchaeus wants to see Jesus, but he's too short to see over the crowd.
■ Zacchaeus climbs a tree so he can see.
■ Jesus stops at the tree and tells Zacchaeus to come down because he needs to go to Zacchaeus' house.

Tell this story outdoors under a tree, if possible. If it's safe, let a child climb the tree to act like Zacchaeus. If you must tell the story indoors, ask a strong adult to act like the tree and hold a small child in his arms or on his shoulders, so the child can represent Zacchaeus.

MEMORY VERSE

"In humility consider others better than yourselves" (Philippians 2:3).

Help the children remember this verse by crowning someone else while they say the verse. Make a crown by forming a strip of paper into circle that will fit on top of people's heads. Tape or staple it in place. Give the crown to one person. While that person says the memory verse, he walks over to another person and puts the crown on that person's head to show that he is honoring that person. Then the person with the crown takes it off, says the verse and places the crown on someone else's head. That person is the next to say the verse and crown someone, and so on until everyone has had a chance to say the verse.

ACTIVITIES

Choose one or more of the following activities to support the story and to provide a springboard for discussion.

FACE SCULPTURES. Give each person a large sheet of aluminum foil. Gently help him mold it around his face and sculpt his features. If you do this activity with children only, line the face sculptures up and let the grown-ups guess who's who. Discuss how each part of our physical bodies does its work. Ask: "How is the church like a body? Who is the head? Is everyone important?"

JOINTS. Describe different types of joints, asking each person to find those kinds of joints on his body: no movement (joints in skull), little movement (backbone), hinges (like knee, elbow), ball and socket (like shoulder). Show a picture of a skeleton if you have one (check an encyclopedia). Point out the joints. Let everyone take turns suggesting and leading exercises or movements that show the working of joint types. Read Ephesians 1:22, 23; 4:16. Say: "Everyone is as important to the body of believers as joints are to our own physical bodies."

STATUE RACE. Mark a start and finish line. Choose one person to be the director. He stands on the finish line facing the others, who line up on the start line. When the director turns his back, the others run toward the finish line. But when the director turns around, everyone must "freeze" as though they were statues. Anyone the director sees moving must return to the start line. The one to reach the finish line first becomes the next director. After the race, sit and rest and discuss how each part of your physical body helped in running the race. Talk about how each person in the body of Christ is important.

FUNNY PEOPLE. Give everyone old magazines and catalogues. (Check to see that any inappropriate sections have been thrown out.) Let everyone cut out heads, arms, legs, and bodies and place them in separate stacks. Then each person chooses the arms and legs, heads and bodies from the different stacks and glues them onto paper to make a new figure. Discuss how each body part does its work both in our physical bodies and in the church. **Option:** cut out only facial features and glue them inside a circle to make a new face.

QUESTIONS

1. Why was Zacchaeus important to Jesus? Why are you important to Jesus?
2. What is the church? How is the church like a body?
3. What does your head do for your body? The Bible says Jesus is the head of the church, his people. What does Jesus do for his people?
4. Why is it important that each of us does our part? Is any one part more important than the others?
5. How did Jesus do what our memory verse talks about?

KIDS' COUNCIL

BRING IT HOME

- Do you ever feel small and insignificant like Zacchaeus? What does the story of Zacchaeus help you learn?
- Read Ephesians 4:16. What are ligaments? Name some of our physical body parts and tell how each does its work. Name some of the different jobs in Jesus' body, the church.
- Which part of Jesus' body of believers do you think you are, or would you like to be? Why?
- Is there someone you know who doesn't feel like an important part of Jesus' followers, his body? How can you let that person know that he's important?

SHARE AND PRAY

- Ask the children to share their concerns and pray for each other.
- Thank God that he cares for people who may not seem important, and that they can be part of his kingdom, his church, his group of believers.
- Ask God to show us how we are important to his people and what our special job is in his body.

ADULT STUDY QUESTIONS

- If Jesus was coming to your town tomorrow and you planned to go watch for him to come, who would be Zacchaeus? Whose house would Jesus visit? Would we complain that Jesus had gone to be a guest of a sinner?
- Which part of Jesus' body of believers are you? If you are not sure, tell which part you think you might be or would like to be. How do you know which part you are?
- Read the entire passage from which the memory verse was taken, Philippians 2:3, 4. Does this mean everyone? Do you find this easy or difficult to do? Can you think of a person you have a hard time considering better than yourself? Are you looking to the interests of others? How can we do this?

SNACK AND FELLOWSHIP

Breadstick Men. Make these ahead of time, or let children make them as an activity early in your group session so they'll be ready for snack time. Use canned, refrigerated breadstick dough. Give each child one or two sticks of dough. Sprinkle the dough with flour. Cut sticks into sections to make legs, body, arms, and head. Arrange these to make a person and pinch the sections together. Bake according to package directions. Talk about how all of us are important parts of Jesus' church just as all the parts of our body are important to us.

Enjoy all the titles in Karyn Henley's new *Families Learning Together* series!

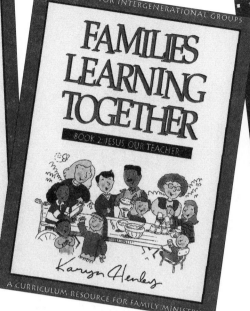

FAMILIES LEARNING TOGETHER SERIES

Karyn Henley. The new *Families Learning Together* series makes learning about the life of Christ a family affair! Each book contains 15 sessions for intergenerational groups in such settings as family nights, Sunday school, small groups, cell groups and family home study. The four titles are:

BOOK 1: JESUS' EARLY LIFE (42055)

BOOK 2: JESUS, OUR TEACHER (42056)

BOOK 3: JESUS, HEALER AND HELPER (42057)

BOOK 4: JESUS' LAST WEEK (42058)

☞ *Also new!*

FUN FAMILY FESTIVALS

24 Super Celebrations for Family Ministry
Nanette Goings. Looking for creative things to do to bring church families together? *Fun Family Festivals* is great for family learning and entertainment. It's a valuable resource packed with ideas for 24 family events/celebrations that are easy to organize and sponsor. (03573)

KARYN HENLEY
is an award-winning children's communicator and author of God's Story, The Beginner's Bible and co-author of My First Hymnal. Karyn also has created a number of teaching resources, such as Child-Sensitive Teaching, Creative Bible Learning: Arts and Crafts, Creative Bible Learning: Science and Cooking and a series of file-folder curriculum units for children's ministry from Standard Publishing.

☞ *All of these great resources are awaiting your family at your local Christian bookstore!*

The Great Green Cookbook

More than 200 irresistible
vegetarian recipes
from around the world

ROSAMOND RICHARDSON

CONTEMPORARY BOOKS

The Cataloging-in-Publication Data for this title is on file with the United States
Library of Congress.

Cover design by Monica Baziuk
Cover and interior photography by Debbie Patterson
Food preparation and styling by Jane Suthering
Interior design by Neil Sayer
Editing by Catherine Ward

This edition is published in 1997 by arrangement with Kyle Cathie Limited.

Photography © 1996 by Debbie Patterson
Layout © 1996 by Kyle Cathie Limited
Copyright © 1996 by Rosamond Richardson
Published by Contemporary Books
An imprint of NTC/Contemporary Publishing Company
4255 West Touhy Avenue, Lincolnwood (Chicago), Illinois 60646-1975 U.S.A.
Printed in Hong Kong
International Standard Book Number: 0-8092-2980-3
18   17   16   15   14   13   12   11   10   9   8   7   6   5   4   3   2

My thanks to Emily for providing several excuses to visit San Francisco; to Peter for doing most of the eating; and to Kyle Cathie and her excellent team for their enthusiasm and tenacity in bringing the book to such a high standard of production.

NOTES TO THE AMERICAN EDITION

Some of the recipes contain certain readily available ingredients whose names as listed might not be familiar to the North American reader. The following list is a glossary of those ingredients:

aubergine	eggplant
baps	any soft rolls, such as hamburger buns
beetleaf	Swiss chard
beetroot	garden beets
broad beans	fava beans
caster sugar	superfine sugar
celeriac	celery root
courgettes	zucchini
cress	watercress
granary flour	all-purpose flour
groundnuts, groundnut oil	peanuts, peanut oil
lambs' lettuce	field lettuce
mangetout	sugar snap peas
pine kernels	pine nuts
pulses	legumes
ratafia biscuits	*amaretti* (cookies)
rocket	arugula
runner beans	pinto beans
salsify	*aka* oyster plant
swedes	rutabaga
sweetcorn	corn
spring onions	scallions; green onions
vol-au-vent	puff pastry
wholemeal flour	whole wheat flour

CONTENTS

INTRODUCTION	6
VEGETABLES THROUGH THE SEASONS	8
SHOPPING & STOCKING THE CUPBOARD	28
ESSENTIAL EQUIPMENT	29
SOME USEFUL TECHNIQUES	30
STARTERS	33
SOUPS	47
EGGS & CHEESE	59
SNACKS, DIPS & BREAD	69
TORTILLAS, PANCAKES & FRITTAS	83
VEGETABLES	
SIDE DISHES	93
MAIN COURSES	98
THE VERSATILE POTATO	111
PURELY PASTA	121
PULSES, RICE & POLENTA	137
SAVOURY PIES & PASTRIES	153
ENTERTAINING	
STARTERS	163
MAIN COURSES	175
SPARKLING SALADS	187
DELECTABLE DESSERTS	209
BASIC RECIPES	218
NUTRITION CHART	219
INDEX	221

INTRODUCTION

This book celebrates the pleasures of cooking with a wide variety of fresh vegetables, herbs and spices that grow through the seasons around the world. Many of the recipes are inspired by international food traditions – regional herbs and spices giving the dishes distinction and vitality. All the vegetables, salads, fruits, nuts, seeds and grains present, with their different flavours and textures, huge possibilities for creative cooking.

But eating well doesn't necessarily depend on complexity or exotica: straightforward, quick recipes using everyday ingredients are a tribute to

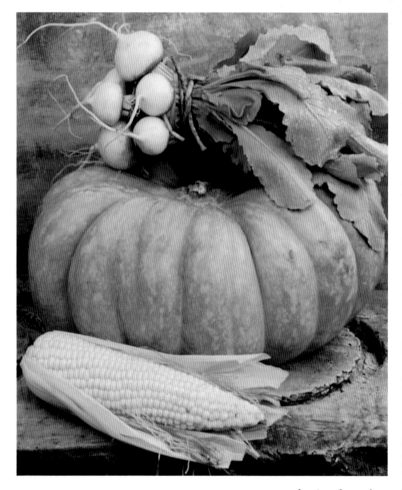

simplicity. A simple cauliflower stir-fry with ginger and garlic can, for me, beat the most elaborate haute cuisine hands down. It's the kind of food that I love. In essence, the beauty of eating like this lies in the skilful but simple use of varied and exciting ingredients. Most people appreciate quick, accessible methods that produce rewarding tastes.

There is a major trend for eating far less meat, poultry and even fish, particularly among the young. This rapidly increasing awareness recognises the benefits of eating more plant foods. After all, it is healthy for the body and good for the bank balance. People are more aware than they ever have been, too, of the ethical issues involved: of compassion in farming and the ecological, health and social problems that rearing meat present. These people are the cooks of the next generation, and this book is for them.

Whether they are young people starting out in life, single or married, couples with small children, students, teenagers, people who have decided to drop meat from their diet, desperate mothers with a sole vegetarian in the family, people who can't afford to eat meat all the time, busy folk who want quick inspired recipes, or anyone who just loves beautiful food – this book will offer both inspiration and practical guidance. There is a comprehensive guide to the ingredients, to nutrition, to essential equipment, and useful hints on shopping and storage.

The recipes are aimed to inspire and satisfy the beginner in the kitchen, as well as the more experienced cook. The more skilful will enjoy the challenges of creating beautiful sauces for stunning new dishes, of making elegant meals for special occasions, while novices will find the recipes full of practical common-sense advice, basic information and simple techniques, yet reap the rewards of wonderful flavours as they go. This is a comprehensive guide as well as a book of inspired recipes. It is the perfect Christmas or wedding present for this generation of young people starting up in life.

When I first started to cook, Elizabeth David was my major inspiration. Her books are the most well-fingered on my shelf. Along with the help of Julia Child and Robert Carrier, I learned some of the basic arts of French and Mediterranean cookery. An Indian friend showed me many of the secrets of Indian and Indonesian cuisine, and she and I travelled the subcontinent together. Wherever I travel I take a notebook. Down go notes of memorable meals and menus, making inspired guesses as to how the dish was made. Re-creating the food as I adapt and simplify it has the bonus of re-experiencing past magic. A mountain walk in Crete or an evening on the edge of the Sahara in Morocco. A memory of the busy streets of Hyderabad or the urban cafés of Paris. Or the tremendous liveliness, variety and quality of the food in San Francisco which has inspired my imagination in recent years.

The cooking universe has expanded with the supermarket revolution. From a world where even in London it was difficult to get hold of garlic and aubergines, the shelves are now stacked with exotic produce from all corners of the globe. I began to experiment with East-Asian food when an ethnic grocery opened nearby, and have learned to stock my larder with their brilliant ingredients – including jars of magical sauces that transform my everyday cookery. Both Far-Eastern and Mexican influences in San Francisco have educated my palate further.

Although I did not realise it at the time, the grounding in classic European cookery was to bring a fabulous dimension to the cooking that I now do all the time. Great sauces from around the world, pasta from Italy, spicy vegetables from India, noodle dishes from Indonesia, tortillas from Mexico, stir-fries from China... The most delicious of these were made with the local vegetables and herbs or spices, and often came with wonderful sauces. So I have translated these regional specialities into recipes that you can make simply, quickly – and often cheaply – at home. Great traditions, great ingredients, great food.

● freezes well

V Vegan

◆ can be prepared ahead of time to this point

VEGETABLES THROUGH THE SEASONS

Vegetables can be classified as green leaves, roots or tubers, pods and seeds, fruits, bulbs, stalks, shoots, thistles and fungi. Throughout the history of man, vegetables have provided important nutrients in the diet and have been recognised as essential to good health. Vegetables are a source of plant protein and the essential minerals and vitamins needed in a balanced diet. They have negligible amounts of fat and a high water content, making them ideal for a society which leads a comparatively sedentary way of life.

Vegetables are always best eaten as soon as possible after they are picked: they lose their nutritive value during long storage and refrigeration. They are always tastiest in season – forced vegetables never have that same intensity of flavour. Always wash your vegetables thoroughly before use, and peel them as little as possible as much of the goodness is frequently found in the skin. Many vegetables are improved with light cooking rather than stewing – with a few exceptions – so stir-frying is one of the best and easiest way to cook them. However, they also lend themselves beautifully to composite dishes, as many of the recipes illustrate.

The story of vegetables is a fascinating one: it is linked closely to the progress of civilisation. Many of the vegetables that we take for granted today, originated in the South-American Andes and the 'fertile crescent' of Mesopotamia. How they came to be grown around the world is a long and intriguing history and there is room for just a tempting taste of it in the following pages.

Vegetables are beautiful things. They are colourful food, they give texture as well as flavour to favourite dishes, and a salad can have the beauty of a still life. The miracle of today is that we are able to buy most of the vegetables on the planet from our supermarkets, fresh for the cooking. The world in your kitchen.

SPRING

BEANSPROUTS

These are the shoots of germinated dried beans such as aduki, alfalfa, soya, fenugreek and mung beans – the latter are the sprouts that we generally buy. They are highly nutritious and contain substantial amounts (35 per cent) of protein, fibre, vitamins A, B and C, minerals and starch. Their unusual flavour and crunchy texture means that they are good eaten raw in salads and sandwiches. They are excellent in stir-fries. Always buy them crisp and white – if they are soft and turning brown they are past it.

You can easily sprout your own at home, either in a sprouter – which will give you full instructions – or in a jam jar. Put 15ml (½oz) of dried beans of your choice into the jar and cover with muslin, securing it with an elastic band. Pour warm water into the jar, rinse by shaking, then pour the water away. Fill the jar with fresh warm water and leave to stand for 24 hours. Then pour away this water and rinse twice, as before. When you have poured off the water, lay the jar on its side, put into a paper bag and leave in a warm place. Rinse and drain the seeds every day – morning and evening – and in about 4 days the jar will be full of sprouts.

CHICORY

Chicory is closely related to the endive lettuce and has a long tradition as a salad plant, particularly in the Mediterranean. Cultivated by the ancient Egyptians, chicory came to be one of the bitter herbs used at Passover. It was grown by the Greeks and Romans and is mentioned by Aristophanes in *The Frogs*, and also by Horace and Pliny.

A perennial, native to Europe and western Asia, chicory has now naturalised in North America where its beautiful blue flowers are often seen on roadside verges. Many varieties are cultivated: the well-known Brussels chicory or Belgian endive, with its tight spindle-shaped heart, is the true chicory. Its botanical name is 'witloof', meaning white leaf (it is grown in darkness to reduce the bitterness of the green leaf), and can be eaten raw or braised. The roasted roots of chicory are used as a coffee substitute, and indeed as an adulterant of coffee. One red variety of chicory is known as 'di Treviso'. The Italian name for chicory is radicchio, a widely available salad leaf that gives colour and freshness to our winter salads. Chicory contains dietary fibre, some folic acid, vitamin C (mostly lost in cooking) and iron.

CHILLI PEPPERS

Chillies' ancestral origins are in Mexico where they have been eaten for 7,000 years. They comprise a huge family of some 200 types, some long and thin, others round, and in many sizes, colours and degrees of hotness. Capsaicin, the compound responsible for the heat, develops in hot weather – so the hotter the climate the hotter the chilli. Capsaicin produces endorphins in the body which block out pain and give a sense of well-being: thus chillies are said to be addictive since it becomes increasingly pleasurable to eat hotter and hotter ones.

When green and unripe, chillies are less hot than when ripe and red – or yellow, or even black. The seeds are hotter than the flesh, so they can be discarded to reduce the effect.

Chillies have long been used to spice Mexican, Chinese, Malay and Indian dishes. Their use in Mexican cooking is very sophisticated. They came to be used in Europe when it was discovered that, dried and powdered, chilli could replace the very expensive black pepper imported from the East Indies.

Tabasco (*Capsicum frutescens*) originates in tropical South America, probably Peru, and has given its name to the most famous of chilli sauces. It is called after a town in southern Mexico in a region where it is widely cultivated. Today, most of the familiar sauce, which is a combination of fermented chillies with spirit vinegar and salt, is produced in Louisiana, a major chilli-growing area in the United States along with Florida, Texas and California.

Cayenne, an ancient cultivar from pre-Columbian times, was first referred to in East Guinea in 1542. Now this tiny, blistering hot chilli is mostly grown in Asia to make a ground pepper which is even hotter than chilli powder.

Of the chilli peppers, two of the most common are the jalapeno pepper, named after the Mexican town of Jalepa and often used for pickling and canning (it is very hot, especially if the seeds are left in), and the Fresno chilli which is not as hot.

Keep the fresh ones refrigerated, or use chillies in their flaked or powdered forms. Dried chillies need to be soaked in boiling water for 20 minutes and then puréed with some of the liquid, or cut into thin strips. Chilli sauces, usually combined with tomatoes and other spices such as cumin or oregano, are useful for flavouring stews and casseroles.

CRESS

Also called garden cress, mustard and cress, and salad cress, this little plant is a native of Europe and grows quickly and freely on damp ground. It is eaten as a seedling and can be grown easily indoors at home on damp wadding. It is sometimes grown with mustard seedlings, which grow faster and therefore have to be planted later. Cress can be used in salads, or as a garnish, and in sandwiches. It is a rich source of vitamins A and C. *Eat cress and learn more wit*, said anonymous sages of old.

Wintercress, also known as yellow rocket, has lobed, dark green leaves and is also easy to cultivate. A hardy wild plant of damp habitat which survives through the winter, it has a strong mustardy flavour and is used widely in salads, and sometimes in soups.

Grown as a salad leaf since the 17th century, and often used as a substitute for watercress, it is still cultivated commercially today. It is also known as American cress because it grows abundantly in the United States.

MUSHROOMS

Mushrooms as we know them on the supermarket shelf have been cultivated in Europe since the 18th century. The French discovered that they could grow them in cellars on horse manure compost, and throughout the 19th century *champignons de Paris* were grown in disused underground limestone quarries around the capital. The Chinese and Japanese have cultivated mushrooms for centuries too, for their distinctive flavour and texture which are fast becoming popular in the West. Enoki, oyster, shiitake and straw mushrooms are the most commonly available.

Little button mushrooms are immature, young mushrooms; 'flats' or open-gilled the most mature with the fullest flavour. The average-size button mushroom is at the halfway stage. Chestnut mushrooms are slightly larger, firmer in texture and brown with a strong flavour. Wild mushrooms can be gathered with care in the autumn and spring, but always be sure what you are eating because poisonous fungi have disastrous consequences. The best of the wild mushrooms – boletus (cèpes or porcini), chanterelles, morels, field mushrooms and puffballs – are easily identifiable (but do check with a good field guide) and can be dried very successfully, then rehydrated for eating when they are out of season. Dried, they are available from some delicatessens and specialist grocers.

Mushrooms are a huge and fascinating subject, being neither animal nor vegetable; they are in a class of their own which harbours lethal substances alongside some of the best tastes in the world. They have a high water content but are rich in vegetable protein, niacin, riboflavin, pantothenic acid and vitamin B12. They contain small amounts of dietary fibre, sulphur and folic acid.

RADISHES

The radish originated in China and is now grown worldwide in many shapes, sizes and colours – red, white and even a black variety known as the Spanish radish. Radishes were grown by the Pharaohs and there is evidence that in 2780BC they were included in rations given to the workers on the Great Pyramid. In the East, they are still an important root vegetable and the daikon or mooli, with its long white root, is commonly used both raw and cooked. It can be used in soups and stews rather in the same way as a turnip, in stir-fries, and made into an oriental pickle. The French and Italians eat the round, red-skinned radish as part of an hors d'oeuvre, with butter, for its pungent peppery taste and crisp white flesh. Radishes have a high water content, no fat, small amounts of iron, copper, vitamins B and C, folic acid, calcium and sodium.

To make a radish flower for garnishing, trim the stalk end and make several cuts toward the root. Leave the cut radish in a bowl of iced water for 30 minutes to open out.

SHALLOTS

Shallots were thought by the ancient Greeks to have originated in Ascalon in Palestine (now Ashqueion in Israel), whence they got their name. They grow as a cluster of small bulbs and are closely related to the onion. However, they are sweeter in taste and far less pungent in odour. Their delicate flavour gives them a favoured place in French cooking, particularly the elongated variety with the blue-grey skin. The round shallot with its papery red skin is the most commonly available, and makes the best pickled onions. Shallots last a long time when kept in a cool place and are abundant during the spring and summer months. Their nutritional value is minimal, with trace minerals and a high water content.

SORREL

Sorrel used to be a popular vegetable in the 18th century but its use has largely died out, except in France where it is admired for its lemony sharpness. It can be used raw in salads, or cooked in soups, purées and sauces – especially for fish. Looking rather like spinach, it is cooked in the same way – simply in the water it is washed in. It makes a superb soufflé, lovely fritters, and is a delicious addition to an Omelette aux Fines Herbes. 'Greensauce' used to be a popular accompaniment to meat and poultry in the 18th century: this consisted of pounded sorrel, vinegar or lemon juice and sugar. A woman in her late nineties told me that a sorrel sandwich for lunch every day was her secret of longevity! However, sorrel contains oxalic acid which inhibits the absorption of certain important minerals, so overindulgence is not advisable.

WATERCRESS

Watercress grows wild in shallow running water but is unsafe to gather unless you are sure that the water is unpolluted. It is an important cultivated vegetable and has been used since Roman times, especially as a valuable source of vitamins to guard against scurvy. Its small green leaves become tinged with bronze as they mature, and the commercial variety is available all year round. It has a slightly hot, peppery flavour and is used in salads, sandwiches, stir-fries, for garnishes and sometimes for soup, to which it gives an inimitable deep green colour. Watercress is rich in vitamin A, and contains folic acid, riboflavin and vitamins C, D and E as well as potassium and calcium. The main season October to May.

Rocket – also known as arugula or ruchetta – is closely related to watercress and grows wild in much of Europe. It is easy to grow in the garden and you are rewarded by its distinctively pungent peppery flavour which adds originality to salads. It has long been popular in the Mediterranean region. Oil extracted from the seeds is said to be an aphrodisiac.

SUMMER

ASPARAGUS

May and June are high season for this most prized of vegetables. Asparagus comes green, purple and white – the latter has never seen daylight, having been grown underground and banked up like celery, and is very tender. 'Sprue' is the name given to very thin, lanky shoots which are delicious in soups or as garnishes.

The Greeks and Romans loved asparagus and in AD77 Pliny mentions elaborate ways of preparing it. Madame de Pompadour thrived on asparagus tips with egg yolks and truffles – presumably because the phallic shape of asparagus and the sensuous mode of eating it reinforce the belief in its aphrodisiac properties.

Asparagus is best cooked in a tall narrow steamer so that the stalks are poached and the tips merely steamed – they are fragile and fall apart if submitted to boiling water. Failing a special steamer, which is an expensive item, place them on the slant in the right size saucepan to achieve the same result. Asparagus is traditionally served with melted butter, sometimes with a sprinkling of Parmesan, or a little added garlic. It is also delicious raw.

Asparagus is a member of the lily family, its natural habitat being seashore and riverbank. It contains vitamins A, B2, C and E, some calcium and other trace minerals.

BEANS: FRENCH

These fast-growing annuals are also known as dwarf, string and snap beans, or haricots verts. As with so many of the bean family, they come from South America where they are still found growing wild in Mexico, Guatemala and the Andes. Cultivated in Peru for nearly 8,000 years, the name haricot is a corruption of the Aztec word for kidney bean, 'ayecotl'. The haricot was brought to Europe in the 16th century. Today, they are always eaten young, as whole pods, and green when they are succulent and delicately flavoured. French beans, as they then came to be known from being widely cultivated in France, contain carotene and vitamin C, and a little dietary fibre.

BEANS: RUNNER

'Scarlet runners' have a wonderful flavour but are not grown commercially because they are climbers and difficult to harvest. They are also frost-prone, so need to be planted late in the season. Yet they are one of summer's treats, picked young and tender and eaten either whole or sliced. Originating in Mexico, where they were cultivated by pre-Spanish civilisations, they were brought to Europe as a decorative plant in the 16th century, and introduced to the public by John Tradescant in an early catalogue. If the beans are allowed to mature, the seeds in the pods are also tasty, with pretty, variegated pink and grey markings. Runner beans are a good source of carotene and dietary fibre.

CARROTS

One of the world's most important vegetables, the carrot has been cultivated for 2–3,000 years and has been popular in Europe since Roman times, when Apicius suggested eating carrots raw in salad, with salt, oil and vinegar. Different varieties from different parts of the world are now available all year round. Carrots can come in shades of red, yellow and white as well as the more usual orange. They are invaluable in soups, stews, casseroles and stocks. Raw, they are excellent in salads and for crudités. They are excellent grated into cakes, including the famous carrot and passion cakes. Carrots can be juiced for a highly nutritious and tasty drink.

They are rich in carotene which converts to vitamin A in the gut, and research has shown this to be a protection against cancer. They also contain small amounts of the B vitamins, calcium, potassium and phosphorus. The best flavour and the vitamin content reside in the skins, so it is better to scrub rather than peel carrots – in which case use only organically grown carrots, which don't contain residues of toxic chemicals in the skins.

New sweet baby carrots are a delicacy – wonderful steamed until tender and then served with butter and chopped parsley.

CHINESE CABBAGE

There are many varieties of this cabbage-like lettuce, used by the Chinese since the 5th century AD. This important staple of the Chinese diet grows prolifically and is loved for its crisp firm texture and slightly mustardy tang. Sweet and delicate in flavour, it is as excellent in stir-fries as it is in salads. It contains good amounts of vitamins A, B1, B2, B3, C and D, some dietary fibre, iron, potassium and calcium and folic acid.

'Pak choi' is a variant of Chinese cabbage which has also been grown for centuries. These 'Mustard greens' grow rapidly in small rosettes of upright leaves, and are often used in oriental pickles – such as sauerkraut – as well as in stir-fries. Pak choi contains iron and vitamin C. You can steam the thick white stems and eat them like asparagus, dipped into melted butter.

COURGETTES

Courgettes, or zucchini, are baby marrows which are usually green and finger-shaped, but can also come yellow or round. 'Courge' is French for marrow; 'zucca' Italian for gourd. Courgettes have smooth, shiny, dark green skins and sometimes come with the yellow flower still attached to one end. This flower is edible and delectable. In Italy they stuff the flowers, dip them in batter and deep-fry them: served with a tomato coulis, they are exquisite.

This member of the squash family is an American species which originated north of Mexico City and was cultivated by the Indians before the arrival of Columbus. It was introduced into Europe in

the 16th century and today it has reached the height of its popularity, often found in haute cuisine and generally accepted as a delicious and versatile vegetable.

Courgettes have a high water content but contain dietary fibre, some potassium and calcium, carotene and vitamins C and B – the latter are depleted on cooking. They are very low in calories.

CUCUMBER

The cucumber comes out of Asia, cultivated in India 3,000 years ago, and became a favourite food of the Romans. The Emperor Tiberius ordered that it make a daily appearance on his tables. It was eaten both raw and cooked – Apicius described it boiled in a sauce to go with game birds, and also stewed with spices. The cucumber found popularity in England in the reign of Edward II (1307–27), but then it somewhat disappeared off the gastronomic horizon. It was introduced to Haiti by Columbus in 1494 and soon spread all over North America, where it was appreciated by the Indian tribes. In the 18th century, John Evelyn championed it and suggested eating it sliced with orange, lemon and oil. Cucumber makes a delicious pickle, a delicate soup, and is mouthwatering fried. It adds its refreshing effect to salads at all times of the year. Mediterranean cuisines mix it with yoghurt and garlic or mint, and it is also served stuffed and baked.

Cucumbers grow on a trailing annual plant and this family of about 25 species includes gherkins and many different shapes, sizes and skin textures. The skin of the cucumber contains vitamin A, some vitamin C, folic acid and fibre, and is high in potassium and sulphur. Most of the nutritional value is lost on skinning since the cucumber comprises 95 per cent water.

GARLIC

Garlic has been grown since the first Egyptian dynasty of 3100BC and there is evidence of its early use in Chinese and Indian cookery. Native to central Asia, it is now grown as far afield as Texas and California as well as in Europe. There are many references to it in the ancient world: it sustained labourers as they worked on the Great Pyramid, it wards off evil, and it is a 'food-remedy' effective for almost every condition known to man. A huge body of folklore has grown up around garlic over the ages: it finds pride of place in medical and herbal literature over the past 700 years.

One thing is known for certain: garlic lowers blood cholesterol and reduces the risk of clotting – old wives' tales always said it was 'good for the blood'. It aids digestion and is generally thought to maintain and improve health, being antibacterial and a powerful antibiotic. It increases the assimilation of vitamins, and itself contains vitamins B and C, calcium, phosphorus, iron and potassium.

There are many varieties of garlic – white, red, pink and purple skinned – the latter said to be the most superior in taste and also known as Mexican or Italian garlic. The strong flavour and pungent aroma of garlic can be used either with discretion – simply rubbing a salad bowl with a cut clove imparts its taste to the salad – or in robuster quantities. But be judicious, because overdoing garlic can completely overwhelm the flavour of the dish.

Garlic can be slivered finely, chopped or crushed – either with a garlic crusher or with the flat blade of a kitchen knife. Its flavour mellows on cooking – roasted garlic becomes delicate, and likewise if you simmer it in water it changes quality completely. My most recent discovery is smoked garlic, hung for 3 weeks in a smoker and aromatic of oak – sublime!

Garlic is planted in the spring and harvested in late July, then dried in the sun before storing. So watch out for garlic in mid-winter and through the early months of the year – it will lose its plumpness and start to dry out, so don't waste your money. Garlic, like all vegetables, is at its best in season.

GLOBE ARTICHOKES

The artichoke is a thistle. This unlikely vegetable is native to North Africa, was imported and adopted by the Greeks and Romans, and is now grown all over Europe and North America. Vast fields of artichokes line the Pacific coast-road north of Monterey where Steinbeck wrote some of his greatest books. Unlike almost any other vegetable it is the flower-bud that is the edible part, the 'heart' of which is highly prized for its delicate flavour and texture. You can buy artichoke hearts canned or frozen and they make excellent additions to salads, egg dishes and stir-fries. Baby artichokes can be eaten whole, fried with oil and garlic, or battered and deep-fried until crisp. A bottled artichoke paste available from delicatessens is superb with poached eggs and a grating of Parmesan.

Globe artichokes were a favourite of King Henry VIII as he found them to be an aphrodisiac: thus is the course of history determined. But Goethe, writing in the 18th century of his Travels through Italy, remarked that he did not take to the thistles that he observed the peasants eating. He is in a minority; artichokes are now commonplace in the Mediterranean diet, and said to be good for flagging livers. They are the basis of the aperitif Cynar, from the organic acid cynarin which is unique to artichokes and which stimulates sweetness receptors on the palate.

There are 2 main varieties of globe artichoke: one purple and one green. They have a high water content but contain protein, potassium and calcium. Eat them as fresh as possible, dipping the fleshy parts of the leaves into melted butter or hollandaise sauce. One of summer's Good Things!

HERBS

One of summer's great pleasures is the variety of fresh herbs that grow freely in the garden and are at the height of their aroma and flavour. Chives and sorrel come early, followed by mint, parsley, fennel, marjoram and rocket. Oregano and tarragon follow up the rear – 2 highly aromatic herbs of midsummer. I grow basil, dill and coriander in pots and keep them on a sunny windowsill – I put them outdoors in a very hot summer, where they thrive. The evergreens – rosemary, sage and bay – are stand-bys throughout the year and are particularly good in casseroles, soups and stocks. I use herbs a lot and whenever I can I garnish dishes with them – just a touch of leaf or flower adds elegance to the simplest of foods.

NEW POTATOES

Native new potatoes are available in the UK from May to August, and are imported at other times of the year. They are surprisingly nutritious, containing more vitamin C than maincrop potatoes, 0.6 per cent potassium, 18 per cent carbohydrate, and dietary fibre. 500g (1lb) of cooked new potatoes provides the daily recommended amount of vitamins C and B1 and riboflavin. They also contain some 2 per cent protein. Most of this goodness is found in the skin, so do not peel new potatoes. Scrub them clean and enjoy the full flavour and goodness with their skins on. New potatoes are best boiled for just a few minutes so that they remain crisp in the centre and retain their waxy texture. There are many varieties, of which Pink Fir Apple is one of the finest.

PEAS AND MANGETOUT

Peas have been grown in southern Europe and the Near East for thousands of years, so they are as old as wheat and barley as a staple crop. They were first cultivated in Turkey; 200kg (440lb) of peas were found in a single container in the ruins of ancient Troy. The Romans brought them to Britain where they became very popular.

Peas are best eaten very young, or else dried when they are old, by which time they are an excellent source of protein. Peas are the seeds of a climbing plant with many varieties and can be eaten as pods before the peas swell. The flat pods of the mangetout or snow pea have long been used in Chinese cooking, and Gerard mentions the 'sugar pea' in his Herbal of 1597. They are prized for their tenderness and sweetness.

'Petits pois' are a dwarf variety specially bred to produce tiny peas which are sweet and tender. They are available frozen or canned. The regular pea harvest is short, and peas are best eaten before maturity, so most of the frozen pea industry harvests them young before their moment is past. To be honest they are hard to beat and usually more tender and tasty than many of the fresh peas on the market. Peas are best cooked lightly, served with a little butter, or used in soups and purées.

Peas contain more protein, sugars, starch and dietary fibre than most other common vegetables, providing calcium, iron, vitamins C, B complex and E, manganese, potassium and phosphorus.

SALAD LEAVES

Salad leaves have been cultivated from wild plants to provide a wide variety of salading throughout the world and throughout the ages.

The origins of the lettuce are uncertain, but they are known to be narcotic in effect, having calming sedative effects in normal doses. The first lettuces came to England in the 16th century. There are numerous varieties which are grown in different places and in different seasons – thin leaf, crisp leaf, red and bronze, curly, plain, thick and juicy, etc. They have a minimal food value, being mainly water and are almost always eaten raw, although they are sometimes used in soups and stir-fries.

Webbs and Iceberg are compact, crisp lettuces; Little Gem, Cos and Romaine have long crisp leaves and a strong flavour; Round or Cabbage lettuces – also known as Butterhead – have soft leaves and less flavour and grow all the year round; Oak Leaf is a deep bronze lettuce with serrated leaves and a distinctive flavour; Lollo Rosso and Lollo Biondo are 2 Italian lettuces with decorative frilly leaves and a good flavour; Four Seasons is also grown in Italy for its round dimpled leaves; and Frisée or Endive lettuces are refreshingly sharp with wavy indented leaves and a good texture.

SWEET PEPPERS

The species Capsicum is native to Mexico and Central America. It has been cultivated since 5000BC and can be seen on pre-Columbian ceramics. Invading Spaniards called sweet peppers pimento in the 16th century, and when they brought them back home found that they grew abundantly in southern Spain. Soon they were grown over a wide region, and incorporated into the Mediterranean diet.

Sweet peppers, also called Bell peppers because of their shape, are now grown in greenhouses all over northern Europe, and in the open in southern Europe, the Middle East and America. They are usually red when ripe but also come white, yellow, green, orange and purplish-black. Peppers can be used raw in salads, and grilled or roasted for hot or cold dishes. They add flavour to casseroles and savoury dishes, make delicious sauces and are excellent stuffed with a rice, nut or cheese mixture and baked. Peppers are a very good source of vitamin C when raw (this is depleted on cooking), vitamins B1 and B2, and carotene, fibre, potassium and folic acid. Paprika is made from dried sweet peppers which are then powdered to make this spice. Hungary is the principal producer.

TOMATOES

A close relative of the potato, the tomato is strictly speaking a fruit, but has always been used as a vegetable. It is usually red although there are – now rarer – yellow forms. Originating in the Lower Andes, tomatoes were widely cultivated at the time of the invasion by Cortes in 1523. They get their name from the Aztec 'tomatl'. They were brought back to Europe by the Spanish, and were regarded with the greatest suspicion because other members of the Solanum family are poisonous – notably the Deadly Nightshade. Gerard, in his famous Herbal of 1597, dismissed them as having a 'ranke and stinking savour'. Yet, today, tomatoes are one of the world's best-selling goods and millions of tons are grown in the United States alone.

The first tomatoes to reach Europe were yellow varieties which were called 'pomo d'oro' or Golden Apple, reflected in the modern Italian for tomato, 'pomodoro'. They were also known as Love Apples or 'pommes d'amour' because tomatoes were thought to be an aphrodisiac. There are now many varieties of tomato cultivated, from the tiny 'cherry' tomato to huge 'beef' tomatoes, the Italian 'plum' tomatoes being among the richest in taste. Tomatoes have a high water content, but contain some carotene and vitamin C. They are high in fibre, potassium and folic acid.

Tomato purée is a thick red paste made from puréed and condensed tomatoes. This is excellent in sauces and soups to add depth and flavour. Sun-dried tomato paste has its own special concentrated flavour and dense texture and is well worth stocking in the kitchen cupboard.

AUTUMN

AUBERGINES

This fruit is commonly known as eggplant, because it is often the shape and size of an egg. The earliest records of this bushy plant come from China in the 5th century BC, and it has probably been grown in India for over 4,000 years. It was introduced into Europe by the Arabs when they brought it to Spain in the 4th century AD, but it did not become widely known in Europe until the 13th century, or cultivated until the 16th. The aubergine gets it name from the Catalan 'alberginia', inherited from the Arabic 'al-badingan' which in its turn came from the Sanskrit.

The aubergine is a member of the Solanum family which includes the potato and the tomato – and Deadly Nightshade. The fruits are mostly a dark purple with a glossy skin, but can be mauve, mauve streaked with white, or even green. They absorb flavours and oils well which makes them ideally suited to Indian cookery. They are widely used for moussaka and ratatouille, and can be stuffed and baked or fried in olive oil. The skin is richer in nutrients than the flesh, and contains vitamins B1, 2 and 3 and vitamin C, plus a little iron, calcium and potassium. A 14th-century manuscript tells us to beware of aubergines because they cause 'males to swerve from decent behaviour.'

BROCCOLI

Broccoli is said to have come to Italy from Crete, and Miller's Gardeners' dictionary of 1724 refers to it as 'Italian asparagus'. Broccoli is closely related to the cauliflower and comes in many types, which are usually green or purple but can be white. Calabrese – the large, firm, dark green heads we most commonly buy in our supermarkets, is 'broccoli from Calabria'. The smaller purplish shoots of sprouting broccoli ('brocco' means little sprout or shoot in Italian) are as tender and tasty as the asparagus to which Miller referred. They require light cooking, as asparagus does, otherwise the tender seedheads disintegrate. Broccoli is now available all year round and is an excellent source of calcium, potassium, carotene and the B vitamins, with 5 per cent protein.

BUCKWHEAT

Although buckwheat is eaten as a cereal grain it is actually the fruit of a plant related to sorrel and rhubarb. It is also known by the romantic name of Saracen Corn. Native to Asiatic Russia, it has been cultivated for at least 1,500 years in the Far East. It came to Europe in the early 15th century, where it was known as 'beechwheat' because the seeds are shaped like tiny beech nuts. In Russia, a porridge made from buckwheat and known as 'kasha' is a national dish, while blinis, the famous Russian pancakes, are also made with buckwheat flour. The Japanese make their soba noodles from buckwheat flour.

Buckwheat has a pleasant and distinctive flavour, enhanced by roasting in which form it is often sold. It makes a happy substitute for rice as a complement to spiced vegetable dishes, stir-fries and curries, and is excellent in stuffings. Buckwheat contains rutin, which is known to be beneficial in guarding against high blood pressure. It is also a good source of starch, protein, dietary fibre, potassium, iron and zinc. It contains the vitamin B complex and E.

FENNEL

Finocchio or Florence fennel is grown for its seeds, feathery leaves and swollen bulb – which actually comprises the expanded leaf stalks at the base of the stem. Its aniseed flavour goes particularly well with fish, so the leaf is used to flavour sauces. The seeds are used as a spice, and are sometimes chewed to relieve hunger pangs. The vegetable – the bulb – can be braised or roasted, or made into a sauce. It is excellent raw – in salads, or served as crudités with cheese instead of celery.

A most popular herb of the ancient world, fennel was cultivated by Assyrian and Babylonian gardeners. The Romans made much use of fennel, and Pliny extolled its virtues. Fennel was introduced to England from Italy and the first records of it being grown there date from the 18th century. In 1824, Thomas Jefferson received fennel seeds for his garden at Montecello in Virginia from the American consul at Livorno. Fennel is found growing wild in Mediterranean Europe and California.

GRAINS

Grains (cereals) constitute the basic food supply of the world. They were first cultivated from wild grasses by ancient tribes and were the chief crop of early agriculture. Thus they could be said to be 'seeds of civilisation'. Certainly they are the staff of life, rich in complex carbohydrates, plant protein, dietary fibre, B vitamin complex and vitamin E – contained in the germ or inner embryo. They contain a substantial amount of iron, plus potassium, calcium, zinc, magnesium, manganese and copper. Much of the goodness is found in the outer husk – the bran. For this reason, processed flour does not have as much goodness as wholewheat.

First cultivated in Mesopotamia, then taken to the New World by the Spaniards, wheat is now a major world crop and comes in many forms. Hard wheat contains a lot of gluten and makes the strong flour that helps bread to rise well. Soft wheat contains more carbohydrate and is better for making cakes and pastries. Cracked wheat or bulgar wheat is boiled and crushed and is the main ingredient of the famous dish Tabbouleh. Wheat forms the basis for breads and noodles and pasta – durum wheat is a very hard wheat that makes the best pasta. Semolina is meal ground from the inside of durum wheat; couscous is semolina coated in wheat flour.

The other major grains in the world food supply are barley, millet, oats, rye and maize (see sweetcorn, page 22).

OKRA

Also known as ladies' fingers, okra are the edible pod of a member of the mallow family and are native to Africa. They came via Egypt to the Mediterranean in the 13th century. African slaves took okra with them to the Caribbean where they are still an integral part of the ethnic cuisine and a vital ingredient of Creole 'gumbo'. They are grown extensively in the southern United States for the canning industry. Okra have a delicate flavour and slightly mucilaginous slimy texture due to a thick gluey sap. This can be modified by soaking prior to cooking, or by adding lemon juice or vinegar to the cooking water. Canned ones are best rinsed before use. Fresh, they are available from supermarkets and Indian or Greek shops, and need to be topped and tailed before cooking. Use them in soups, casseroles, mixed vegetable dishes and curries. Okra contain some sugars, dietary fibre, a little protein, iron, calcium, magnesium and potassium, along with a small amount of vitamin C and beta carotene.

RICE

Rice is the most important cereal in the world, the staple food of over half the world's population. The seed of an aquatic grass, rice comes in numerous varieties – said to number over 10,000. It is grown in paddy fields in hot moist climates, particularly in India, Java, China, Japan, the United States and Europe – notably in the Po Valley in northern Italy, where it was introduced by the Venetians in the 17th century. Ninety per cent of the world crop is still grown and consumed in the monsoon regions of Asia.

Rice was first cultivated in southern Asia a very very long time ago, and has been established in India and China for at least 5,000 years. It arrived in Egypt around 400 or 300BC and thence travelled to the Middle East. The Arabs took it to southern Italy and Spain, but not until AD1000. By Elizabethan times, it was being imported to England.

Rice is sold as brown or white – the brown retaining its bran husk, the white milled to remove the bran, and polished. Rice is an excellent source of protein, carbohydrate, vitamins and minerals. It contains no fat. Brown rice is a good source of dietary fibre.

SPINACH

Spinach originated in South-West Asia and was first cultivated by the Persians. Its name comes via the Arabic from the Persian 'espenaj'. It arrived in Europe in the 11th century, in England in the 16th. It had reached North America by the 19th century, when Thomas Jefferson grew it in his kitchen garden at Montecello, Virginia. Spinach is available all the year round, and is usually an annual although there are perennial varieties. 'Florentine' denotes its use in recipes, and it can be eaten either cooked, or raw in salads. Spinach is a good source of dietary fibre and contains more protein than many other vegetables. It is high in carotene and also riboflavin, vitamins A, C, E and K, and contains iron, calcium, potassium, magnesium and phosphorus. It has a high concentration of beta carotene, thought to be protective against some cancers.

SQUASHES

This vigorous family of trailing and climbing plants originated in the Americas, and was an important food to the pre-Columbian culture. Its name comes from the American-Indian 'askutasquash'. 'Squash' is a term that covers marrows, pumpkins and winter and summer squashes, including the courgette (see page 13). The fast-growing vines, both annual and perennial, bear large, brightly coloured and often curiously shaped fruits which give them names such as turban squash, crookneck, banana, etc. They are delicious and versatile, although it is true to say that it would take an expert to know the difference in flavour between one squash and another. They can be roasted, stuffed, fried, baked in stews, made into soups and even jams. They are best young and freshly picked – older squashes become watery and some taste bitter as they mature. Squashes have a high water content with small amounts of protein,

some dietary fibre, minerals and beta carotene. The highly nutritious seeds can be roasted and eaten.

'Winter' squashes, with their thick skins, include acorn, crown prince, butternut, onion, spaghetti and turban. Pumpkin, the largest and best known of the winter squashes, is traditionally served at American Thanksgiving made into a spicy dessert pie. Hallowe'en is another festival where pumpkins make their distinctive mark, hollowed out, cut into faces and lit from inside. Pumpkins can weigh up to 50kg (100lb), big enough to be transformed into the mythical coach of Cinderella – with its accompanying curse that has passed into the language. The deep orange-yellow flesh of pumpkin with its earthy taste contains vitamin A, folic acid, potassium, a little of the B vitamin complex, dietary fibre and iron. Pumpkins are available from October to December, and make one of the best winter soups in the world.

'Summer' squashes, with their thinner skins, are gathered when immature and include the yellow courgette, gem squash, courgette and patty pan.

SWEETCORN

Cultivated by Mexicans and Peruvians for over 3,000 years, maize or sweetcorn was first mentioned in the Sacred Book of the Quicke Indians of Guatemala. It tells how the gods ate it so that man might become strong, and calls it the 'mother and father', the source of life. It has since become a staple food for many cultures worldwide. The flour is used for thick mealy porridge, or for tortillas. The grain contains more sugar than starch and is highly valued as a source of energy: it was the principal cereal of the Aztec, Maya and Inca civilisations – who discovered popcorn!

Columbus first spotted maize in Cuba in 1492, but it wasn't until the 16th century that the Spaniards brought it back to Europe. It arrived in Sicily and then spread into Italy. Now it is grown all over the world in many forms – red, blue, cream, white, yellow, brown

and even variegated. It is best eaten just after picking, before its sugars turn to starch, and cooked very briefly in boiling water – for no more than 3–4 minutes, otherwise it goes tough. Baby sweetcorn is eaten whole and is a great delicacy.

Sweetcorn is grown extensively in northern Italy where it is enjoyed in the form of polenta: ground maize cooked until it is thick, cooled and served in slices – often with cheese or flavourings. Sweetcorn contains starch, some protein and dietary fibre, a small amount of sugars, phosphorus, potassium and sulphur, and vitamins A, B, C and E.

TURNIPS

A member of the Brassica family, turnips are related to cabbages, Chinese cabbage, swedes and radishes. They are delicious when young, disgusting when old – the delicate mustard flavour becomes overpowering and the texture coarse. Since Roman times, old turnips have been used as cattle fodder and this has affected their reputation. Since they grow well on poor soil and don't mind harsh conditions, they have long been regarded as food for the poor, being cheap and filling. However, the young greens from turnip tops are a delicious spring green, cooked like cabbage, and young turnips are delicious roasted, stir-fried or lightly boiled and served with butter. Raw grated turnip is wonderful in salad and a great addition to coleslaw. Cooked, turnips add flavour to vegetable stews and soups and add an original touch to a stir-fry. Turnips also make an excellent pickle. The small French purple-topped turnip is now widely available on the markets, popular for its delicate spicy flavour and crisp texture. There are also yellow-skinned, white and green as well as purple types.

Turnip tops have a high content of vitamins A B and C. Turnips themselves are 90 per cent water with traces of vitamins and minerals, and a little dietary fibre. They are low in calories.

WINTER

BEETROOT

Beetroot belongs to a family that includes sugar beet (from which much of our refined sugar is obtained), mangold (used as a winter feed for stock), chard and perpetual spinach. 'Red chard' was mentioned by Aristotle and thought to be grown by the Greeks, whereas red beetroot was developed by the Romans – Apicius recommends a salad of beetroot with mustard, oil and vinegar. In the late Middle Ages it was called 'Roman Beet'. Gerard regards beetroot with great suspicion in his Herbal of 1597.

It is an important vegetable in Polish and Russian cuisines – beetroot is famously made into Borscht, the great Russian soup. It

can be grated into salads; young beetroot can be boiled and served with butter to make an exquisite dish; or it can be used to make excellent preserves. The leaves of beetroot, which can be cooked like greens, are high in vitamin A and contain more iron, calcium and vitamin C than spinach. The roots are rich in potassium, dietary fibre and oxalic acid. The juice can be used as a food dye.

CABBAGE

The cabbage family derives from *Brassica oleracea* and includes cauliflower, broccoli, brussels sprouts and kohlrabi. Closely related are the swede, turnip, Chinese cabbage and oil-seed rape. The earliest records of the cultivation of cabbage from a wild species is in about 600BC, when kale gets a mention in Greek literature. Pliny records a vegetable akin to kohlrabi, claiming that there was little that the cabbage did not cure. The Romans were responsible for bringing cabbage to the British Isles, but the cabbage as we know it today originated in Germany, where red and white varieties were being grown by AD1150. Savoy cabbage, which probably originated in Italy, was recognised as a distinct type of cabbage by 1543.

The various types of cabbage give us a steady supply through the year: spring, summer and autumn cabbages, winter white, savoy, January king and red cabbage cover the spread of the seasons. They can be eaten raw in salads, pickled, boiled and served with butter or cream, the outer leaves can be rolled and stuffed, or they can be cooked in casseroles. Raw cabbage was said in folklore to be a protection against inebriation, and chewing the seeds would, it was said, keep you sober. The medicinal value of cabbage is apparently huge: it will get rid of headaches and give immunity from common ailments of all kinds: *He who sows cabbages and fattens a pig will get through the winter.* Research in the 1930s showed that if rabbits ate cabbage leaves before a high dose of radiation they would survive it, and recent research shows it to protect against colon cancer. Its vitamin C content was well known in the past: Captain Cook took sauerkraut (which retains the vitamin) on his voyages and claimed that it prevented scurvy and kept his crew healthy. Cabbages are also a good source of potassium, folic acid, calcium and iron, and contain in addition vitamins A, B1, B2, B3 and D.

CELERY & CELERIAC

Celery and celeriac are close cousins. Celery grows wild in Europe and Asia, in marshes or along the edge of tidal rivers. 'Smallage' as this wild version is called is used in European country cooking for soups and casseroles to which it imparts a strong celery flavour. It was first cultivated in Italy in the 16th century, and John Evelyn, writing in the 1690s, considered it a new vegetable. Celery is excellent braised, as a side vegetable or in casseroles, but is principally used in salads and as crudités. It has no nutritional or calorific value, just a small amount of dietary fibre.

Celeriac on the other hand has a substantial carbohydrate content, and contains vitamin C and some of the B vitamins. It is high in iron, and has other trace minerals. It was not known in Europe until the 1720s, introduced from Alexandria by a certain Stephen Switzer and offered in his catalogue. Celeriac is a swollen stem base, not a root as it might appear. It is excellent in soups and salads, and makes an exquisite purée for winter meals.

JERUSALEM ARTICHOKES

The root artichoke is so-called because its delicate flavour is said to be like the globe artichoke. Its origins lie in North America and it is related to the sunflower, the Italian for which is 'girasole',

meaning 'turning to the sun'. A corruption of this led to the name 'Jerusalem'. The sunflower was called the 'marigold of Peru' by a 17th-century herbalist, John Goodyer, which led to some confusion about the origins of the artichoke. But North American it is, cultivated by the Native Americans before the 16th century.

Its arrival in Europe did not arouse much enthusiasm. The same herbalist said that they 'cause a filthie loathesome stinking winde within the bodie, thereby causing the belly to be muche pained and tormented'. True, there is nothing quite like the flatulence caused by eating artichokes and this is due to a starch it contains which is indigestible to most human stomachs, with a few exceptions. Yet it is a seductive vegetable, with a sweet and nutty taste and crisp texture. It is delicious roasted, or fried in batter. Boiled, it can be eaten buttered or in a sauce. Artichokes are excellent fried in the same ways as potatoes, mashed, or made into an excellent soup. They are rich in potassium, and contain a little protein and some dietary fibre. They are tastiest with their skins on, simply scrubbed. If you do peel them, you will need to put them into water with some vinegar or lemon juice added, to stop them discolouring before you cook them.

LAMBS' LETTUCE

The pleasant delicate flavour of lambs' lettuce makes it a popular winter salading. It has a sweet nut-like taste when picked young and tender, and a slightly chewy texture. A native of Turkey and eastern Europe, it was introduced into North America at the beginning of the 19th century and nowadays is more widely grown in the United States than anywhere else. The Americans call it 'corn salad'; the French call it 'mache'.

LEEKS

Wild leeks – 'Levant garlic' – were found in the remains of Jericho around 7000BC, but the earliest records of its cultivation are from Egypt in 3200BC. The Romans liked them – Nero ate them several days a month to improve his oratory, in the belief that leeks cleared and strengthened his voice. Old wives' tales have long said that they clear the lungs. The Romans probably brought them to Britain where they are often associated with early Christian sites, possibly cultivated by the monks. Leeks were popular in the Middle Ages and became the national emblem of Wales in memory of an ancient victory when they stuck leeks into their caps like feathers.

Leeks are related to onions and garlic and have lots of goodness in them – vitamins B, C and E, carotene, calcium, iron, phosphorus, potassium, sodium, sulphur and traces of copper. They contain antiseptic oils and have a high protein content. Leeks are very versatile – you can use them in soups, casseroles or quiches. They make a marvellous hors d'oeuvre, cold, with walnuts in walnut oil dressing. Young, they can be shredded into stir-fries or salads – the latter were a favourite dish of the Romans. Leeks are harvested from November to March and are at their best in season

rather than forced: as with all vegetables, the flavour is better when allowed to develop naturally.

ONIONS

Onions are the most commonly grown vegetable in the world. They have been cultivated in China and Japan since time immemorial and belong to the lily family – the Alliums – which includes leeks, garlic, chives and shallots. Spring onions or scallions are young slim onions with a delicate favour and higher nutritional content than fully grown onions, which nonetheless contain vitamins B, C and E, carotene, calcium, iron, phosphorus, potassium, sodium, sulphur and traces of copper. Onions contain an antiseptic oil which is not destroyed on cooking, and which reduces the risk of heart disease – just 1 tablespoon of onion per day will substantially lower blood cholesterol. Onions make the basis of stews and casseroles, soups, composite dishes, burgers and quiches. Onion rings fried in batter are delicious, pickled onions with cheese are the heart of the Ploughman's lunch, and thinly sliced onions are delicious in salads. They are much used in Mediterranean cooking, and are sold through the winter plaited into strings. Onions come with various coloured skins, which have particular flavours and slightly varying shapes. Brown-skinned are the ones we usually buy. Others include yellow, white and Spanish (large mild onions), and red or purple, which are mild, slightly sweet and excellent in salads.

Onions were mentioned in the Bible as being a favourite food of the Israelites, who longed for them in the wilderness. An inscription on the Great Pyramid tells of 1,600 talents spent on onions, radishes and garlic for the labourers, and they have always had a reputation for imparting strength and vigour. The more pious suspected that they incited lust and so some religious leaders banned them. A legend arose that onions grew where Satan put his right foot on earth when cast out of Paradise.

PARSNIPS

People either love or hate the distinctive taste of parsnips. This long tapering root with its creamy white flesh was developed from a wild parsnip found growing in the Caucasus. It was probably grown by the Greeks and Romans – who brought them to Britain along with the carrot and the radish. They were found to grow very successfully in Britain, for the parsnip is hardy and can withstand bitter winters. They were definitely being grown in Germany by the mid-16th century, had reached the West Indies by 1564 and Virginia by 1609, and 100 years later were being grown by the Native Americans.

Parsnips are loved for their sweetness, and were often roasted with meat before the arrival of the potato. They make excellent fritters, can be fried like potatoes either as hash-browns or in the form of chips, and are delectable mashed with butter. Boiled until tender, they are also delicious sliced into salads. The high sugar content was exploited to make a fine country wine, jam and 'honey' – a parsnip-flavoured syrup. Parsnips contain starch, dietary fibre, folic acid, the B vitamins and vitamin C.

POTATOES

The world's best known vegetable is native to the shores of Lake Titicaca in Peru and was an important staple to the Incas, as evidenced by remains dating from 4000BC. Potato-shaped pottery urns of AD1000 were found in a Peruvian burial site, showing that the natives had discovered how to freeze them at high altitudes.

The potato first gets a mention in 1563 and there is a legend that Sir Francis Drake's botanist brought some back to his master's estate in County Cork in 1586, where they took to the Irish climate and soil and were to play a major part in Irish history. From these small beginnings the potato has become the world's fourth largest crop after wheat, maize and rice. Irish immigrants took them to America in 1719, the Portuguese took them to India where they arrived in 1615, and Louis XIV and his courtiers wore a potato flower as a buttonhole.

The potato caught on fast in Europe: recorded in Seville in 1573, it travelled to Italy and thence to Germany where it remains a hugely successful vegetable. From Gerard's receiving his first potato in 1588, *The Times* of 1845 reports that in England the 2 main meals of a working man's day consisted of potatoes, not the expected bread and cheese. In spite of Scottish preachers denouncing them as unfit since they were not mentioned in the Bible, potatoes still constitute 20 per cent of the average UK diet.

The Irish became dependent on the potato to the extent that a crop failure in 1727 caused rioting, and a disastrous failure in 1739 caused by early frost in November resulted in the death of one-third of the population. Worse was to come: in 1845 potato blight spread through the island and the Irish experienced the worst famine in their history. By June 1847 over 3 million people were receiving emergency rations from government soup kitchens, and the population of Connaught had declined by over 28 per cent.

The potato is a member of the Solanum family, related to the tomato and the aubergine – and to Deadly Nightshade. There are over 400 varieties and it is worth trying out the different types: the Pink Fir Apple is my personal favourite. Potatoes are lifted in September/October and sold over the ensuing 8 months. (For New Potatoes, see page 17.)

Sneered at as being tasteless food for the poor by Brillat-Savarin, Neitszche and Diderot, the potato is nonetheless a highly nutritious vegetable. 500g (1lb) of cooked potatoes provides the recommended daily allowance of vitamin C, as well as a good amount of potassium. Potatoes are 18 per cent carbohydrate, 2 per cent protein, with some dietary fibre and B vitamins. They have a high water content and are low in calories. Their nutrients are lost on long storage and on peeling since most of the goodness is in the skin. The skins are delicious, leave them on: scrub your potatoes rather than peel them. They are extremely versatile: you can mash them, chip them, fry them, turn them into hash or gratins, crisps or pie toppings, or they can be sautéed, steamed or baked.

PULSES

Pulses or legumes are the edible seeds of beans, peas and lentils and cover a wide variety of colours, shapes and sizes. The oldest evidence of beans is to be found in Peru, dating from around 8000BC, and they have been used in North America since 5000BC. Staple food for millions ever since, they are convenient to store in their dried state, and highly nutritious. Pulses are a good source of protein (the soya bean is 40 per cent protein), starch and dietary fibre, and are low in fat. They contain calcium, the B vitamins, iron, manganese and carotene as well as the essential amino acid Lysine. The famous flatulence that they cause is due to indigestible starches. Pulses are wonderful in soups, pies, burgers, curries and dhal, and are much used in Indian cooking. Store dried pulses in a cool place for between 6 and 9 months.

All dried pulses need soaking for several hours or overnight to soften the skins. Give them plenty of water to cover. The exceptions are whole lentils and large split peas which need to be soaked for only 2–3 hours. Very fine red lentils and finely split peas need no soaking at all.

To cook, drain and rinse the soaked pulses, cover with water, add a bayleaf, a sprig of rosemary and a slice or two of onion for flavour. Add a dash of olive oil and simmer, covered, for the amount of time given in the packet instructions. Add salt at the end of the cooking time – it toughens the skins and hardens them if you add it earlier.

Canned pulses are quite soft and do not need long cooking – it's best to add them towards the end of cooking a casserole, for example, so that they don't go mushy. Drain them well and rinse them under running cold water before you use them.
Dried pulses double their weight on soaking and cooking, so when using canned pulses in place of dried, multiply the amount given in the recipe for dried pulses by 2: use 250g (8oz) canned for every 125g (4oz) dried.

SOYA BEAN PRODUCTS

The soya bean is the seed of the soya plant. It has been used as a staple in the Chinese diet for more than 4,000 years.

Tofu is soya bean curd made from coagulated soya milk, which is cooked, mashed and strained before being pressed into shape. Add to soups to make them thick and creamy.

Tempeh is a fermented soya bean paste made from cooked soya beans. Good source of vitamin B12.

Miso is a fermented condiment made from soya bean, grain (rice or barley), salt and water.

Soya sauce (shoyu) is made by fermenting soya beans with cracked roasted wheat, salt and water.

Tamari is similar to shoyu but slightly stronger and made without wheat.

Soya milk is made by soaking and boiling soya beans in water and then straining them to remove the fibre. It is sugar-free and low in fat. You can use soya milk very successfully in place of dairy milk in most recipes.

Soya creem (SIC) is a non-dairy cream alternative made from soya milk and corn syrup. It is like single cream in that it does not whip stiff and can be used in place of it.

Soya cheeses are now available, flavoured with onions, garlic, herbs, pepper and chilli.

Soya oil and margarine are widely available. They are high in polyunsaturated fats and low in saturated fats.

TVP is de-fatted soya flour, processed and dried to produce a spongy-textured substance which can be flavoured to resemble meat. A good source of fibre and high-quality protein, TVP is also fortified with vitamin B12. Wheat protein, which has a greater similarity to meat and is used in many meat substitutes, is derived from wheat gluten and then processed to resemble meat.

SWEDES

The Swedish turnip or rutabaga (its American name) is larger than the turnip and probably came into cultivation in Bohemia in the 17th century. The skins can be white, purple or yellow, the flesh orange-yellow or white. The swede is sweeter and drier than the turnip, with a nutty flavour and a high water content. It contains some sugars, minimal dietary fibre, calcium, the B vitamins and C. It was introduced from Sweden to England in 1755 – hence its name – and was used to feed cattle as well as people. In Scotland, mashed swedes are traditionally eaten with haggis in mid-winter.

SHOPPING AND STOCKING THE CUPBOARD

LOCAL PRODUCE

Undoubtedly the best way to buy vegetables is fresh, and in season. If you can find a source of garden or allotment produce, or an organic grower or retailer, it will be hard to beat in terms of flavour and freshness. At certain times of the year individual growers are more than happy to sell their excess – and usually for a very good price. Their vegetables have the unmistakable flavour of the home-grown as opposed to the mass-produced or forced.

Street markets often have good fresh vegetables, and at noticeably cheaper prices than large stores. The high street greengrocer, too, may have local produce to sell which has escaped the cocktail of chemicals meted out to mass-marketed foods.

ORGANICALLY GROWN

Above all, search for organically grown vegetables and fruit. This is the only way that you can be sure of true flavour and at the same time of not digesting toxic chemicals from the fertilisers, pesticides and hormones used to grow plant foods. Organic vegetables are delicious: it is a relief to taste a carrot or a potato once more as they were meant to taste. The more we, the public, demand them, the more that the organic market will increase. The goods are more expensive, but it is worth buying quality rather than quantity.

ETHNIC GROCERS

One of the few genuine pleasures of shopping is chez the ethnic grocer. Authentic Indian, East Asian, Thai, Malaysian and Japanese foods are now available from these shops which have sprung up in towns and cities everywhere. Not only can you get interesting, exciting ingredients (some of which you may never have even tried before!), but they are priced low and are amazingly good value. My advice is to stock up with a range of ethnic goods that appeal to you (my personal favourites are a selection of different noodles, black bean sauce, chilli and garlic sauce and dark sesame oil), and you will find that they liven up your everyday cooking enormously.

SUPERMARKET SHOPPING

The bigger supermarkets also sell some of the products that you will find in the oriental grocer, but not necessarily the best or most authentic brands. Undoubtedly, they will be at a higher price.

Some also sell organic fruit and vegetables, so make a point of searching them out, and asking for them if you can't find them. Although you'll pay that bit more, it really is worth it both for the flavour and for your health.

A general note: read the label on processed foods. They may contain more additives and preservatives than you would want to put into your system, quite a few of which may be derived from animal products.

STOCKING THE STORE CUPBOARD

Here is a basic list of stores for the kitchen cupboard, with which you will be able to put together great meals very simply and quickly. Keep goods dry and cool, in sealed containers.

Canned produce: tomatoes; baked beans and other beans – haricot, butter beans, red kidney, flageolet etc.

Sauces and seasonings: mustards (see page 170), vegetable stock cubes, marmite, curry powder, tomato purée, soya sauce, tamari, coconut cream powder, black bean and garlic sauce, yellow bean sauce, chilli and garlic sauce etc. from ethnic grocers. Taco sauces and hot relishes from the Mexican department. Pesto and favourite pasta sauces.

Oils: olive oil; sunflower, grapeseed, groundnut, dark sesame oil and walnut oil.

Vinegars: red and/or white wine, tarragon, raspberry, sherry and balsamic vinegars.

Nuts and seeds: almonds, dried coconut, hazelnuts, peanuts, pine kernels, walnuts, pumpkin seeds, sesame seeds and sunflower seeds.

Dried pulses: black beans, black-eye beans, borlotti beans, lentils (red, green and brown), butter beans, cannellini beans, flageolet beans, mung beans, red kidney beans, yellow split peas, chick peas.

Cereals: roasted buckwheat, ground maize (polenta), oats, rice, wild rice, Chinese noodles, rice vermicelli, wholemeal and plain pasta various shapes.

Herbs and spices: the complete range.

Dairy produce: milk, butter, cheeses – cheddar, Parmesan or Pecorino.

Free-range eggs.

Lots of **fresh fruits** and **vegetables** in season, organic where possible.

ESSENTIAL EQUIPMENT

The good workman who never blamed his tools presumably always invested in good ones. Quality is always the best policy: not only do the tools perform better, they also last for years on end. If you can't afford them all at once, collect them gradually, and drop hints around Christmas and birthday times...

Food processor: This may be the most expensive item you will invest in, and probably the one you use the most. You can choose between a free-standing or hand-operated machine: either will chop, slice, purée, blend and shred in a few seconds. You can make breadcrumbs and mayonnaise in a matter of minutes. The best present that anyone can buy for you!

Set of quality knives: Get the best that you can afford – you will never regret it (or get someone to give them to you for Christmas). These are the most important tools of the trade and make a huge difference in the kitchen. Knives that have balance – with fine, sharp blades – will serve you well for many years as you cut, slice and chop. You will need a good knife sharpener too.

Microwave oven: Although not a necessity, once you have owned one you tend to regard it as such. A microwave oven 'steams' vegetables to perfection, retaining their flavour, texture and colour in a way that cooking over open heat does not. It reheats dishes extremely successfully, keeping them moist and fresh. Then there is the added attraction of not having to wash up saucepans – you can cook vegetables in the dish in which you serve them at the table.

Good saucepans: Good quality saucepans are a boon to the good cook. Thick-bottomed, heavy pans cook evenly and steadily - whether you are simmering or frying – and a small, heavy pan is essential for making good sauces. This may mean a bit of an outlay at the time, but it is a good investment – quality pans will last for many years, if not a lifetime.

Electric hand whisk: Ideal for beating eggs, making light cakes and whipping cream.

Other essential items:
wooden chopping board(s)
wok
selection of wooden spoons
cheese-grater with coarse and fine, and a slicer on the side
electric whisk
hand beater
wire whisk
lemon zester
salad spinner
set of scales (wall-mounted if you don't have much surface area)
plastic spatulas, various sizes
measuring jug(s)
selection of mixing bowls
selection of baking sheets, loaf tins, cake tins, flan tins, etc.
large sieve, small sieve
pastry brush
slotted spoon
pepper mill
food thermometer

SOME USEFUL TECHNIQUES

STEAMING

This gentle way of cooking is excellent for vegetables, since it retains all their flavour, texture and moisture.

Put water into the lower pan of the steamer and bring it to the boil. Put the vegetables in the steamer part, place over the hot water and cover tightly. Cook the vegetables for the time stated in the recipe, testing with a sharp knife before the end of the cooking time to make sure that they do not overcook. Most vegetables are improved with undercooking, which should leave them slightly crisp in the centre.

If you don't have a steamer, put 1cm (½in) water into a pan, bring to the boil and put in the vegetables. Lower the heat to a simmer. Cover very tightly with a lid so that the minimum of steam escapes. Shake the pan occasionally, and test after 5 minutes for young and tender vegetables, 8 minutes for larger ones.

You can also steam vegetables very successfully in the microwave. Put them into a dish with a little water. Cover with a lid or plate (remember, nothing metallic in the microwave oven) and cook on full power for the time stated in the recipe. Allow to stand for a few minutes to complete the cooking before you serve them.

DEEP-FRYING

Frying at very high temperatures seals food and cooks it – effectively steaming it inside.

Heat your oil – groundnut or soya are good because they are tasteless – in a wok or deep-fryer. Use a thermometer if you have one and bring the oil to chip heat. To test, drop a piece of food into the oil and when bubbles appear around it and the food cooks to crisp quickly, the oil is hot enough to deep-fry.

Don't add too many items to the oil at one time, as it will cause the temperature to drop. Make sure the food is dry before you drop it in, otherwise the oil will spit. When the food is cooked – you can usually tell by its light golden-brown colour – lift it out with a slotted spoon and drain on absorbent kitchen paper. Always be careful not to let hot oil drop on to the stove as it can cause a fire.

When you have finished cooking, leave the oil to cool before straining it through a sieve lined with absorbent kitchen paper and storing in a jar. You can reuse it 3 or 4 times.

BAKING BLIND

Baking blind means partly or entirely baking a pastry shell before it is filled.

Roll out the pastry on a lightly floured board and use to line a greased flan tin. Press it gently into the corners and edges, and trim the rim. Prick with a fork in several places, then spread a piece of foil over the surface so that it overlaps the rim by 5cm (2in). Fill the middle with baking beans. You can buy ceramic baking beans, or

you can simply use dried kidney beans or butter beans which you store for this use alone, since once baked they are useless except for baking blind. Store them in a screw top jar – clearly labelled, otherwise you may mistake them!

Put the lined, weighted dish into the preheated oven at 200°C/400°F/gas mark 6 for 20 minutes. Turn off the oven, remove the foil and beans, and return to the oven for 10 minutes to crisp the pastry. Cool on a rack.

SKINNING PEPPERS

Cut peppers into quarters and de-seed. Cut each quarter into 2 or 3 strips and place skin-side up under a hot grill for 5–6 minutes. When the skin has blistered and blackened, remove and cool. The skin will then peel off easily.

Alternatively you can use a very simple microwave method: prick the pepper with a sharp knife and microwave on full power for 3–4 minutes, depending on the size of the pepper. Allow to cool, and cut into quarters. The skin will peel off easily.

SKINNING TOMATOES

Put tomatoes into a large bowl and cover with boiling water. Leave to stand for about 5 minutes. Lift out one by one, piercing them with a sharp knife as you do so. The skin should now peel off easily.

This technique also works for skinning peaches.

STRIPPING CORN OFF THE COB

Remove the outer leaves and husks from the corn. Holding the corn cob upright with the flat end firmly on a board, take a sharp knife and run it down between the kernels and the cob, to strip them away.

KEEPING SALAD FRESH

Cut or torn lettuce leaves, washed and dried in a spin-dryer, keep crisper for longer stored in an airtight bag or container in the refrigerator. But remember that any vegetables stored for a long period of time lose their nutritive value, and much of their flavour and firmness.

ONIONS

Peeling pungent onions makes your eyes run, so it's handy to be near a cold water tap and run your hands under it when the tears pour as it stems the flow.

Softening onions in oil or butter, which is a basic step in many recipes, is best done by first tossing the sliced onions in the oil or butter over a medium heat until well coated, then turning the heat down, covering with a lid, and leaving to cook very gently for about 10–12 minutes. After this time, the onions become soft and sweet as this process steams them rather than browns them. Stir once or twice during this time.

Browning onions takes less time and is done over a higher heat, uncovered. The taste of browned onions is much stronger than softened ones.

STIR-FRYING

A quick and tasty way of cooking vegetables, this is best done in a wok, or failing that in a large frying pan. Cut your fresh vegetables into bite-size pieces, diagonally if you prefer, or in some cases shred or slice them in the food-processor (see 'Cutting Vegetables').

Groundnut oil is best for stir-frying because it is tasteless and doesn't burn easily: add the tasty oils like dark sesame towards the end of the cooking time. Heat a very little oil in your wok or pan and smear it over the surface. Get the oil – and the pan – really hot before you toss in the vegetables, letting the heat sear them as you stir them in the pan. When they are evenly heated through and beginning to cook, turn the heat down a little and stir briskly until they are tender but still crisp. At this point, add the seasonings in the recipe. In some cases you then turn the heat right down, add a little water, cover with a lid and allow the vegetables to steam to a finish.

Always serve stir-fried vegetables as soon as possible after cooking as they are at their best crisp and hot from the pan.

CUTTING VEGETABLES

Chopping vegetables can be done in a number of different ways, using a sharp knife (see page 29) and a wooden chopping board. A marble slab will blunt your knives.

You can chop coarsely or roughly for vegetables that will later be blended or stewed. For a soup or sauce that is not going to be sieved or a decorative dish, cut into thin slices, then into tiny cubes – or into thicker slices and larger cubes, to suit the recipe.

Dicing vegetables generally means cutting into 1cm ($\frac{1}{2}$in) slices, then into cubes.

You can cut sliced vegetables into squares or oblong pieces. For stir-frying or steaming, it looks nice if you slice vegetables diagonally. To julienne vegetables, slice them thinly and then cut into fine matchsticks. You can buy a blade attachment for the food processor which will do this for you very effectively.

Shredding leafy vegetables means cutting them into fine shreds. Roll up a pile of leaves and cut across the roll with a sharp knife.

STARTERS

You can get a meal off to an inspired start with a wide variety of colourful and tasty dishes: a cheese dish, or light filo delicacies; fresh salad compositions or mushrooms in various guises. A delectable morsel of goat's cheese melted over fried bread with sun-dried tomatoes; a simple salad of yellow peppers with mozzarella dressed in a balsamic vinaigrette, or a stir-fry of cauliflower with ginger and garlic – all these launch a memorable meal in style. There are some stunning flavours in this section which reflect cuisines from West to East – some make good, light meals on their own.

GRILLED YELLOW PEPPER & MOZZARELLA SALAD WITH BALSAMIC DRESSING

A simple, dainty salad that makes a classy starter. Serve it with a fresh Plaited Cob (page 81) for an extra-special occasion.

SERVES 4

3 large yellow peppers, quartered and deseeded

75g (3oz) good Mozzarella cheese, sliced

2 teaspoons Dijon mustard

4 tablespoons balsamic vinegar

4 tablespoons olive oil

finely chopped fresh dill, to garnish

Place the peppers skin-side up on a baking tray and set under a very hot grill for 7–8 minutes, or until the skins blister and turn black. Cool, then peel off the skin and slice the flesh into long, thin strips. Arrange with the Mozzarella in a serving dish.

In a separate bowl, mix the mustard and vinegar together, then gradually stir in the oil to make a well-amalgamated dressing. Pour over the peppers and cheese, tossing well together. Sprinkle with finely chopped dill and serve at room temperature.

CRISP THAI VEGETABLE PATTIES WITH LEMON GRASS & DIPPING SAUCES

Little morsels that melt in the mouth and are full of flavour, these are exotic and more-ish. Lovely finger food to dip into East-Asian sauces.

MAKES 20 SMALL PATTIES

350g (12oz) courgettes
250g (8oz) cauliflower
250g (8oz) carrots
50g (2oz) peanuts, chopped finely
10–12.5cm (4–5in) piece fresh lemon grass, bruised and chopped very finely
1 fresh red chilli, chopped very finely
4cm (1¹/₂in) piece fresh root ginger, peeled and grated finely

1 teaspoon salt
1 whole egg, plus 2 egg yolks
100g (4oz) fresh wholemeal breadcrumbs (see page 42)
rice flour or plain flour, for dipping
groundnut or sunflower oil for frying

Grate the courgettes, cauliflower and carrots using the coarse blade of a food processor, if you have one, or else grate by hand. Mix with the peanuts, lemon grass, chilli, ginger and salt.

Now break the eggs and yolks into the bowl and beat lightly together. Stir in the breadcrumbs, then gently fold into the vegetables.

Shape into little patties with your hands, squeezing them gently to hold the mixture together. Roll the patties in a plate of rice flour – this is lighter than ordinary flour – so that they are lightly coated on both sides. ◆

Heat a little oil in a frying pan and shallow-fry the patties over a medium heat for 5–6 minutes on each side, or until light golden-brown and crisp. Drain on kitchen paper and keep warm in a low oven while you fry the remaining patties.

Serve with a garnish of shredded lettuce, and the dipping sauces.

DIPPING SAUCES

SPRING ONION AND GINGER
2 tablespoons spring onions, chopped very finely
2 teaspoons freshly grated root ginger
1 tablespoon soy sauce
4 tablespoons sesame oil
Mix together. Use immediately or store in the refrigerator for 2–3 days.

CHILLI
3 tablespoons chilli oil
1 tablespoon soy sauce
Mix together. Use immediately or store in the refrigerator for up to 1 month.

GARLIC AND RASPBERRY VINEGAR
2 tablespoons soy sauce
1 tablespoon raspberry vinegar (see page 188)
1 clove garlic, peeled and crushed
Mix together the soy sauce and vinegar and season to taste with garlic. Use immediately or store in the refrigerator for 2–3 days.

SHERRY AND GINGER
75ml (3fl oz) sherry
2 tablespoons freshly grated root ginger
Mix together. Use immediately or store in the refrigerator for 2–3 days.

SATAY SAUCE
This peanut-based sauce from Indonesia, spiked with chilli, is one of my great favourites and a must for the kitchen cupboard.

You can buy jars of very good satay sauce from oriental grocers and supermarkets, but make sure you choose a good brand because some are much better than others. There is also an excellent dried version, which you can make up to the desired consistency with water.

Satay sauce is delicious served with these patties. To thin the sauce for dipping, mix with dark sesame oil and a little soy sauce to bring to the desired consistency.

MELTING CROÛTONS WITH GOAT'S CHEESE & SUN-DRIED TOMATOES

Sun-dried tomatoes have a wonderfully rich flavour which has great impact in this dish. They come either dried, in which case you rehydrate them by soaking them for an hour or two, or in oil – which I prefer, so I have used them here.

MAKES 12 SMALL CROÛTONS

TO SERVE

mixed salad leaves, tossed in a little
    vinaigrette (see page 204)
a handful of alfalfa sprouts (see page 9)

FOR THE CROÛTONS

12 small or 6 large slices wholemeal bread
olive oil, to brush
175g (6oz) round goat's cheese, cut into
    12 slices
6 sun-dried tomatoes in oil, cut in half
freshly-ground black pepper
4 sprigs parsley or chervil, to garnish

Arrange the tossed salad leaves on 4 medium serving plates and sprinkle with the sprouts.

Using a round fluted pastry cutter, 6.5cm (2½in) in diameter, cut out 12 rounds of bread. Brush them with olive oil on both sides, and grill until golden. Place a slice of cheese on each one, and top it all with a piece of sun-dried tomato.

Bake in the oven at 220°C/425°F/gas mark 7 for 15 minutes, or until melted and golden-brown. Sprinkle with freshly ground black pepper.

Arrange 3 croûtons on each plate of leaves, garnish with a sprig of herbs, and serve immediately.

SPICED AUBERGINES

This simple way of cooking aubergines with ground spices is delicious either hot, warm or cold. If you choose to eat it hot, serve with a spoonful of fragrant jasmine rice (see page 143). Warm or cold, it is delicious on a bed of soft mixed leaves tossed in vinaigrette.

SERVES 3–4
V

2 large aubergines, sliced
3 tablespoons olive oil
2 teaspoons each ground cumin, coriander,
    turmeric and cardamom

1 teaspoon sea salt
1 tablespoon lemon juice
150ml (¼ pint) vegetable stock

Cut the aubergine slices into 1cm (½in) strips. Heat the oil in a wok, add the aubergines and soften over a medium heat for 5 minutes.

Sprinkle the spices and salt over the aubergines and stir-fry for a further minute or two. Then add the lemon juice and stock and cover with a lid. Turn the heat down low and cook gently, stirring occasionally, for 20–25 minutes, or until the aubergines are completely tender, even soft to the point of breaking up.

Stir-Fried Cauliflower with Ginger & Garlic

As is the case with most very simple dishes, this is brilliant. The hit of ginger on the palate and the rich flavours of yellow bean sauce and dark sesame oil, bring magic to the cauliflower. AND it takes only a matter of minutes to make.

Serves 3–4

V

1 medium cauliflower, cut into small florets
3 tablespoons groundnut or sunflower oil
2.5cm (1in) piece fresh root ginger, peeled and sliced very finely
1–2 cloves garlic, peeled and sliced very finely
1 fresh chilli, sliced very finely (optional)

2 tablespoons yellow bean sauce
1 tablespoon dark sesame oil
a little soy sauce, to taste
3 tablespoons chopped chervil or coriander, to garnish

Cut the cauliflower florets into thin slices. Heat the oil in a wok and stir-fry the cauliflower, ginger, garlic and chilli (if using) for 3 minutes. Then add 2 tablespoons water and turn the heat down low. Cover with a lid and steam for 5–6 minutes, shaking the pan or stirring from time to time.

Stir in the yellow bean sauce and sesame oil, then season to taste with soy sauce. Serve sprinkled with the chervil or coriander.

Baby Tomatoes Guacamole

Little tomatoes filled with the traditional Mexican recipe guacamole – an avocado purée flavoured with garlic and lemon – is a sophisticated way to start a meal, yet very easy to prepare. Serve with pitta bread, or if you want to keep to the Mexican theme why not make the Best Cornbread on page 80 – it is sublime.

Serves 4–6

For the guacamole
12 medium tomatoes
2 ripe avocados, cut in half and stones removed
1 clove garlic, peeled and crushed
2 tablespoons lemon juice
2 tablespoons natural yoghurt
2 tablespoons very finely chopped green pepper
2 tablespoons very finely chopped celery
1 tablespoon chopped parsley
1 teaspoon cayenne pepper (or ¼ teaspoon chilli powder, if you like your food hot!)
salt
chopped chives

To serve
a handful of lambs' lettuce leaves
vinaigrette dressing (see page 204)

Slice the tops off the tomatoes and scoop out the flesh and the seeds. Stand upside down on kitchen paper to drain.

Scoop the flesh out of the avocados and mash well. Add the garlic, lemon juice, yoghurt, green pepper, celery and parsley. Mix well and season to taste with cayenne and salt. ◆

Fill the tomatoes with the avocado mixture and sprinkle the tops with chopped chives. Serve on a bed of lightly dressed lambs' lettuce, allowing 2–3 tomatoes per person.

Opposite: Stir-fried Cauliflower with Ginger & Garlic and Best Cornbread (page 80)

Filo Wafers with Courgettes, Basil & Pine-nuts

This recipe is quite complex to make but worth the toil. These wafers are brilliant. They are crisp, tasty and light and make a mouthwatering appetiser.

MAKES 12 WAFERS

USING FILO PASTRY

Filo pastry freezes well and is useful to keep in store. Defrost completely before using. You can re-freeze any leftovers after use.

Keep any filo pastry you are not using immediately wrapped in clingfilm, or place under a damp cloth to prevent it drying out and becoming brittle.

When brushing the pastry with olive oil, don't be too heavy-handed. Use just enough to lightly cover the surface and keep it crisp; too much oil will make the pastry soggy.

You can use off-cuts of filo pastry for decoration. Brush them with olive oil, then scrunch them up lightly with your hands and set on a greased baking tray. Bake at 200°C/400°F/gas mark 6 for 10–15 minutes, or until golden-brown. They look wonderful as a garnish, and are tasty too.

PINE-NUTS

These are not nuts at all. They are the seeds of the Mediterranean stone-pine tree. They have a resinous flavour and oily texture and are delicious either eaten raw or lightly browned under the grill.

FOR THE FILO WAFERS
500g (1lb) medium courgettes
4 spring onions, sliced
1 tablespoon olive oil
3–4 cloves garlic, peeled and crushed
2 tablespoons chopped basil
3 tablespoons chopped parsley or chervil
175g (6oz) Ricotta cheese
sea salt and freshly ground pepper
200g (8oz) packet filo pastry
*75g (3oz) pine-nuts, lightly browned under
   the grill*
olive oil, to brush

TO SERVE
salad leaves
sun-dried tomatoes
lime vinaigrette (see page 205)

Grate the courgettes on the coarse side of the grater, then pat dry on kitchen paper. In a sauté pan, soften the spring onions in 1 tablespoon of olive oil over a low heat for about 2 minutes. Add the courgettes, toss well in the oil and sauté over a medium heat for 3–4 minutes. Now add the garlic and herbs and cook for 4–5 minutes, stirring constantly. Remove from the heat and leave to cool for a few minutes before mixing in the cheese. Season to taste with salt and pepper. ◆

Cut the filo pastry into 8.5cm (3½in) squares. Brushing each one with olive oil as you go, make layers with 5 of the oiled sheets, then place a circle of pine-nuts on top. Cover with another layer of filo, brush with olive oil and place a tablespoon of the filling in the centre. Cover with another layer of filo, brush with oil and press lightly around the edges to seal. Make an indentation with your finger in the centre and put 4 or 5 more pine-nuts into this 'nest'. Cover with 3 more layers of the filo, brushing each one lightly with oil.

Place the filled filo nests on an oiled baking sheet, set in the oven at 200°C/400°F/gas mark 6 and cook for 25–30 minutes, or until golden-brown and crisp.

Serve hot or warm, on a bed of salad leaves tossed in a lemony vinaigrette dressing. Garnish with sun-dried tomatoes.

SPICED VEGETABLES WITH YELLOW BEAN SAUCE 'MU-CHOO'

A mouthwatering dish in which gently spiced vegetables are wrapped in the pancakes that are usually served with Peking Duck. Delicious with Lemony Brown Rice (see page 144).

SERVES 4

V

175g (6oz) cauliflower
250g (8oz) broccoli
100g (4oz) courgette or squash, peeled
100g (4oz) mangetout
2 large spring onions
half a yellow pepper
75g (3oz) beansprouts

75g (3oz) waterchestnuts, sliced thinly
6 Chinese leaves, shredded finely
3 tablespoons yellow bean sauce
1–2 teaspoons chilli sauce
soy sauce
12–15 Chinese pancakes (see below)

Finely chop the first 6 vegetables, then mix with the beansprouts, the finely sliced waterchestnuts and the Chinese leaves. Steam until tender – either in the steamer or in the microwave. Leave to cool a little, then toss in the yellow bean sauce and the chilli sauce. Season to taste with soy sauce. ◆

Warm the pancakes by steaming them for 1 minute in a steamer, or for 30 seconds in the microwave. Cover with a napkin to retain the heat.

Serve each helping of vegetables with 3 or 4 pancakes. To serve, wrap a spoonful or two of the vegetables in a pancake and eat with your fingers – it's a slightly messy operation but wonderfully memorable, informal food!

CHINESE PANCAKES

These are sometimes called 'Mandarin Wrappers'. They are small, papery pancakes about 10cm (4in) in diameter. They are sold by the packet in oriental stores and some supermarkets.

CELERIAC & TOMATO SALAD WITH CELERY & MUSTARD

The very mustardy dressing on this salad makes it a warming salad starter for cold weather. For me, celeriac rates highly among the winter vegetables, so this recipe is a firm favourite.

SERVES 6

V

FOR THE DRESSING
2 tablespoons Dijon mustard
2 tablespoons balsamic vinegar
5 tablespoons olive oil

FOR THE SALAD
250g (8oz) celeriac, peeled and cut into
   julienne strips
250g (8oz) celery hearts, chopped very finely
300g (10oz) small tomatoes, sliced thinly
a little finely chopped tarragon, to garnish
   (optional)

Mix the mustard with the vinegar until smooth. Gradually stir in the oil until you have a thick dressing.

Mix the celeriac with the celery and toss in the dressing. Place some of the sliced tomatoes in the centre of a serving dish and heap the celeriac mixture in a ring around the outside. Fill the ring with more slices of tomato.

Garnish with chopped tarragon or celery leaves, and serve with warm bread.

BALSAMIC VINEGAR

This dark brown, thick vinegar is made from fermented grape juice and has a fine well-balanced flavour. It comes from Modena in Italy, where it is matured in wooden barrels for many months. It has a scented aroma and a rich sweet-sour taste that gives a distinctive touch to salad dressings.

FENNEL & FRENCH BEAN SALAD WITH CROÛTONS

If you can get hold of yellow courgettes for this dish, they look much prettier than the ordinary green ones. Served with the Basil and Garlic Bread on page 81, this makes a sophisticated starter with a wonderful combination of flavours.

SERVES 6

V

FOR THE SALAD

2 large slices bread, cut into dice

groundnut oil for deep-frying

2 heads fennel, trimmed and sliced thinly

2 tablespoons olive oil

1 large yellow courgette, trimmed

1 large yellow pepper, quartered and deseeded

300g (10oz) French beans, cooked 'al dente'

6 spring onions, chopped finely

the juice of half a lemon

a little chopped tarragon

FOR THE DRESSING

2 tablespoons dark sesame oil

1 tablespoon raspberry vinegar (see page 188)

First make the croûtons: fry the cubes of bread in groundnut oil until golden-brown, then drain them on kitchen paper and keep warm in a very low oven.

Sauté the sliced fennel in the olive oil over a medium heat until soft but still crisp – about 4 minutes. Remove from the pan and cool.

Steam or microwave the courgette until it is cooked through but still crisp. Cool and slice.

Place the pepper quarters skin-side up on a grill tray and set under a hot grill until the skins blister and turn black. Turn them over and grill the underside for a minute or two. Peel off the skin and cut the flesh into strips. Arrange the prepared vegetables in a serving dish and toss with the lemon juice.

To make the dressing, heat the sesame oil in a small pan and when hot add the vinegar. Let it sizzle for a few seconds, then pour over the salad and toss quickly. Sprinkle with chopped tarragon and croûtons and serve immediately.

GREEK SPINACH FILO TRIANGLES

These tiny, crisp triangles of filo pastry are filled with a scrumptious spinach and dill mixture and baked to golden. They are a mouthwatering way to start a meal – finger food which everyone loves.

MAKES 14 TRIANGLES

500g (1lb) fresh spinach

6 spring onions, trimmed and sliced finely

2 tablespoons olive oil

3 tablespoons chopped dill

2 tablespoons chopped parsley

salt, pepper and nutmeg

2 eggs, beaten

100g (4oz) Feta cheese, crumbled

100g (4oz) filo pastry

olive oil, to brush

Wash the spinach and cook in its own water for 3–4 minutes, then drain thoroughly and chop finely.

Sauté the spring onions in the olive oil until soft – about 4–5 minutes – then stir in the spinach. Cook gently for 5 minutes, then add the herbs. Mix well,

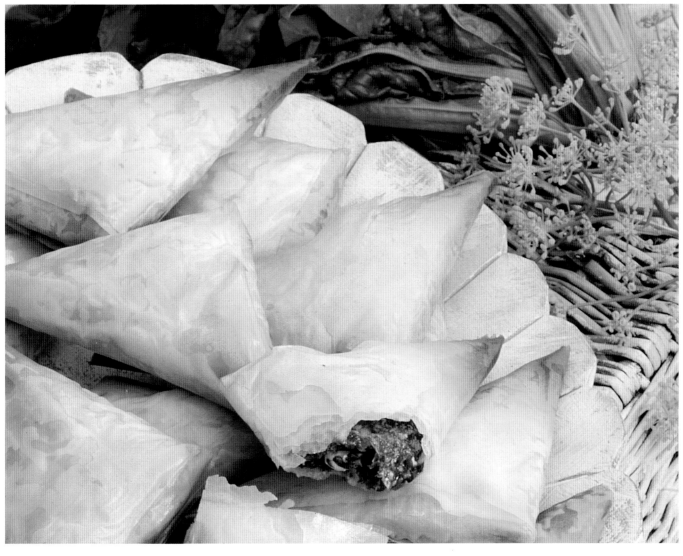

season with salt, pepper and nutmeg and set aside to cool.

Drain off any excess liquid from the spinach, then mix into the beaten eggs. Finally, fold in the crumbled cheese. ◆

Cut the filo sheets in half lengthways so that they measure 8.5 x 30cm (3½ x 12in). Brush one sheet with olive oil, then set another one on top. Brush with oil again. Spoon 1 tablespoon of the spinach mixture onto the top corner of the strip. Bring the adjacent corner over the filling and press it onto the opposite side of the strip to make a diagonal fold. Press the edges together to seal. Fold over again and again until you reach the end of the pastry strip, finishing with a tight triangular package. Brush the top with olive oil. Make all the triangles in this way, then place on a greased baking sheet.

Bake in the oven at 190°C/375°F/gas mark 5 for 20–25 minutes, or until golden-brown. Set on a wire rack to cool slightly. Serve warm.

ROASTED AUBERGINES & GRUYÈRE
WITH A LIGHT TOMATO & PECORINO SAUCE

This is a truly scrumptious way to eat aubergines. They have a crunchy garlicky topping finished with melting cheese, and look beautiful on the plate served with a spoonful or two of the creamy tomato sauce.

SERVES 6

MAKING BREADCRUMBS

The simplest way of making breadcrumbs is to put pieces of day-old (or older) bread into the food processor and run the machine. (Fresh bread is soft and because it is moist the crumbs tend to stick together.)

Use the resulting crumbs fresh, or dry them on a baking tray in a very low oven (140°C/275°F/gas mark 1) for 40–50 minutes, shaking from time to time. Cool on a rack and store in an airtight container.

1 x 350g (12oz) aubergine, sliced and sprinkled with salt
olive oil
3 cloves garlic, peeled and crushed
100g (4oz) fresh wholemeal breadcrumbs (see below)
100g (4oz) Gruyère cheese, sliced thinly
6 sprigs of parsley, to garnish
full quantity Light Tomato and Pecorino Sauce (see page 179)

Leave the sliced and salted aubergine to sweat for 20 minutes, then pat dry on kitchen paper. Brush lightly with oil. Mix the crushed garlic into the breadcrumbs, stir in 2 tablespoons of oil and mix well together. Place the aubergine slices on a baking tray and spread with the breadcrumb mixture.

Bake at 190°C/375°F/gas mark 5 for 25–30 minutes, or until the aubergines are soft. Place the cheese on top and return to the oven for a further 3 minutes, or until the cheese melts.

Serve hot, garnished with a sprig of parsley, and pour some Tomato and Pecorino Sauce around each helping.

STEAMED COURGETTES WITH CRISP WALNUTS
& CRÈME FRAÎCHE

This is a great favourite of mine – partly because I love simple food, but also because I have a weakness for courgettes. It is brilliant in its simplicity – a perfect summer starter served with little Sesame Toasts (see page 78).

SERVES 3–4

500g (1lb) courgettes, trimmed
50g (2oz) walnut pieces, chopped roughly
175g (6oz) crème fraîche
a little finely chopped dill, to garnish

Steam the courgettes until well-cooked but still slightly crisp. Plunge into cold water to cool, then slice thinly.

Crisp the walnuts under a hot grill: spread on a grill tray and set under the grill for 2–3 minutes, tossing them occasionally. Take care not to let them burn. Cool.

Mix the nuts into the sliced courgettes, then combine with the crème fraîche and coat well. Sprinkle with chopped dill.

Eat and enjoy!

GARLICKY TAPENADE OF BLACK OLIVES WITH CHILLI

The inspiration for this recipe comes from Provence, land of sun-baked olive groves and blue skies. Serve the tapenade with thin toast or crackers, and some fresh crudités such as raw carrots, mushrooms, courgettes and celery.

SERVES 4–6

FOR THE TAPENADE
100g (4oz) black olives, stoned
50g (2oz) whole almonds with their skins on, chopped
2 eggs, soft-boiled for 2 minutes, cooled and shelled
a tiny slice of green chilli
1 clove garlic, peeled and sliced
1 tablespoon soy sauce

1 tablespoon white or red wine vinegar
about 50ml (2 fl oz) olive oil
a pinch of dried tarragon
sea salt and freshly ground black pepper

TO SERVE
lettuce leaves
sliced tomatoes

Put the first 7 ingredients into the food processor and blend until smooth, adding enough olive oil to make the mixture spreadable. Season to taste with tarragon, salt and pepper.

Place a helping in the centre of a crisp lettuce leaf and serve surrounded by slices of tomato.

CREAMY MOZZARELLA MUSHROOMS ON CROÛTONS

A delicious starter: a large mushroom filled with a garlicky, nutty mixture of Mozzarella and herbs, then baked until the mushroom is soft. It goes well with a glass of red wine.

SERVES 4

5 large flat mushrooms for stuffing
2 tablespoons olive oil
2 cloves garlic, peeled and chopped finely
50g (2oz) walnuts, chopped finely
175g (6oz) Mozzarella cheese, cut into thin strips
sea salt, freshly ground black pepper and ground mace

1 tablespoon chopped parsley
1 tablespoon chopped basil or tarragon
1 egg, beaten
25g (1oz) fresh wholemeal breadcrumbs (see page 42)
4 circles of fried bread (see page 75)
4 basil or tarragon leaves, to garnish

MOZZARELLA CHEESE
This Italian curd cheese is occasionally made without animal rennet (see page 66). It is white, egg-shaped and soft, and comes packed with its whey. It is best eaten fresh, within a day or so of purchase. You can also buy smoked Mozzarella, which is a delicacy and well worth trying in this dish.

Remove the stalks carefully from the mushrooms, reserving 4 of the caps for stuffing. Chop the stalks finely along with one whole mushroom. Sauté the chopped mushrooms in the olive oil with the chopped garlic and walnuts. Remove from the heat and mix in the mozzarella strips. Season to taste with salt, pepper and mace, add the herbs, then stir in the beaten egg and mix well. Add the breadcrumbs and stir to a paste. Fill the 4 whole mushroom caps with this mixture and set on a greased baking tray.

Bake in the oven at 200°C/400°F/gas mark 6 for 15 minutes. (Alternatively, arrange on a plate, cover with another plate and microwave on full power for 2 minutes.)

Serve piping hot on circles of fried bread (see page 75). Garnish with a single basil or tarragon leaf.

SPINACH & OYSTER MUSHROOMS WITH PROVOLONE & WARM SESAME DRESSING

Unusual and elegant, this starter is exceptional – lovely flavours and textures combine to make something very special. Perfect with the Basil and Garlic Bread on page 81.

SERVES 4

250g (8oz) oyster mushrooms
3 tablespoons yellow bean sauce
1 tablespoon curry powder
250g (8oz) baby spinach
2 yellow peppers, grilled (see page 30)
100g (4oz) Provolone or Pecorino cheese (see page 135 and page 122)

FOR THE DRESSING
60ml (2fl oz) raspberry vinegar (see page 188)
5 tablespoons dark sesame oil

Toss the oyster mushrooms thoroughly in the yellow bean sauce and curry powder and marinate for 1 hour.

Arrange the spinach in a large salad bowl. Skin the peppers and slice into long strips. Add to the spinach.

Just before serving, microwave the mushrooms for 3 minutes. Cut the cheese into thin slivers with a sharp knife, or on the side of the grater. Spoon the mushrooms with their juices over the salad.

Heat the sesame oil in a small pan and when hot stir in the vinegar. Heat through and pour over the salad. Toss quickly, cover with the slivers of cheese and serve immediately.

SALAD OF TINY BROCCOLI FLORETS WITH DARK SESAME OIL, GINGER & CORIANDER

Sublime simplicity: this is one of those dishes that you'll want to make over and over again for its rich flavours and hint of the East. And it is SO easy and cheap to make. If purple sprouting broccoli is in season, use that instead of ordinary calabrese. You can get dark sesame oil from oriental grocers. Always store a piece of root ginger in the freezer – it keeps well and can be grated from frozen.

SERVES 4

V

2.5cm (1in) piece fresh root ginger, peeled and grated finely
5 tablespoons dark sesame oil
a small bunch of fresh coriander, chopped finely

1kg (2lb) broccoli
a sprig of fresh coriander, to garnish

To make the dressing, mix the finely grated ginger into the oil with the chopped coriander. Leave to stand while you prepare the broccoli.

Cut the end stalks off the broccoli and set aside for other use – in soup or vegetable stock, for example (see page 218). Cut the heads into tiny florets or slices and steam them for 1–2 minutes, or until soft but not mushy. Remove from the heat and leave to cool. If you are using purple sprouting broccoli, steam the whole stems for 2–3 minutes, then cool. ◆

Toss the cold broccoli in the prepared dressing and arrange in a serving dish. Garnish with a sprig of fresh coriander. Serve at room temperature.

SOUPS

Soups make wonderful winter food, although I have included a fabulous spring vegetable soup here, as well as several soups for summer. Soups freeze extremely well and so I tend to make large batches at a time, when the vegetables are at their best in high season, and store them for later use. Using large yoghurt cartons is good for this, each carton being roughly the equivalent of one good serving. So enjoy using the seasonal plenty as the year turns, using as many organic vegetables as possible.

CREAMY BROCCOLI SOUP WITH A HINT OF BLUE CHEESE & CUMIN

*S*uch a simple soup to make, this mixture is exquisitely warming and has the most wonderful flavours. Since broccoli is readily available throughout the year, it is a soup for all seasons. You can use purple sprouting when it is in season, to ring the changes.

SERVES 4

625g (1¼ lb) broccoli
1.2 litres (2 pints) vegetable
  stock (see page 218)
100g (4oz) mature Stilton,
  crumbled

2 teaspoons cumin seeds,
  pounded in a mortar
2 tablespoons crème fraîche
freshly ground black pepper

Steam the broccoli until very tender and leave to cool a little. Then chop roughly and spoon into the blender with half the stock, the crumbled cheese and the pounded cumin seeds.

Blend to a smooth soup, gradually adding the rest of the stock until it is all used up. Stir in the crème fraîche and season with freshly ground pepper.

Creamy Broccoli Soup, Chilled Almond Soup (page 49), and Olive Focaccia (page 79)

CHINESE SOUP

*L*ight and tasty, this delicate soup is great *as a starter to a three-course meal. I also love it as a simple supper on a cold night. It is excellent if you are watching your weight, as it is filling and satisfying, but light on calories.*

SERVES 4

V

1.2 litres (2 pints) vegetable stock (page 218)
3 medium spring onions, trimmed and sliced
　finely
2.5cm (1in) piece fresh root ginger, bruised
175g (6oz) small button mushrooms, sliced
　very finely

50g (2oz) rice vermicelli
a squeeze of lemon juice
1–2 tablespoons soy sauce
chopped fresh coriander, to garnish

Pour the stock into a large saucepan and bring to the boil. Add the spring onions, bruised ginger and sliced mushrooms, lower the heat and simmer gently for 3–4 minutes. Stir in the vermicelli, then draw off the heat and leave to stand for 5 minutes. Season to taste with lemon juice and soy sauce, and remove the ginger.

Pour into soup bowls and sprinkle with chopped coriander.

SPINACH & COURGETTE SOUP WITH GARLIC CROÛTONS

*T*his lovely soup has subtle flavours *and a most beautiful green colour. Served with the garlic croûtons on page 218 and some warm granary bread, it makes a perfect lunch.*

SERVES 4

250g (8oz) fresh spinach
500g (1lb) courgettes
50g (2oz) butter or margarine
1 small onion, sliced very finely and then
　chopped
3 tablespoons wholemeal flour
1.2 litres (2 pints) vegetable stock (page 218)

4 tablespoons single cream, or skimmed or
　soya milk if preferred
sea salt, freshly ground black pepper and
　nutmeg
4 sprigs of marjoram, to garnish
garlic croûtons (made from 2–3 slices of bread,
　see page 218), to sprinkle

Wash the spinach, then cook in its own water until tender – about 3–4 minutes. Drain thoroughly.

Steam the courgettes until soft – about 4–5 minutes in the microwave – then leave to cool.

Melt the butter or margarine, add the onion and soften over a very low heat for 5 minutes. Then stir in the flour. When blended, gradually pour in half of the stock, stirring constantly to make a smooth roux base. Bring to the boil and simmer gently for 6–7 minutes in order to cook the flour.

Put the spinach and courgettes into the blender with the rest of the stock and whizz to a purée. Gradually add this to the roux, stirring all the time, then add the cream and season to taste with sea salt, freshly ground black pepper and nutmeg.

Pour into soup bowls, float a sprig of marjoram in the centre of each and sprinkle with a handful of garlic croûtons.

TOFU

Tofu was invented by the Chinese, made from a pressed purée of soya beans. It is white, moist and bland, but absorbs flavours well. Silken tofu is very soft and you can mash it to make dips or use it to thicken soups. Firm tofu is heavily pressed with a cheese-like texture and can be sliced or diced, then marinated and fried. You can also obtain smoked tofu.

Tofu is a nutritious food, high in protein and containing iron, calcium and the B vitamins. It is very low in fat, so can add creaminess to soups and sauces without making them too rich. (Also see Soya Products, page 27.)

SWEETCORN & PEPPER SOUP WITH CHILLI

A lovely thick soup to warm you on cold days. This soup is made with milk instead of stock, which gives it a soothing quality. It is full of flavour, and freezes very well.

SERVES 4

V

1.2 litres (2 pints) skimmed or soya milk
1 medium onion, diced finely
1 bay leaf
4 sprigs of parsley
a large sprig of thyme
8 peppercorns

1 large red pepper
350g (12oz) tomatoes
2 x 500g (1lb) cans sweetcorn
sea salt and chilli powder
chopped chives, to garnish

Bring the milk to the boil with the onion, bay leaf, parsley, thyme and peppercorns. Turn the heat right down and allow to stand, covered with a lid, for half an hour.

Cut the pepper into quarters and deseed it. Grill skin side up under a hot grill until the skin burns and blisters. Then steam or microwave, covered, until completely soft – about 2–3 minutes. Cool, then skin and chop roughly.

Pour boiling water over the tomatoes and let them stand for a few minutes before piercing with a sharp knife and peeling them. Chop roughly.

Put the pepper, tomatoes and sweetcorn into the blender and strain the milk over them. Blend to a thick soup, then season to taste with sea salt and a pinch or two of chilli powder. Sprinkle each helping with a few chopped chives.

CHILLED ALMOND SOUP

For hot summer days, and for sophisticated parties, this is your soup. It is exquisitely delicate, with original and unusual flavours. Serve it with the Olive Focaccia on page 79 and it is sensational.

SERVES 3–4

V

175g (6oz) blanched almonds
100g (4oz) wholemeal bread, crusts removed
1–2 cloves garlic, peeled and crushed
the juice of half a lemon
4 tablespoons virgin olive oil

900ml (1½ pints) cold vegetable stock (see page 218)
25g (1oz) flaked almonds, toasted under the grill (see page 57)
4 sprigs of mint, to garnish

Grind the almonds to a fine powder in the food–processor. Soak the bread in cold water and squeeze dry. Add to the almonds in the machine with the garlic and lemon juice and process until smooth.

While the machine is running, gradually pour in the oil in a thin stream. When well-amalgamated, pour in half the stock and blend until smooth. Pour into a large serving bowl and stir in the rest of the stock. Chill thoroughly.

To serve, sprinkle the flaked almonds over the top of each helping, and decorate with a sprig of mint.

SUMMER COURGETTE SOUP WITH CURRY SPICES

A fabulous way to cook courgettes, spicing a delicate vegetable. This is an excellent way of using summer's annual glut of courgettes, because the soup freezes very well. I am lucky enough to have a source of organic courgettes each summer, and their flavour is fantastic in this soup.

SERVES 4

V

FRESH HERB GARNISHES

Out of season, fresh herbs are not only expensive but nothing like as aromatic and tasty as those grown in season. For this reason, the garnishes for all my recipes are optional. However, I love to use fresh herbs freely through spring and summer, giving a touch of elegance to the food. Growing your own herbs is a simple business – whether in the garden or in pots or window-boxes – and is worthwhile for their exceptional and distinctive flavours as well as for their prettiness as plants.

---

750 g (1½lb) courgettes
40g (1½oz) butter or margarine
1 large onion, sliced finely
whole curry spices: 1 teaspoon each cumin seeds, coriander seeds and mustard seeds; plus 4 cloves and ¼ teaspoon cardamom pods
powdered curry spices: ½ teaspoon each ground cinnamon and turmeric; ¼ teaspoon cayenne pepper
1cm (½in) piece root ginger, peeled and grated finely
1 pint (600ml) vegetable stock (see page 218)
sea salt
sprigs of coriander, to garnish

Steam the courgettes until tender – about 5–6 minutes – or cook in the microwave on full-power for 7–8 minutes.

Melt the butter or margarine in a large pan, stir in the sliced onion and cook gently until it softens.

Pound the whole spices together in a mortar until they are ground fine; remove the husks and discard. Add to the pan with the powdered spices and grated ginger and stir well.

Chop the cooked courgettes and add to the pan, coating them well with the mixture. Cook for 5 minutes, then pour in the stock. Cover and simmer gently for 8–10 minutes, or until the vegetables are tender.

Purée until smooth in the blender and check the seasoning.

Pour into bowls and serve garnished with a sprig of fresh coriander in the centre of each soup bowl.

LIGHTLY CURRIED ARTICHOKE SOUP

Simplicity itself. A huge favourite all through the winter. I adore the taste of Jerusalem artichokes, and here it is in all its purity. I leave the skins on since that is where much of the nutritional goodness lies.

SERVES 4

1kg (2lb) Jerusalem artichokes, washed
1.2 litres (2 pints) vegetable stock (page 218)
5 tablespoons crème fraîche
sea salt and freshly ground black pepper
finely chopped parsley, to garnish

Simmer the artichokes in a covered saucepan until completely soft. Cool in their liquid, then drain.

Liquidise with half of the stock until smooth, then gradually add the rest of the stock. Stir in the crème fraîche and season to taste.

Sprinkle each helping with a little chopped parsley.

PUMPKIN SOUP WITH GRUYÈRE

This creamy, sumptuous soup is warming and rich – the perfect answer to cold, winter evenings. Serve it with warm granary bread and you have a complete meal.

SERVES 4–6

1kg (2lb) pumpkin or squash, such as butternut, turban, patty pan, etc.
40g (1½oz) butter or margarine
1 medium onion, chopped finely

1.2 litres (2 pints) vegetable stock (page 218)
sea salt and freshly ground black pepper
75g (3oz) Gruyère cheese, grated finely
chopped parsley or chives, to garnish

Cut the pumpkin (or squash) in half, scoop out the seeds and place cut-side down on a lightly oiled baking sheet. Bake in the oven at 200°C/400°F/gas mark 6 for about 1 hour, or until the flesh is soft. Alternatively, microwave on full-power for 10–15 minutes. Cool, then peel.

Melt the butter or margarine in a large saucepan or casserole, add the onion and cook gently for about 5 minutes until it softens. Stir in the chopped flesh of the pumpkin or squash and half of the stock. Bring to the boil, cover partially with a lid and simmer gently for 15–20 minutes.

Liquidise in the food-processor to a creamy puree, then stir in the rest of the stock. Season to taste with salt and freshly ground black pepper, then stir in the grated cheese. Serve garnished with chopped parsley or chives.

SPICY CARROT & ORANGE SOUP

A soup of wonderful fresh flavours that needs no extra seasoning. You can make it throughout the year, using organic carrots in season for better flavour. These are easy to get hold of and are always a better buy in terms of quality.

SERVES 4–6

40g (1½oz) butter or margarine
3 medium onions, sliced finely
500g (1lb) carrots, scrubbed clean and sliced
600ml (1 pint) vegetable stock (see page 218)

the grated rind and juice of 1 large orange
150–300ml (¼–½ pint) skimmed or soya milk
finely chopped mint, to garnish

Melt the butter or margarine in a pan, add the sliced onions, cover with a lid and soften over a gentle heat for 10 minutes, or until cooked and slightly sweet. Add the sliced carrots and toss them in the oil until well-coated. Cook for 3–4 minutes.

Pour in the stock and simmer, covered, for 15 minutes. Add the orange rind and cool a little, then add the orange juice.

Pour into a food processor and blend to a smooth soup, thinning to the desired consistency with the milk.

Heat through gently and serve sprinkled with a little chopped mint.

LEMONY SPRING VEGETABLE SOUP WITH CRÈME FRAÎCHE

A beautiful soup using early vegetables, with a touch of lemon for extra freshness. For a real treat, serve this with the Basil and Garlic Bread on page 81.

SERVES 6

CRÈME FRAÎCHE

This is a thick pasteurised soured cream that has been matured and fermented to produce a faintly sharp, acid taste. It is quite heavy in texture and keeps longer than fresh cream – 10–14 days on average in the refrigerator. Crème fraîche is widely used in French cuisine for its delicate tang, which can be attractive in savoury and sweet dishes alike. It is slightly richer than single cream, but with more protein and considerably less fat than double cream. I like its freshness, and use it in soups to enrich them without making them heavy. Healthier!

40g (1½ oz) butter or margarine
1 medium onion, chopped
175g (6oz) small new potatoes, washed and chopped
100g (4oz) leek, sliced
175g (6oz) baby carrots, sliced
250g (8oz) courgettes, sliced
100g (4oz) peas
100g (4oz) spinach, washed (or half and half with sorrel)

1.2 litres (2 pints) vegetable stock (page 218)
a small bunch of fresh mint
grated rind of 1 lemon
15g (½oz) cornflour
2 egg yolks
90ml (3fl oz) crème fraîche or single cream
the juice of quarter of a lemon
sea salt and freshly ground black pepper
chopped chives, to garnish

Melt the butter or margarine in a large pan, add the onion, cover with a lid and soften over a low heat for 6–8 minutes. Then add the other prepared vegetables and toss well. Cook over a gentle heat, covered, for a further 8 minutes. Then add the stock and simmer for 10 minutes. Spoon into a food processor and blend until smooth, then stir in the chopped mint and grated lemon rind.

Sift the cornflour into the egg yolks and whisk until smooth. Gradually stir in the crème fraîche. Pour into the pan with the puréed soup and simmer for 5 minutes, or until the soup thickens. Finally, stir in the lemon juice and season to taste with sea salt and black pepper. Sprinkle with the chopped chives and serve.

FRESH BEETROOT SOUP

This is the simplest of soups – a straight purée of freshly cooked beetroot, served with chopped dill and yoghurt. Beetroot is an epicurean vegetable and often severely underrated: just the smell of it as it boils is mouthwatering. This soup is the most sublime magenta to red colour, turning to a stunning pink as you mix in the yoghurt.

SERVES 4
(omit yoghurt garnish) V

1.5kg (3lb) beetroot, scrubbed clean
600ml (1 pint) vegetable stock (see page 218)

chopped dill or chervil, to garnish
4 tablespoons Greek yoghurt

Put the beetroot into a large saucepan and cover with cold water. Bring to the boil and simmer for 50–60 minutes or until tender. If you are using small beetroot the cooking time will be shorter. Leave to cool in the water, then lift out and peel off the skins.

Chop roughly and put into the blender. Liquidise with the stock until the purée is as smooth as it will go – it will have a slightly grainy texture. It needs no seasoning.

Spoon into 4 bowls and sprinkle with dill or chervil. Put a dollop of yoghurt in the centre and serve.

WINTER VEGETABLE SOUP

This is a serious soup. It needs serious time to prepare and is seriously warming. It is easy to make a big batch because a little of each of the vegetables goes a long way. Since it freezes very well, it is worth having a good session in the kitchen – you will reap the rewards for some time.

SERVES 8

V

●

MIXED DRIED HERBS

The quality of dried herbs varies greatly. You can detect their excellence by their aroma, so always have a good sniff before you buy. Some mass-packaged herbs are devoid of flavour and add nothing to your cooking. Personally, I like to obtain herbs from the places where they are known to grow best – such as the Mediterranean – so I bring back bags of dried herbs from my holidays.

75g (3oz) dried cannellini or flageolet beans
75g (3oz) chickpeas
1 onion, cut in half
a sprig of rosemary
1 bay leaf
50g (2oz) fresh root ginger, cut in half and bruised
100g (4oz) parsnips, cut into julienne strips

250g (8oz) turnips, cut into julienne strips
300g (10oz) seakale or cabbage, sliced
175g (6oz) beetroot, cut into julienne strips
250g (8oz) carrot, cut into julienne strips
250g (8oz) leek, sliced
1–2 vegetable stock cubes (optional)
500g (1lb) potatoes, scrubbed

Soak the pulses for 6–8 hours, or overnight if possible. Drain. Put into a saucepan with the onion, rosemary, bay leaf and ginger and cover with water. Bring to the boil and simmer for 45 minutes.

Meanwhile, prepare all the vegetables: wash them thoroughly but leave the skins on – they're the best part of the vegetable nutrition-wise and add to the flavour of the soup. Use a julienne cutter on the food processor if you have one – it will save a lot of time! Add the vegetables to the pan and simmer for a further 30 minutes. If necessary, add a little water to cover and a stock cube or two, to taste.

Meanwhile, cover the potatoes with water in a separate pan. Bring to the boil and simmer for 25–30 minutes, or until very soft. Purée in the blender with a little of the cooking liquid to a medium-thick purée. Stir into the soup to thicken it, remove the root ginger and check the seasoning.

CARROT & LENTIL SOUP WITH CORIANDER

I love this soup on winter days for a warming lunch, served with the Soda Bread on page 80. It is hard to beat. You can also make it with mint instead of coriander and that is excellent too.

SERVES 4

V

●

'Herbes de Provence' are among the best mixed herbs; Greek thymes and marjoram are hard to beat; Moroccan souks sell wonderful dried mountain herbs; and French markets never fail. So bring back little packs from your travels to enjoy at home.

175g (6oz) red lentils, soaked for half an hour
750 g (1½lb) carrots (organic if possible), scrubbed clean and trimmed
1 large onion, sliced
1.2 litres (2 pints) water or vegetable stock (see page 218)

1 tablespoon dried mixed herbs
large bunch fresh coriander, chopped finely
salt and pepper
4 sprigs coriander, to garnish

Drain the lentils. Put into a saucepan with the carrots and onion and cover with the water or stock. Bring to the boil and add the herbs. Simmer, covered, for 45 minutes.

Pour into the food processor and blend to a purée. Season to taste with salt and pepper, then stir in the chopped coriander.

To serve, warm through, pour into soup bowls and garnish with a sprig of fresh coriander in the centre of each.

RED PEPPER & TOMATO SOUP

This classy soup is a wonderful red, its flavour distinguished. I love to serve it for special suppers 'a deux', along with the Plaited Cob on page 81. It is as good hot as cold.

SERVES 2–3

V

If you want to enrich soups, try using silken tofu: just add it at the liquidising stage and it makes the soup creamy without making it heavy. This is a good source of protein and an easy way of obtaining it.

2 large red peppers
500g (1lb) ripe tomatoes
3 tablespoons olive oil
2 teaspoons mixed dried herbs
2 cloves
1 bay leaf
1 sprig rosemary

4 cloves garlic, peeled and chopped
1 medium onion, chopped
1 leek (white part only), chopped
300ml (½ pint) vegetable stock (see page 218)
1 teaspoon sea salt
150ml (¼ pint) crème fraîche
sprigs of rosemary, to garnish

Steam or microwave the red peppers until soft – about 5–6 minutes. Leave to cool, then deseed and slice. Cover the tomatoes with boiling water, leave to stand for 3–4 minutes, then prick with a sharp knife and remove the skins.

Heat the oil in a pan, add the herbs, cloves and bay leaf and soften over a low heat for 2 minutes. Then stir in the rosemary, garlic, onion and leek. Cover with a lid and cook gently over a low heat for about 10 minutes, or until the mixture is well-softened. Remove the bay leaf and rosemary and discard.

Purée the skinned tomatoes with the cooked red peppers and add to the pan. Stir well, then add the stock and season with salt. Cover the pan, bring to the boil and simmer gently for a further 8–10 minutes. Return to the blender and purée until smooth.

Stir in the crème fraîche just before serving and pour into bowls. Garnish with a small sprig of rosemary.

SOUPE À L'OIGNON GRATINÉE

I first ate this great French classic soup in the old market place of Les Halles in Paris in the 1960s, and the memory is still vivid after 30 years. It is a wonderful meal in itself, served with warm French bread, so if you want to transport yourself to that great city, this is one way of doing it.

SERVES 4

4 large mild onions, sliced thinly
75g (3oz) butter or margarine
900ml (1½ pints) vegetable stock (see page 218)

sea salt and lots of freshly ground black pepper
4 slices bread
250g (8oz) Cheddar cheese (low-fat if preferred), grated

Cook the sliced onions in the melted butter or margarine over a very gentle heat, covered with a lid, for about 30 minutes until soft and sweet, stirring from time to time.

Now add the stock and simmer for 5–8 minutes, seasoning to taste with salt and pepper. Pour into 4 heatproof soup dishes.

Trim the bread and toast it. Float on top of the soup, cover with grated cheese and put under a hot grill until the cheese melts and bubbles.

NUTTY CELERY SOUP WITH SHALLOTS & LEMON GRASS

An elegant soup with an exotic touch, this makes a good first course for a special dinner or an informal supper party. Serve it with the Garlic Bruschetta on page 78, for added style.

SERVES 6–8

4 celery hearts, chopped roughly
2 thick stalks lemon grass, bruised
the pared rind of 1 lemon
2 vegetable stock cubes
250g (8oz) shallots, sliced very finely
50g (2oz) butter

1 heaped tablespoon wholemeal flour
2 teaspoons soy sauce
75g (3oz) slivered almonds, browned (see below)
chopped chives, to garnish

TO BROWN ALMONDS
Spread the almonds in a thin layer on a metal baking tray and put under a medium grill. Toss frequently as they begin to brown, keeping a close watch over them so that they don't burn. When lightly and evenly browned all over remove from under the grill and leave to cool in the tin.

Put the celery, lemon grass and lemon rind into a large saucepan and cover with water. Bring to the boil and simmer for 30–40 minutes, or until the celery is completely soft.

Crumble in the stock cubes and leave to stand for 15 minutes off the heat. Then lift out the lemon grass and lemon rind and discard.

Purée the celery in a little of the cooking liquid. If it is stringy, pass it through a sieve.

Soften the shallots in the melted butter, covered, for 10–15 minutes over a very low heat. Stir from time to time. Then add the wholemeal flour and make a roux with some of the cooking liquid. Bring to the boil and simmer gently for 7–8 minutes to cook the flour.

Now stir in the celery purée, mix well, and season to taste with soy sauce. Add as much of the cooking liquid as you like to bring the soup to a fairly thin consistency.

Heat through and serve sprinkled with browned flaked almonds and chopped chives.

SPICY CAULIFLOWER BLENDER SOUP WITH LENTILS

Easy, quick and utterly delicious, this is a great favourite in my family. It is extra nutritious because of the protein in the tofu, which also gives the soup a lovely creamy consistency.

SERVES 3–4

1 medium cauliflower
100g (4oz) red lentils
sea salt
100g (4oz) tofu
900 ml (1½ pints) vegetable stock (see page 218)

1 tablespoon garam masala paste
single cream or crème fraîche (optional)
chopped chervil, to garnish

Steam the cauliflower until tender, and leave to cool.
Cover the lentils with water in a pan and simmer for 10 minutes, or until mushy. Season with a little salt.

Blend the cauliflower and tofu to a smooth purée in the food processor with 600ml (1 pint) of the stock. Add the garam masala paste, whizz again, then stir in the lentils with the rest of the stock. Check the seasoning and add a little cream if desired. Sprinkle each bowl with a little chopped chervil.

EGGS & CHEESE

The beauty of cooking with eggs is that they are versatile, cheap, and quick to prepare. They are also excellent vehicles for herbs and spices, so very tasty meals can be made up in virtually no time at all.

PUMPKIN SOUFFLÉ

This is sublime autumn food, served with Oil-roasted New Potatoes (see page 118) and a Spinach Salad (see page 198). Each helping should come out with a light crust – that is, if you prepare your soufflé dish by greasing it first, then dusting the inside with finely grated Pecorino cheese.

SERVES 4

750g (1½lb) pumpkin or squash
25g (1oz) butter or margarine
2 tablespoons flour
125ml (¼ pint) skimmed or soya milk
1 egg yolk
1 teaspoon ground cinnamon
50g (2oz) Cheddar cheese (low-fat if preferred), grated
salt
4 egg whites

Wrap the pumpkin or squash in foil and bake it at 190°C/375°F/gas mark 5 for 1½ hours, or until soft. Allow it to cool, uncovered, then skin and seed it. The cooked flesh should weigh about 350g (12oz). Scoop into a saucepan and simmer until much of the water has evaporated – about 5–10 minutes. Set aside.

Melt the butter or margarine over a gentle heat, stir in the flour and then stir in the milk gradually. Simmer for 3–4 minutes until thick and smooth, then remove from the heat and beat in the egg yolk. Fold in the pumpkin, cinnamon and half of the cheese. Season with salt.

Whisk the egg whites until stiff. Gently fold one tablespoon into the pumpkin mixture, then carefully fold in the rest.

Turn the mixture into a prepared soufflé dish (see below) and sprinkle with the rest of the cheese.

Bake at 190°C/375°F/gas mark 5 for 30 minutes, or until well-risen and set but still moist in the centre. To test, stick a skewer into the centre – if a little of the mixture adheres to the skewer the soufflé is ready.

Serve immediately.

ALTERNATIVE FILLING: SPINACH

Follow the master recipe for the soufflé above, using:

350g (12oz) fresh spinach, washed
2 shallots, sliced

15g (¹/₂oz) butter or margarine

Cook the spinach in its own water; drain thoroughly, then chop. Soften the shallots in the butter or margarine and mix into the chopped spinach.

Fold into the soufflé with the cinnamon and half the cheese.

PREPARING A SOUFFLÉ DISH

Brush the inside of your soufflé dish all over with melted butter or margarine. Sprinkle liberally with finely grated Parmesan, rolling it around so that the entire surface is coated. This creates an appetising crust for the soufflé, and prevents it sticking to the dish.

WHISKING EGG WHITES

To obtain maximum volume from your egg whites, always make sure that your beater, and the bowl, are completely clean and free from grease. Otherwise the egg whites won't beat frothy and stiff. Use an electric whisk, if you have one, to beat the maximum amount of air into them. Hand beaters can do the job as well, but it is harder work and takes longer.

Don't over-beat whites: if you put too much air into them they will collapse – rather like a balloon bursts when you put too much air into it. Egg whites are fully beaten when they make soft peaks which hold quite firmly.

CHEESY 'KOOKOO' WITH COURGETTES

A kookoo is a Persian dish, a form of baked omelette full of vegetables which is served cut in wedges. This one has delicate flavours and looks gorgeous with its lovely greens and yellows. Serve with your favourite salad (see pages 187–198).

SERVES 4

1 green pepper, quartered and seeded
500g (1lb) courgettes, grated
4 spring onions, chopped finely
3 tablespoons chopped parsley and rosemary, mixed

salt and pepper
5 eggs, beaten
175g (6oz) Cheddar, Lancashire or Mozzarella cheese (low-fat, if preferred), grated

Grill the pepper skin-side up under a hot grill until the skin burns and blisters. Cool, then peel off the skin. Slice finely.

Add to the grated courgettes with the spring onions, herbs, salt and lots of pepper. Mix well.

Stir the mixture into the well-beaten eggs. Spoon half the omelette mixture into a round ovenproof dish and cover with grated cheese. Pour the rest over the top and cover with foil.

Bake at 180°C/350°F/gas mark 4 for 40 minutes, then remove the foil and increase the heat to 200°C/400°F/gas mark 6. Cook for a further 15 minutes, or until the top browns and the centre is lightly set.

GOUGÈRE WITH MUSHROOMS IN SAFFRON MAYONNAISE

Gougère is such a treat – an inspired piece of French cuisine that always looks and tastes spectacular. The ring of cheesy choux pastry is filled here with minced mushrooms spiced with saffron. This is irresistible, but expensive: turmeric makes a tasty alternative.

SERVES 4–6

FOR THE GOUGÈRE

scant 300ml (½ pint) skimmed or soya milk
50g (2oz) butter or margarine, cut into small pieces
salt and freshly ground black pepper
100g (4oz) flour, sifted
4 eggs
75g (3oz) Gruyère cheese, cut into tiny cubes

FOR THE FILLING

10 threads saffron
1–2 tablespoons hot water
2 tablespoons crème fraîche
230ml (8fl oz) mayonnaise, preferably home-made (see page 206)
500g (1lb) button mushrooms

Bring the milk to the boil, then leave to cool for a minute. Add the butter or margarine, salt and pepper and return to the heat. Bring to the boil again. When the butter has melted, pour in the sifted flour. Beat vigorously until the mixture comes away clean from the sides of the pan.

Put the mixture into the food processor and break the eggs in one at a time while it is running, giving them time to be thoroughly absorbed. When the pastry is shiny, fold in the cubes of cheese and leave to cool.

Drop tablespoons of the mixture in a large circle onto a greased baking sheet, leaving a hole in the centre about 7.5cm (3in) across. Spoon a second layer of choux pastry on top until the mixture is all used up. Bake at 190°C/375°F/gas mark 5 for 45 minutes, or until golden. Cool on a rack.

Meanwhile, make the mayonnaise. Put the threads of saffron into a cup and pour the hot water over them. Leave to infuse for 10 minutes. Spoon the threads, with their soaking liquid, into the crème fraîche, then stir this mixture into the mayonnaise.

Note: If you are using powdered saffron or ground turmeric, simply add the spice to the mayonnaise – allowing 1–1½ teaspoons, according to taste. ◆

Mince the mushrooms in the blender, one third at a time, being careful not to run the machine too long – they take only moments to mince, and quickly turn to mush if you overdo it!

To serve, mix the mayonnaise into the mushrooms and pile into the centre of the cooled gougère.

SAFFRON

Saffron has always been, and is still, the most precious spice in the world. It comes from the stamen of the saffron crocus flower, which has to be picked out by hand; there are no mechanical devices for this process. 4,500 crocuses are required to yield a single ounce of the spice.

Always buy the stamens if you can afford them; powdered saffron is always mixed with other compounds and lacks the pure, inimitable flavour of real saffron. However it is an acceptable and less expensive substitute. Indeed, if you travel to North African countries such as Morocco or Egypt, their powdered saffron is excellent.

The spice gives the food with which it is cooked a beautiful golden-yellow colour, so a small supply in the spice rack is worth its weight in gold.

AN ALTERNATIVE TO SAFFRON

The poor man's version of saffron is turmeric, an orangey-yellow powder with a spicy, slightly hot flavour. It is delicious in rice dishes, and makes a good alternative in the saffron mayonnaise above.

SOUTH INDIAN CURRIED EGGS

An authentic recipe from my Indian friend whose family comes from Bangalore. She is a superb cook and the combination of spices she uses here is wonderful. Serve this with plain rice or noodles and a crisp side salad.

SERVES 4—6

1 large onion, chopped finely
4 tablespoons sunflower oil
3 cloves garlic, peeled and crushed
5cm (2in) piece fresh root ginger, grated
2 tablespoons ground almonds or pine-nuts
½ teaspoon chilli powder
½ teaspoon ground turmeric
2 teaspoons ground coriander

a little water
50g (2oz) coconut powder, dissolved in
    350ml (just over ½ pint) water
1 x 400g (14oz) can tomatoes
2 bay leaves
salt
6 large hard-boiled eggs, shelled
sprig of coriander, to garnish

Place the onion in a frying pan with the oil, cover with a lid and soften over a low heat for 10 minutes.

Mix the garlic, ginger, ground nuts, chilli powder, turmeric and coriander with a little water to make a paste. Add this to the onions when soft, and cook gently for 3–4 minutes. Pour over the coconut milk.

Stir in the tomatoes with their juices and the bay leaf. Simmer for about 15 minutes, or until the sauce thickens and the tomatoes disintegrate. Season to taste with salt. ◆

Cut the eggs in half and place on top, spoon some of the mixture over them and garnish with a sprig of coriander.

LEEK & NOODLE TIMBALE

A timbale is a savoury egg 'custard', which is baked in the oven standing in a dish of hot water until it is lightly set. This one, with leeks and noodles, is a soothing, comforting dish: satisfying for supper served with the Light Tomato and Basil Sauce on page 174.

SERVES 4–6

100g (4oz) egg noodles
350g (12oz) leeks, washed and sliced
4 eggs
150ml (¼ pint) soured cream

a medium bunch of parsley or tarragon,
    chopped finely
salt, pepper and nutmeg

Butter a soufflé dish well. Cook the noodles according to the packet instructions until soft; drain well and place in the bottom of the dish.

Steam the leeks until tender – about 10 minutes – drain and leave to cool.

Put them into the blender with the eggs, soured cream and herbs, season well and blend to a thin purée. Pour this mixture over the noodles. ◆

Bake in a bain-marie (that is, standing in a tin of hot water in the oven) at 170°C/325°F/gas mark 3 for 30–35 minutes, or until set.

BROCCOLI & POTATO FRITTATA

A frittata is a cake-like omelette thick with vegetables, pan-fried until set. You can use purple sprouting broccoli for this recipe when it is in season. The frittata is brilliant served hot or warm with mixed salad and spicy noodles. You can also serve any cold leftovers in a bap as a snack for lunch the next day.

SERVES 3–4

2 shallots, chopped finely
2 tablespoons olive oil
250g (8oz) broccoli, cut into tiny florets
175g (6oz) potatoes (organic if possible),
    peeled and diced small
salt and pepper

4 eggs
50g (2oz) Cheddar or Jarlsberg cheese, grated
15g (½oz) butter or margarine
1–2 tablespoons Parmesan or Pecorino cheese
    (see page 122), grated finely
a little chopped mint, to garnish

Sauté the shallots in the oil. When they begin to soften, add the broccoli and potatoes and mix well. Cover with a lid and steam over a gentle heat for 12–15 minutes, or until the vegetables are cooked but still slightly crunchy. If necessary, add a little water from time to time to stop the vegetables sticking. Season to taste with salt and pepper. Cool a little. ◆

Beat the eggs well, then stir in the cheeses and the cooked vegetables.

In a heavy frying pan, melt the butter or margarine until it sizzles. Pour the omelette mixture into the foaming butter and then lower the heat as much as possible. Cover with a lid. Cook very slowly, covered, until the eggs are set but still a little loose in the centre – about 15 minutes.

Sprinkle with the Parmesan or Pecorino and put under a hot grill for one minute to brown lightly.

Slide onto a serving plate and leave to rest for several minutes before serving. This releases the flavours, which come out better when it is warm rather than piping hot.

Serve sprinkled with finely chopped mint.

EGGS 'FOO YONG'

*L*ovely with buttered pasta and a mixed
salad, this simple dish is based on a
Chinese classic, adapted for simplicity. Just
right for Sunday supper!

SERVES 2–3

It's important to use eggs that are fresh: stale eggs lose their bounce and tend to go flat and disintegrate on cooking. Buy free-range eggs: battery hens are submitted to gross indignities and their eggs often taste of the fish feed they are given. Use your eggs at room temperature – they will bind better in the cooking. So store them in a cool place, not in the fridge, and away from strong smells since the shells are porous.

FOR THE SAUCE

100g (4oz) mushrooms
100g (4oz) peas
25g (1oz) butter or margarine
150ml (¼ pint) vegetable stock (see page 218)
soy sauce

FOR THE EGGS

4 eggs
3 spring onions, sliced finely
*75g (3oz) beansprouts, blanched in boiling
water, then strained*
salt and pepper
2 tablespoons olive oil

First make the sauce. Mince the mushrooms in the blender (see page 77). Cook the peas in boiling water until tender, about 4 minutes. Drain.

Melt the butter or margarine in a pan and stir in the minced mushrooms. Cook until the juices run, about 5 minutes. Then add the peas and mix. Stir in the stock and then purée in the blender. Add soy sauce to taste.

Now prepare the eggs. Beat them thoroughly, then stir in the spring onions and beansprouts. Season well with salt and pepper.

Heat the oil in a frying pan and when hot pour in the egg mixture. Draw the vegetables towards the centre with a spatula and as the edges begin to set, bring them towards the centre.

Continue until you have a thick round 'omelette', then turn and cook on the other side until the eggs are set in the middle.

Turn out onto a warm platter and serve with the sauce.

SOFT EGGS WITH STEAMED COURGETTES & CRÈME FRAÎCHE

*J*ust the answer when you want something
quick but delicious. This is an elegant
rendering of poached eggs (see below), with
lightly spiced courgettes on a bed of noodles.

SERVES 4

POACHED EGGS

Bring some water to the boil in a saucepan with a few drops of lemon juice. Break the egg into a cup and slip it into the boiling water. Remove from the heat immediately and allow the egg to poach in the hot water for 3–4 minutes. Lift out carefully with a slotted spoon.

100g (4oz) egg noodles
500g (1lb) courgettes
1–2 teaspoons green garam masala paste

200ml (7fl oz) crème fraîche
salt
4–6 eggs

Cook the noodles according to the packet instructions, then spoon into the bottom of an ovenproof dish.

Steam the courgettes, leave to cool and then slice thinly lengthways. Cut into 2.5cm (1in) lengths.

Mix the masala paste into the crème fraîche, then fold in the courgettes. Spoon over the bed of noodles.

Heat through at 170°C/325°F/gas mark 3 for 10–12 minutes from cold, or 6–9 minutes from warm.

Meanwhile, poach the eggs (see left).

To serve, spoon the poached eggs over the courgettes. Eat immediately with fresh, warm granary bread.

CLASSIC SPANISH OMELETTE

A perfect supper dish. The word omelette comes from a 17th-century form meaning 'thin plate'. However, in this case it is a thick plate. This is beautiful food which goes really well with the New Potatoes with Capers on page 118. It will be the best Spanish omelette you will have ever had!

SERVES 2

2 tablespoons olive oil
half a red onion, chopped
1 clove garlic, peeled and chopped
1 medium to large courgette, sliced thinly
1 medium potato, sliced thinly
150g (5oz) aubergine, microwaved whole for
    3 minutes or simmered in boiling water for
    4–5 minutes

2 tomatoes, chopped
½ teaspoon dried oregano, or 1 tablespoon
    fresh, chopped
salt and pepper
2 eggs
1 egg white

Heat 1 tablespoon oil in a medium saucepan, add the onion, cover with a lid and soften over a low heat for 5 minutes, stirring from time to time.

Then add the garlic, courgette and potato, stir thoroughly and cover again. Cook over a low heat for 7–8 minutes, or until the vegetables are tender but still crisp.

Cut the cooked aubergine into cubes and add with the tomatoes to the pan. Stir in the oregano, season to taste with salt and pepper and leave, covered, over the lowest possible heat while you prepare the eggs. ◆

Beat the eggs with the egg white, and season with salt and pepper. Heat the remaining olive oil in an omelette pan. Beat the eggs, then stir in the warm vegetables and pour into the pan. Cook over a medium heat for 4–5 minutes, then finish under a hot grill for a further 2–3 minutes until the omelette is set.

Slide on to a platter and serve at once.

OEUFS ST. GERMAIN

Eggs baked on a purée of peas is a lovely dish inspired by a French recipe. For a simple lunch, with fresh bread and a side salad, it takes some beating.

SERVES 2 AS A STARTER

250g (8oz) peas
50g (2oz) butter or margarine
salt

2 eggs
a little chopped mint, to garnish

Cover the peas with water, bring to the boil and simmer until soft – about 5 minutes. Drain, reserving some of the cooking liquid.

Spoon the peas, along with a little of their cooking water, into the blender, season with a pinch of salt and whizz to a rough purée. Add the butter and blend again until smooth. ◆

Place in the bottom of 2 ramekins, break an egg over the top of each one, and bake at 200°C/400°F/gas mark 6 until the egg is lightly set – about 6–8 minutes.

Sprinkle a little finely chopped mint over the top just before serving.

CHEESE FLAN 'MADAME RECAMIER'

An elegant recipe from France, this classic cheese flan has a layer of cheesy 'meringue' on top which makes it very original. Quite a party piece for a small but special dinner. Delicious with the French Bean and Tomato Salad (see page 189).

1 x 20cm (8in) flan tin, lined with shortcrust pastry and baked 'blind' (see page 30)
2 shallots, sliced very finely
a small bunch of parsley, chopped finely
40g (1½oz) butter or margarine
25g (1oz) wholemeal flour
300ml (½ pint) skimmed or soya milk

salt and freshly ground black pepper
75g (3oz) Cheddar cheese (low-fat if preferred), grated
2 eggs, separated
25g (1oz) finely grated fresh Parmesan or Pecorino cheese (see page 122)

THE NUTRITIONAL VALUE OF CHEESE
Cheese is a good source of protein, calcium, zinc and vitamin B12. However, it has no carbohydrate or fibre and is a very poor source of iron. Too high a consumption of cheese should be avoided as it is a major source of saturated fat and can lead to high cholesterol levels.

Sprinkle the chopped shallots and parsley over the base of the cooked pastry.

Melt the butter or margarine and stir in the flour. Gradually add the milk and stir to a thick sauce. Simmer very gently for 5 minutes, season with salt and pepper, then stir in the Cheddar cheese. Leave on a low heat for 5 more minutes, then remove from the heat and stir in the well-beaten egg yolks.

Pour into the prepared flan tin and bake at 190°C/375°F/gas mark 5 for 20 minutes. Cool for 10 minutes on a wire rack.

Beat the egg whites until very stiff, then fold in the grated Parmesan cheese. Pile this on top of the flan and return to the oven at 220°C/425°F/gas mark 7 for 10–15 minutes, or until the topping is cooked through. Serve immediately.

CHEESE
Most cheeses are made with rennet. Rennet is a substance containing an enzyme usually obtained from the stomach-lining of newly born calves. Rennet coagulates milk, separating it into curds and whey, and is essential in the manufacture of many cheeses. Advances in genetic engineering have led to the synthesising of a product identical to animal rennet and this may soon replace it.

Cottage cheese is always made without rennet, as are most cream cheeses and soft cheeses (but not all). Mozzarella is occasionally made without rennet. Most major supermarkets stock vegetarian versions of Cheddar, Cheshire, Double Gloucester, Stilton, Brie, Dolcelatte, blue cheese, Feta, Ricotta and others. Parmesan is almost always made with animal rennet, although an alternative vegetarian version is emerging.

SNACKS, DIPS & BREAD

For food in a hurry, or for when you don't feel like spending ages in the kitchen, these snacks are great stand-bys. They are ideal family food and many of the recipes are popular with children. They don't take long to prepare and don't use exceptionally unusual ingredients, so it is likely that you will be able to cobble them together from what you have in the fridge and the kitchen cupboard. They are highly tasty since a lot of them use herbs and spices, belying the short time spent on them. Very rewarding cooking!

The dips are highly versatile food, and again so quick and easy to prepare. You can use them as snacks or as a nibble to go with drinks before a meal, or serve them for lunch with some salads and warm breads. They are satisfying, nutritious food: some of them, like the Red Bean Dip and the Creamy Cannellini Dip, are warming in winter, whereas the cooling Garlicky Greek Tsatziki is perfection on a hot summer's day, for lunch in the shade or to go with evening drinks.

GARLICKY GREEK TZADZIKI

I never tire of this famous Greek dish. Made with good-quality Greek yoghurt, organic cucumber and lots of garlic, it takes some beating.

SERVES 2–3

half a cucumber, grated coarsely (skin included)
175g (6oz) thick Greek yoghurt (low-fat if preferred)

2 cloves garlic, peeled and crushed
sea salt
chopped fresh mint, to garnish

Pat the grated cucumber dry on kitchen paper. Mix with the yoghurt, then stir in the garlic and sea salt.

Chill well, sprinkle with chopped mint and serve with pitta bread or toast.

Garlicky Greek Tzadziki and Cretan Tirasalata (page 74)

SAVOURY PUFF PASTRY 'TATIN'

Raid the larder for a can of ratatouille and the freezer for some puff pastry, and you will have one of the best snacks you have ever tasted. It's brilliant, and there are endless variations of vegetables that you can use, including leftovers (leeks are wonderful).

SERVES 3–4

1 x 400g (14oz) can ratatouille
a little curry paste

250g (8oz) puff pastry, defrosted
1 egg yolk, beaten

Mix the ratatouille with curry paste to taste, and chop in any leftover vegetables you may have in the refrigerator. Spoon into a 23cm (9in) flan tin.

Roll out the pastry to a circle just a little larger – by about 2.5cm (1in) – than the circumference of the flan tin. Gently lay it over the ratatouille, tucking in the edges lightly. Brush with beaten egg yolk.

Bake at 220°C/425°F/gas mark 7 for 20–30 minutes, or until well-risen and crisp golden-brown. Remove from the oven, run a knife around the edges and invert onto a serving plate. Serve immediately, cut in wedges.

MELTING FOCACCIA WITH MOZZARELLA, SUN-DRIED TOMATOES & PESTO SAUCE

This is a great idea, and rings the changes from eternal toasted sandwiches or cheese on toast. More luxurious, admittedly – but treat yourself!

SERVES 2

4 long slices focaccia bread, buttered on both sides
pesto sauce

10–12 sun-dried tomatoes, preserved in olive oil
100g (4oz) Mozzarella cheese, sliced

Spread a little pesto onto one side only of the buttered focaccia. Lay the sun-dried tomatoes over the top and cover with the slices of Mozzarella.

Bake at 190°C/375°F/gas mark 5 for 10 minutes. Serve hot, straight from the oven.

ITALIAN BREADS

Focaccia
The origins of focaccia go back to Roman times when a flat bread was baked on hot hearthstones under the ashes of the fire. The word means 'flat bread'. Today, focaccia is made primarily in northern Italy, where the dough is leavened with yeast and baked in the oven. Many versions are available, some studded with olives, onions or sun-dried tomatoes, others flavoured with pungent herbs like rosemary and sage.

Ciabatta
This crusty, open-textured white bread is often made with unbleached wheat flour. Its distinctive quality comes from the olive oil, which is used to moisten the dough. It has a light and pleasant taste, and is best served warm. Ciabatta means literally 'a slipper', because of its long flat shape.

Pugliese
This bread has a looser texture than ciabatta, and is hand-moulded into a round cob loaf. It is made with extra-virgin olive oil and is delicious served with cheese.

CRISPY VERMICELLI

I often serve this as a nibble to go with a drink before a meal – it disappears like melting snow! Served alongside the Crispy Seaweed (see below), they make an interesting combination.

V

rice vermicelli
groundnut or sunflower oil for deep-frying
salt

Heat about 1cm (½in) oil in a deep pan until it is hot enough to puff the rice: test the temperature after a couple of minutes by dropping one piece of vermicelli into the hot oil – it should puff and crisp immediately.

To deep-fry the vermicelli, drop small amounts into the oil and cook very briefly, turning so that all the pieces puff up. Do not put too much in at one time since it expands considerably. Remove with a slotted spoon immediately the vermicelli crisps up, but before it starts to brown. Drain on kitchen paper and sprinkle with a little table salt.

Keep warm in a low oven until ready to eat.

CRISPY 'SEAWEED'

The world's cheapest food!

V

1 large outer cabbage leaf per person, for example Savoy
groundnut or sunflower oil for deep-frying

5-spice powder
salt

FIVE-SPICE POWDER
This aromatic powder is made from ground fennel, star anise, cloves, cinnamon and Sichuan peppercorns. You can buy it from supermarkets and oriental grocers.

Remove the woody part of the stem from the cabbage leaves and discard. Shred the cabbage extremely finely using a sharp knife.

Heat 1cm (½in) oil in a deep pan until very hot – test by dropping one or two shreds of cabbage into the oil. If they crisp up and turn brown very fast, it should be hot enough. Fry all the cabbage in this way, a little at a time, turning as you cook. Be careful not to overcook the cabbage, as it burns easily.

Lift out immediately it begins to brown and drain on kitchen paper. Sprinkle with 5-spice powder and salt while still warm, and serve as soon as possible.

TASTY MUSHROOM BURGERS

These are a great alternative to the traditional burger and are truly delicious. The perfect healthy snack for any time of the year.

MAKES 6 BIG BURGERS

FOR THE BURGERS
350g (12oz) button or chestnut mushrooms
100g (4oz) fresh granary breadcrumbs (see page 42)
1 tablespoon dried mixed herbs

2 egg yolks
sea salt and freshly ground black pepper

TO SERVE
6 soft baps, buttered

Put the mushrooms into the blender and mince finely (see page 77), or chop them very finely with a sharp knife. Mix with all the other ingredients and season to taste with salt and pepper. Shape into burgers with your hands and place on a well-greased baking tray.

Set under a hot grill and cook for about 5 minutes on each side. Place inside buttered soft baps and serve with your favourite relishes.

CRETAN TIRISALATA

This is equally good served as a snack or as a starter. It is very simple to make, so long as you have a little blender (see page 29). I had it in the mountains of Crete in a tiny village, and it always reminds me of the thyme-scented slopes, the glaring heat of midday, and Sunday lunch in the shade of a simple inn.

SERVES 3–4

75g (3oz) Feta cheese, crumbled
75g (3oz) low-fat cottage cheese
4 tablespoons olive oil

a small bunch of fresh oregano or marjoram, chopped finely

Purée all the ingredients to a fairly thick consistency in the blender.

Serve with the Garlic Bruschetta on page 78, and some crudités such as raw baby carrots and celery to nibble.

MEXICAN TOMATO RELISH

This very simple version of salsa can be made in a few minutes. It tastes wonderful.

SERVES 3–4
V

4 medium tomatoes, peeled (see page 30) and roughly chopped
quarter of a small onion, chopped

quarter to half of a fresh green chilli, chopped
1 tablespoon chopped fresh parsley or chervil
salt

Place all the ingredients in a blender and whizz to a smooth sauce. Heat through before serving.

SPICY SCRAMBLED EGGS WITH FRIED BREAD TRIANGLES

A sophisticated and interesting version of scrambled eggs which makes a perfect light supper, served with a tomato and onion salad.

SERVES 2

4 thin slices of bread
sunflower oil for frying
half an onion, chopped very finely
2 tablespoons olive oil
1 teaspoon each of ground cumin, coriander
and cardamom

½ teaspoon each of turmeric and
cayenne pepper
salt
4 eggs, beaten

Cut the crusts off the bread, then cut each slice in half diagonally to make a triangle. Heat a little oil in a frying pan and fry the bread triangles until golden-brown and crisp on both sides. Drain on kitchen paper and keep warm.

Heat the olive oil in a small saucepan, add the onion, cover with a lid and soften over a very low heat for about 10 minutes. Add the spices and cook gently, stirring all the time, for 3–4 minutes. Increase the heat to medium and stir in the beaten eggs. Cook gently, stirring from time to time, until the eggs scramble and set lightly.

Serve immediately on warm plates, surrounded by the fried bread.

MUSHROOM SANDWICHES

One of Life's Best Things. Who would have thought it, a mushroom sandwich? It's sublime – try one and see. Vegans can make these omitting the cheese and using a non-dairy spread.

MAKES 8 GENEROUS SANDWICHES

350g (12oz) fresh mushrooms, sliced
8 slices fresh granary bread

175g (6oz) Ricotta or low-fat cream cheese
sea salt and freshly ground black pepper

Steam the mushrooms in the microwave, or in a steamer, until tender – about 3 minutes. Cool completely and pat dry with kitchen paper.

Spread the slices of granary bread with a generous layer of Ricotta. Divide the mushrooms between 4 of the slices, cover with the remaining 4 and trim the crusts. Cut in half and you have a feast on your hands!

GUACAMOLE

This ever-popular Mexican dip is simple to make, and a delicious filling for Tacos (see page 86).

SERVES 4–6

2 large avocadoes, diced
2 tomatoes, skinned (see page 30) and
chopped
the juice of 1 large lemon

1 small red chilli, sliced very finely
1 clove garlic, sliced finely (optional)
4 spring onions, sliced finely (optional)
sea salt and freshly ground pepper

Combine all the ingredients in the blender and purée until very smooth. Season to taste.

SMOKED CHEESE & GARLIC SPREAD WITH CRUDITÉS

The smoked cheese flavour gives this spread its special quality. Its texture is appetising; the hint of garlic irresistible. Serve it with toast, in baps, or with crudités.

SERVES 4–6

100g (4oz) smoked cheese, grated
175g (6oz) quark or low-fat cream cheese
100–150ml (4–5fl oz) olive oil

2 cloves garlic, peeled and crushed
freshly ground black pepper

Mix the grated cheese with the cream cheese. Put into the small bowl of the blender, pour over the olive oil and blend until smooth. Add the garlic and blend again, then season to taste with freshly ground black pepper.

RED BEAN DIP WITH CHEESE

A surprising mixture that is extremely tasty and popular – everyone I give it to loves it. It is very versatile: you can eat it cold with tortilla chips, or with celery or other crudités, or heat it through gently and serve it as a topping for baked potatoes.

SERVES 3–4

250g (8oz) canned kidney beans
70 ml (2¹/₂fl oz) soured cream
2 tablespoons tomato purée
2 cloves garlic, peeled and crushed
¹/₂ teaspoon chilli powder

1 teaspoon ground cumin
40g (1¹/₂oz) finely grated Cheddar cheese
    (low-fat if preferred)
salt

Drain the beans and put them into the small bowl of the blender. Add the rest of the ingredients and whizz until completely smooth. Season to taste with salt.

CREAMY CANNELLINI DIP WITH CUMIN

A dream! Eat this simply with salad, on pitta bread, or as a dip to go with crudités. You'll love it.

SERVES 4

1 x 250g (8oz) can cannellini beans, drained
100g (4oz) Greek yoghurt (low-fat if preferred)
3 tablespoons mayonnaise

2 teaspoons ground cumin
crushed garlic
¹/₂ teaspoon sea salt

Bring a pan of water to the boil, add the beans and simmer gently for 12–15 minutes, or until completely soft. Drain through a sieve, allow to cool, then liquidise in a small blender.

Add the rest of the ingredients and blend to a smooth, thick purée. Check the seasoning. Chill well before serving.

PERUVIAN VEGEGRILLS WITH MEXICAN TOMATO RELISH

*M*y daughter ate these in a café in deepest Peru and described them to me with such enthusiasm that we re-created the Andes experience in our little kitchen. This is the result. They are delicious.

MAKES 6 VEGEGRILLS

FOR THE VEGEGRILLS
250g (8oz) outer leaves of iceberg lettuce, minced in the food processor (see below) or chopped very finely
2 small tomatoes, diced very small
75g (3oz) grated Cheddar cheese, low-fat if preferred
100g (4oz) fresh breadcrumbs (see page 42)
1 tablespoon dried mixed herbs
1 large clove garlic, peeled and crushed
1 egg, plus 1 egg yolk
sunflower oil for shallow-frying

TO SERVE
6 baps, buttered
Mexican Tomato Relish (see page 74)

Place the minced lettuce, tomatoes and cheese in a bowl and mix well together. Stir in the breadcrumbs, herbs and garlic, break in the eggs and egg yolk and mix thoroughly. Shape into burgers with your hands.

Heat the oil in a heavy-based frying pan and fry the burgers over a medium heat until golden-brown – about 5 minutes on each side.

Place inside the fresh, buttered baps, serve with the relish and eat!

MINCING SOFT VEGETABLES IN A FOOD PROCESSOR

You can use the basic puréeing blade of your food processor or blender to 'mince' soft vegetables such as lettuce and mushrooms. It chops them very finely indeed and begins to pulverise them – so fast in fact that you need to be watchful that you don't run the machine too long and mash them to a pulp. The safest method of doing this is to use the pulse action.

THE BREAD BASKET

Making your own bread sounds like hard work, a daunting prospect taking hours of kneading and rising and baking. Some breads do, of course, but not all. The recipes here show you how to make the most mouthwatering loaves in minimum time. I have included one classic bread – the Plaited Cob – simply because it is such a personal favourite that I couldn't omit it. The dough is rolled into 3 threads and plaited. It is a masterpiece for special occasions.

The Cornbread recipe, which is more like making a cake than making bread, is an instant success with everyone. It is light and moist, has that inimitable hit of chilli on the palate, and is lusciously cheesy. I have been making the Soda Bread recipe for years and it never fails. Made in a matter of minutes and baked in 30, it is sublime eaten hot and fresh from the oven, but also makes deliciously nutty toast.

The Basil Bread, Bruschetta and Sesame Toasts add a delicate touch to any home-made meal. They, too, are simple to make, and mouthwatering. So enjoy the smell of baking bread in your home as you prepare to enjoy your meal!

GARLIC BRUSCHETTA

Bruschetta means 'grilled bread'. It's a crusty, toasted version of garlic bread which is traditionally grilled over hot coals. Use the finest quality olive oil that you can afford.

V

1 loaf Italian bread – ciabatta if possible (see page 70)

1 clove garlic, skinned and cut in half
olive oil

Cut the bread into fairly thick slices and grill on both sides – preferably over charcoal – until golden-brown. Drizzle olive oil over the cut surfaces and rub a clove of garlic into the bread. Sizzle under the grill or return to the coals for a few more seconds, then serve immediately.

SESAME TOASTS

These strips of grilled bread with a crust of sesame seeds on one side are mouthwatering when served with dips and spreads – or just as a snack in their own right.

wholemeal or granary bread, cut into thin slices

butter or margarine, to spread
sesame seeds, to sprinkle

Put the slices of bread under a hot grill and toast them on one side only. Butter the untoasted side generously with butter or margarine and sprinkle with a thick layer of sesame seeds. Press them down with the flat edge of a knife and return to the grill to brown. Some of them will pop.

When they are golden-brown, remove from the grill and press down again. Cut the bread into long thin slices, and cool.

OLIVE FOCACCIA

A superb bread which is irresistible eaten fresh from the oven while the aroma of baking bread is still in the kitchen. The succulent olives give the bread its special style, which is nothing less than sensational.

MAKES 1 LOAF

V
●

15g (¹/₂oz) dried yeast
230ml (8 fl oz) warm water
350g (12oz) organic plain white flour
5 tablespoons olive oil

100g (4oz) black olives, stoned and sliced
1 teaspoon salt
a little maize meal, to dust

Dissolve the yeast in the warm water in a large bowl. Allow to stand for 10 minutes in a warm place until the yeast has dissolved and the mixture is creamy.

Fold in 250g (8oz) of the flour and beat until the dough is sticky and smooth. Gradually add the remaining flour, turning it out onto a floured board as soon as it is smooth enough to handle. Once all the flour is incorporated, knead to a smooth, elastic dough which is no longer sticky.

Put into an oiled bowl and cover with cling film. Allow to rise in a warm place, such as an airing cupboard or the top of the boiler, for 1 hour. Then knock it back with your fists, add 4 tablespoons of the olive oil and knead in the sliced olives and salt.

Knead again on a floured board until smooth, then place on a well-greased baking sheet which you have dusted with maize meal. Press into a circle about 25–30cm (10–12in) in diameter. Brush the dough with the remaining oil and leave to rise for a further hour in a warm place. After this time, it should have doubled in bulk. The dough spreads considerably as it rises, so I place it in a Swiss-roll tin which has edges to contain it.

Bake at 200°C/400°F/gas mark 6 for 30 minutes, or until the top is golden. Cool on a wire rack for at least 5 minutes before cutting.

BEST CORNBREAD

This is unbelievably lovely fresh from the oven. It is moist and spicy-hot, and completely irresistible. You can reheat it successfully wrapped in foil in a medium oven for about 10 minutes.

MAKES 1 LOAF

1 tablespoon, plus 4 tablespoons olive oil
1 tablespoon sesame seeds
175g (6oz) maize meal
150g (5oz) plain white flour
3 tablespoons granulated sugar
4 teaspoons baking powder
½ teaspoon salt

225ml (8fl oz) plain low-fat yoghurt
50ml (2fl oz) skimmed or soya milk
1 egg, beaten lightly
1–2 fresh jalapeno chilli peppers (according to how hot you like it!), chopped very finely
3 tablespoons chopped fresh coriander

Put 1 tablespoon oil into a 20cm (8in) square baking tin and warm over a low heat on top of the hob. When hot, stir in the sesame seeds and heat for 10–20 seconds. Remove from the heat, scoop out most of the seeds – leaving some on the bottom – and reserve until later.

Combine the maize meal, flour, sugar, baking powder and salt in a large mixing bowl. Add the yoghurt, milk, egg, chilli, coriander and 4 tablespoons olive oil and mix thoroughly until the dough starts to come together.

Shape into a round and press into the tin, then scatter the reserved sesame seeds over the top.

Bake at 200°C/400°F/gas mark 6 for 25–30 minutes. Cool on a rack for 10–15 minutes before turning out.

SODA BREAD

I have been making this simple yeastless bread for years. It is delicious eaten warm, fresh from the oven, but also makes divinely nutty toast.

MAKES 1 LOAF

500g (1lb) self-raising flour
1 teaspoon salt
300ml (½ pint), plus 2 tablespoons skimmed or soya milk

2 tablespoons water
poppy seeds or sesame seeds, to sprinkle

Sift the flour and salt into a large bowl. Make a well in the centre, pour in the milk and water and mix to a soft dough with a fork. Turn onto a floured board and knead lightly for a minute or two until the dough is light and smooth.

Shape into a round with your hands and score the top with a cross, using a sharp knife. Brush with a little more milk to glaze and sprinkle with the seeds.

Bake at 220°C/425°F/gas mark 7 for 30–35 minutes, or until the bread sounds hollow when tapped underneath. Allow to cool a little on a wire rack. Serve warm.

PLAITED COB

This is an enticing way to serve home-made bread – in a plait-shape and sprinkled with sesame seeds. This recipe is easy to make as it requires almost no kneading and no interim rising time – that takes place in the oven.

MAKES 1 LOAF
(omit garnish) V

350g (12oz) granary flour
100g (4oz) plain flour
2 heaped teaspoons sea salt
25g (1oz) fresh yeast

300ml (¹/₂ pint) warm water
2 tablespoons skimmed or soya milk
1 egg yolk, beaten
poppy or sesame seeds, to sprinkle

Mix the flours with the salt. Activate the yeast by mixing it with a little of the warm water. Make a well in the centre of the flour, pour in the yeast and mix to a soft dough with the rest of the water. Transfer to a floured board and knead with your hands to a smooth dough.

Cut the dough into 3 equal parts. Roll each one into a long sausage shape, tapering the ends. Plait the 3 strands together, pinching the ends to seal. Brush the top with the milk and beaten egg yolk, sprinkle with poppy or sesame seeds and set on a greased and floured baking sheet.

Bake in a pre-heated oven at 230°C/450°F/gas mark 8 for 10 minutes, then turn the heat down to 190°C/375°F/gas mark 5 and bake for a further 30–40 minutes, or until the loaf is golden and sounds hollow when tapped on the base. Cool slightly on a wire rack. Serve warm.

BASIL & GARLIC BREAD

A variation on plain garlic bread, this loaf has an aromatic touch of basil, which works wonderfully with soups or at dinner parties. You can also make it using dill, for another lovely summer flavour.

MAKES 1 LOAF

100g (4oz) butter or margarine
2 cloves garlic, peeled and crushed

2 tablespoons chopped fresh basil
1 long baguette

Melt the butter or margarine and stir in the garlic and basil. Leave to cool and set slightly. ◆

Slice the baguette lengthways and spread the cut sides with the herb butter. Sandwich together, then wrap in foil. Bake at 180°C/350°F/gas mark 4 for 15–20 minutes, or until heated through.

Cut into slices and serve immediately.

TORTILLAS, PANCAKES & FRITTERS

This section is full of wonderful family food, food that children enjoy and come to love, and that is quick to prepare yet nutritious and satisfying for all ages. The Mexicans use tortillas – their version of a pancake – in inspired ways which we can adapt to our preferences. Children rarely like chilli, for example, so simply omit it from the recipe and season with a little black pepper instead. There are equally brilliant thing you can do with classic pancakes too, which always make delicious meals. And fritters make some of the most tempting meals around.

SPICY CHIMICHANGAS

*C*himichangas are tortilla envelopes filled with a refried bean mixture and fried until golden. You can buy chilli sauces from supermarkets, or get them from ethnic grocers.

SERVES 2

4 small tortillas (see page 85)
2 tablespoons refried beans
2 tomatoes, sliced
50g (2oz) Cheddar cheese (low-fat if preferred), grated

2 tablespoons chilli sauce
1 fresh chilli, sliced finely (optional)
extra grated cheese, to sprinkle

Place equal amounts of refried beans, sliced tomato, grated cheese, chilli sauce (and extra fresh chilli if you like your food REALLY hot!) in the centre of each tortilla. Roll up the tortillas, folding in the edges to make a closed parcel. Secure with cocktail sticks. ◆

Heat about 1cm (½in) oil in a frying pan and deep-fry the tortillas until golden-brown on both sides, removing the sticks once one side is cooked so that the tortillas cook to golden all over. Drain well on paper towels.

Serve as soon as possible, with salsa (see page 84) if desired, and a sprinkling of grated cheese.

Spicy Chimichangas and Bean Burritos (page 84)

Bean Burritos

Mexican food in San Francisco is the nearest I have got to Mexico itself, but even in their native country it would be hard to beat these bean burritos. Hugely satisfying and nourishing food, spiced with chilli to warm you through, this is brilliant food.

Serves 2–3

4 large soft tortillas
1 x 400g (14oz) can spicy kidney beans
175g (6oz) Cheddar cheese, grated
half an iceberg lettuce, shredded finely

half a large avocado, sliced
4 tablespoons soured cream
300ml (½ pint) Quick Salsa sauce (see below)

Lay the tortillas out flat on a work surface and spoon a quarter of the beans along the centre of each. Pile with grated cheese, shredded lettuce and avocado and roll up to make a parcel, tucking in the ends. Put into a baking dish and top each one with a spoonful of soured cream. ◆

Bake at 200°C/400°F/gas mark 6 for 10–15 minutes, or until heated through. Serve with salsa to hand around.

Quick Salsa

This ridiculously easy recipe for salsa is incredibly good. The fresh, authentic flavours go wonderfully well with all the Mexican recipes in this section.

V
●

1 x 200g (7oz) can tomatoes in juice
half a red onion, chopped
1 fresh chilli, chopped finely

a small bunch of coriander
a little sea salt

Put all the prepared ingredients into the food processor and run the machine for 30 seconds, or until the salsa is well-blended. ◆

Vegetable Fajitas

Fajitas are the simplest way of all of using tortillas. You just heat a filling of your choice, warm the tortilla and roll the former up inside the latter – and eat it!

Makes 6 filled tortillas
V

2 x 400g (14oz) cans spicy Thai vegetables, chilli beans or ratatouille (or equivalent leftover vegetables), mixed with grated cheese (low-fat if preferred)

6 large tortillas
crisp chopped lettuce, to garnish
salsa, soured cream or low-fat yoghurt

Heat the filling gently – either in the microwave or in a pan on the hob. Warm the tortillas separately in the microwave for 30 seconds just before assembling the fajitas.

Spoon 3–4 tablespoons of the vegetable mixture into the centre of each tortilla. Roll up into a thick cigar shape and eat immediately, with a little salsa, soured cream or yoghurt spread over the top.

CALIFORNIAN QUESADILLAS

Quesadillas are tortillas folded into parcels and filled with an appetising stuffing before being fried until golden. I first had these in San Francisco where wonderful Mexican food is found. They are an exceptionally mouthwatering snack, delicious with salsa and a garnish of chopped crisp lettuce. You can also make delicious stuffings using mushrooms or spinach.

MAKES 4 FILLED TORTILLAS

150g (5oz) smoked cheese, cut into cubes
300g (10oz) sweetcorn
1 red onion, chopped
a bunch of chives or coriander, snipped small
5 tablespoons soured cream
1/2–1 teaspoon chilli powder
4 large tortillas
150ml (1/4 pint) Quick Salsa sauce (see page 84)
olive oil for deep-frying

Combine the cubed cheese, sweetcorn, chopped onion and chives or coriander in a bowl. Stir in the soured cream, season to taste with the chilli powder and mix well together. ◆

Place one quarter of the mixture onto one side of the tortilla and fold the other half over to cover. Moisten the edge with a little water and press together to hold in place.

Heat 1cm (1/2in) oil in a deep frying pan or wok, add the tortillas and fry in batches for a minute or so on each side, until crisp and golden. Drain on kitchen paper.

Serve as soon as possible, with the salsa (see page 84).

TORTILLAS

These soft, flat Mexican pancakes are made from cornmeal, flour, water and salt. They are available from most supermarkets and ethnic grocers. They bear no resemblance to the Spanish 'Tortillas de Huevos' (egg pancakes).

TORTILLA SHELLS

You can fill tortilla shells with salad, chilli beans, guacamole, salsa, soured cream (or low-fat yoghurt if you prefer) and cheese in whatever combination you like. They make substantial, healthy fast food which children love.

tortillas
vegetable oil for deep-frying

Heat the oil in a deep-fryer, to chip heat. Insert a tortilla and press down with a ladle into the hot oil. Hold it down for about 35 seconds, then remove the ladle and let the tortilla cook for a further 30 seconds, or until light golden-brown in colour. Remove and drain on kitchen paper. Serve warm with any of the above.

SOFTENING CORN TORTILLAS FOR FOLDING

To soften tortillas for folding, microwave for 15 seconds or place in a warm oven for a few minutes. After softening, they will fold more easily without breaking.

BRINGING UP CHILDREN ON A VEGETABLE-BASED DIET

It is perfectly safe to bring up children on a vegetable-based diet, so long as you make sure that they are getting the right levels of protein for their age, enough minerals and vitamins, and a wide variety of foods. The guidelines in the Nutrition Chart on page 219 are an invaluable aid to gauging nutritional balance. However, nutrition is an evolving science and parents are advised to read the latest publications on the subject to keep up to date.

MINI TACOS WITH AUBERGINE CAVIAR

These little tacos filled with a smooth aubergine purée make a delicious snack to go with an aperitif. A French friend from Provence gave these to me one balmy summer's evening, and I admired the Mediterranean flavours so much that she gave me her recipe.

MAKES 12 MINI TACOS

V

1 large aubergine

4 large tomatoes (fresh or canned), skinned (see page 30) and chopped

2 cloves garlic, peeled and crushed

salt, pepper and chilli powder (optional)

a little fresh thyme

12 mini taco shells (see below)

Simmer the aubergine in a little water until quite tender – about 10 minutes. Alternatively you can microwave it: pierce with a knife first, then cook on full power for 5–6 minutes. Cool, then chop finely.

Heat the chopped tomatoes in a small pan and stir in the aubergine. Add the crushed garlic, cover and simmer gently for 10 minutes, or until cooked down to a soft pulp.

Pour into the bowl of the food processor and blend to a fine purée. Failing that, pass through a sieve. Season to taste with salt, pepper and freshly chopped thyme. Cool and chill. ◆

Fill the mini-taco cases just before serving to prevent them going soggy.

TACOS

V

A favourite snack of the Mexicans, tacos are folded corn tortillas that are fried until crisp, then filled with traditional savoury stuffings such as black beans or guacamole (see page 75). They are served with a topping of grated cheese (low-fat if preferred), crisp shredded lettuce and chopped mint.

GRATED COURGETTE FRITTERS

A mouthwatering supper dish when courgettes are at their height in the summer, these fritters are perfect served with new potatoes and a tossed salad.

MAKES 8 FRITTERS

500g (1lb) medium courgettes, grated coarsely

grated rind of quarter of a lemon

2 tablespoons chopped chives or dill

2 spring onions, sliced finely

50g (2oz) Feta cheese, crumbled finely

4 tablespoons fresh wholemeal breadcrumbs (see page 42)

1 egg, plus 1 egg yolk, beaten

salt and freshly ground black pepper

1–2 tablespoons olive oil

Mix the grated courgettes with the lemon rind, herbs, spring onions, Feta cheese and breadcrumbs. Stir in the well-beaten eggs and season to taste with salt and pepper. Heat the oil in a heavy-based frying pan so that the mixture sizzles when it goes in. Pour in the fritter mixture and cook until golden-brown on both sides – about 4–5 minutes on each side. Eat as soon as possible.

Buckwheat crêpes with mushrooms & soured cream

A party piece! This stunning dish takes a while to prepare but it is well worth the effort. It is wonderful, memorable food with the brilliant flavour of buckwheat – distinctive, earthy and really lovely.

Makes 6 pancakes

Cooking pancakes

Ideally use a heavy pan no more than 20cm (8ins) in diameter so that the edges of the pancake are moulded by the edge of the pan rather than thin and ragged. Always get the pan really hot first – my experience is that the first pancake is always a rehearsal, then once the pan is evenly and thoroughly hot they begin to work.

Alternative filling: spinach

For 6 pancakes

1 small red onion, chopped finely
2 cloves garlic, peeled and chopped finely
1 teaspoon dried thyme
2 tablespoons finely chopped fresh parsley
3 strips lemon peel, sliced very finely
4 tablespoons olive oil

625g (1¼ lb) mushrooms, sliced thinly
150ml (¼ pint) white wine
salt, pepper and lemon juice
150ml (¼ pint) soured cream
6 crêpes (see below)
chopped chives

Sauté the onion, garlic, herbs and lemon peel in 2 tablespoons of the olive oil. Stir-fry for 2 minutes, then cover and cook until soft over a low heat for about 8 minutes. Add the rest of the oil, toss in the mushrooms and stir-fry over a medium heat. When the juices start to run, pour in the white wine and simmer gently until the mushrooms are soft and the liquid reduced.

Season with salt, pepper and lemon juice to taste. Leave to cool. ◈

Drain off the juices and stir into all but 3 tablespoons of the soured cream. Divide the mixture between the crêpes and roll up. Place seam-side down in an ovenproof dish.

Bake at 200°C/400°F/gas mark 6 for 8–10 minutes. Serve with an extra dollop of soured cream on top, and sprinkle with chives.

1kg (2lb) spinach, washed
300ml (½ pint) béchamel sauce (see page 218)

nutmeg, freshly ground pepper and cayenne

Cook the spinach in its own water for 5–6 minutes. Drain thoroughly, pressing it against a sieve with a wooden spoon to release all the cooking liquid. Then chop finely on a wooden board, letting more juices run away. Mix into the béchamel sauce and season to taste. ◈

Warm the filling over a low heat, then divide between the pancakes and roll up. Bake as above.

Buckwheat crêpe batter

This classic pancake recipe can be served sweet or savoury. Any leftover crêpes can be frozen between sheets of greaseproof paper.

Makes 8 crêpes

150ml (¼ pint) water
150ml (¼ pint) skimmed or soya milk
2 eggs

50g (2oz) buckwheat flour
½ teaspoon salt
50g (2oz) butter or margarine, melted

To make the batter, put all the ingredients into the bowl of the food processor and blend until smooth. Allow to rest for 1 hour before using.

Thin out the batter with a little more milk, if necessary (buckwheat flour is quite absorbent, so the mixture may have thickened). Melt a little butter or margarine in a crêpe pan and cook as for normal pancakes (see above). ◈

TEMPURA OF SUMMER VEGETABLES WITH DIPPING SAUCES

This classic recipe from Japan – of tender vegetables cooked in a light batter – makes one of the most appetising meals in the world. Lovely with the simple dipping sauces on page 34 and the Lemony Brown Rice on page 144, you can make it with any vegetables you happen to have in the store cupboard – and at any time of the year.

SERVES 4

FOR THE FILLING
250g (8oz) courgettes, sliced thickly
250g (8oz) small button mushrooms, cut in half
250g (8oz) baby carrots, cut into short lengths
100g (4oz) broccoli florets

FOR THE BATTER
100g (4oz) plain white flour
1 egg
200ml (7fl oz) water
a large pinch of salt
vegetable oil for deep-frying
2–3 tablespoons finely chopped mint or coriander, to garnish

Prepare the vegetables. Put the batter ingredients into the blender and run it until smooth.

Heat about 7.5cm (3in) oil in a deep saucepan or wok to 175°C/320°F. Dip the vegetables separately into the batter, then place carefully into the hot fat using a slotted spoon. Do not fry too many pieces at once. Turn until light golden-brown all over – each batch takes only a couple of minutes – then transfer to kitchen paper to drain. Keep these pieces hot in a warm oven while you fry the next batch.

Serve as soon as possible, sprinkled with a little finely chopped mint or coriander. Hand around some of the dipping sauces on page 34.

CORN FRITTERS WITH CHIVES & CRÈME FRAÎCHE

These golden morsels melt in the mouth. The crisp rounds filled with crunchy sweetcorn are spiced with a hint of chilli and are memorable served with salsa or a pepper relish.

MAKES 12 FRITTERS

100g (4oz) plain white flour
1 large egg (separated), plus 1 egg white
1 tablespoon olive oil
150ml (¼ pint) crème fraîche
scant 60ml (2fl oz) skimmed or soya milk

250g (8oz) sweetcorn kernels
half a chilli, chopped very finely
a small bunch of chives, snipped small
sunflower oil for deep-frying

First make the batter. Sift the flour into a bowl and make a well in the centre. Add the egg yolk, oil, and crème fraîche and mix thoroughly together. Thin out to a dropping consistency with the milk. Chill for an hour.

In a separate bowl, beat the egg whites until stiff with electric beaters.

Stir the corn, chilli and chives into the cold batter, then gently fold in the egg whites. Heat about 1cm (½in) oil in a deep pan or wok. When hot, drop in the batter in large spoonfuls – one on each side – turning until golden-brown on both sides. Drain on kitchen paper and keep warm in a low oven while you fry the rest.

Chilaquiles

*T*hese are scraps of tortilla that are fried until crisp, then folded into a spicy egg mixture. A fabulous snack or supper dish, served with a tossed salad.

SERVES 2–3

4 medium tortillas
groundnut or sunflower oil for deep-frying
3 eggs, beaten
150ml (¼ pint) Quick Salsa sauce (see page 84)

75g (3oz) Cheddar cheese (low-fat if preferred), grated
extra grated cheese, to sprinkle
a sprig of fresh coriander, to garnish

Tear the tortillas into 4cm (1½ in) pieces. Heat 1cm (½ in) oil in a pan and deep-fry the tortillas pieces in it for 30–40 seconds each, or until golden and crisp. Drain on paper towels.

Pour away the hot oil in the pan, leaving one tablespoon remaining. Take care – the oil will be very hot. Stir in the eggs, add the tortillas and cook until the eggs are set and lightly scrambled, stirring all the time.

Stir in the salsa and cheese and simmer for 15 minutes, uncovered.

Sprinkle with grated cheese just before serving, and garnish with a sprig of fresh coriander.

ENCHILADAS WITH CHEESE & CHILLI

In this recipe, the tortillas are stuffed just like pancakes with cheese and mushrooms, topped with yet more cheese and baked in the oven until golden. A wonderfully tasty and satisfying supper dish, particularly in cold weather.

SERVES 2

4 medium tortillas
300ml (½ pint) Quick Salsa sauce (see page 84)
half a red onion, chopped
175g (6oz) grated cheeses such as Cheddar (low-fat if preferred) and Bel Paese

1 mild green chilli, sliced very finely
250g (8oz) mushrooms, steamed and sliced
4 tablespoons soured cream
grated Pecorino, to sprinkle

Brush one side of each tortilla with the salsa. Brush the bottom of an ovenproof dish with salsa.

Mix together the red onion, cheeses, chilli, mushrooms and soured cream and divide between the tortillas. Roll up the tortillas, folding in the edges to create closed parcels, and pack into the dish. Sprinkle with Pecorino cheese. ◆

Bake at 180°C/350°F/gas mark 4 for 20 minutes, or until golden-brown on top. Serve with the rest of the salsa, and salad.

CRISPY MUSHROOM ROLLS 'DRAGON INN'

Inspired by an excellent restaurant in London's Chinatown, these crispy rolls are full of the rich dark flavour of the mushrooms. They make a stylish starter in their own right, or a light lunch or supper dish, served with rice and a green salad.

MAKES 6 CRISPY ROLLS
V
●

2 tablespoons olive oil
500g (1lb) mushrooms, sliced finely
3 spring onions, sliced finely
2.5cm (1in) piece fresh root ginger, grated finely
2 cloves garlic, peeled and sliced finely

1 tablespoon soy sauce
25g (1oz) rice vermicelli
6 spring roll wrappers (available from Chinese grocers)
vegetable oil for deep-frying

Heat the olive oil in a large pan, toss in the mushrooms and spring onions and coat in the oil. Stir-fry for a minute or two, then cover with a lid and cook for 3–4 minutes. Add the ginger and garlic and steam, covered, for a further 3 minutes. Season to taste with soy sauce and toss thoroughly. Leave to cool.

Soak the rice vermicelli in hot water for 5–8 minutes, then drain and chop roughly. ◆

Drain the mushroom mixture thoroughly, discarding the cooking liquid, and mix with the vermicelli. Place 1–2 tablespoons on each wrapper and roll up into a cigar-shape, tucking in the ends before the last turn to prevent the filling from falling out.

Heat 1cm (½in) oil in a deep frying pan or wok and fry the rolls in batches until golden-brown on all sides. Drain on kitchen paper and keep warm until ready to serve.

Note: you can freeze these rolls. To reheat from frozen, bake at 190°C/375°F/gas mark 5 for 20 minutes.

VEGETABLES: SIDE DISHES

There are several vegetables that are so good in their own right – particularly when they are young – that it is a shame to add to them in the cooking. In this category I include runner beans, baby broad beans and baby beetroot which are all sublime as side vegetables, with a little melted butter. Corn on the cob is irresistible simmered lightly, stripped off the cob and tossed with garlic butter. Mange-tout, peas and petits pois all make exquisite side vegetables, with a knob of butter and a sprig of mint.

In winter I love the cabbages with their varying colours and leaf shapes. NEVER overcook cabbage: it is best crunchy and lightly buttered. Raw red cabbage is fantastic in salads, as is fresh celery, raw grated carrot and shredded raw brussels sprouts. Puréed leeks and brussels sprouts also make great accompaniments.

AL SHAMI'S BROAD BEANS

A wonderful dish for summer, from a Lebanese restaurateur who kindly gave me his recipe. Use the youngest, freshest baby broad beans possible – they require very little cooking, and are succulent and delicate. You can also make this dish using cauliflower – or try it with potatoes, it is sublime.

SERVES 2

300g (10oz) shelled baby broad
    beans
2 cloves garlic, peeled and sliced
    finely

2 tablespoons olive oil
a bunch of fresh coriander,
    chopped
a few coriander leaves, to garnish

Sauté the broad beans and slivers of garlic in good olive oil until 'al dente' – about 6–8 minutes. Toss in the coriander and cook, covered, for 2–3 minutes more.

Garnish with a scattering of fresh coriander leaves and the dish is ready to serve. It is lovely with pitta bread.

LEMON BROCCOLI

A simple starter for all seasons. The lemony sauce goes beautifully with broccoli. You can serve this warm or cold, with fresh granary bread.

SERVES 4

625g (1¼lb) broccoli florets
1 egg

the juice of 1 lemon
sea salt and freshly ground pepper

Trim the broccoli florets and steam them until tender – about 5–6 minutes. Alternatively, cook them in the microwave for 4–5 minutes. Keep warm, reserving the cooking liquid.

Beat the egg with the lemon juice and put into the blender. With the machine running, slowly pour in about 150ml (¼ pint) of the hot cooking liquid in a thin stream.

Pour into a heavy-based saucepan and stir constantly over a medium heat, with a wooden spoon, until the sauce thickens. Be careful not to let it come to boiling point, otherwise it will curdle.

Remove from the heat, season to taste with salt and pepper and leave to settle for 10–15 minutes. Then spoon over the warm broccoli and serve.

FRIED MUSHROOMS WITH GARLIC & BLACK PEPPER

A lovely supper dish. Serve this with fragrant jasmine or basmati rice or egg noodles to mop up the juices, and a salad of your choice (see pages 187–198).

SERVES 2

V

2 tablespoons soy sauce
2 cloves garlic, peeled and crushed
3 spring onions (white parts only), shredded
  lengthways
masses of freshly ground black pepper

350g (12oz) large button mushrooms,
  quartered
250g (8oz) aubergine, cut into slices
  0.5cm (¼in) thick
2 tablespoons olive oil

Mix the soy sauce, garlic and spring onions together and season liberally with freshly ground black pepper. Leave aside while you prepare the rest. ◆

Place the mushrooms on a plate, cover with another plate and steam in the microwave (without added water) for 4 minutes on full power. Keep warm, reserving the juices.

Brush the cut surfaces of the aubergine with olive oil and place in a single layer on a baking sheet. Bake at 180°C/350°F/gas mark 4 for 15 minutes. Cool, then slice into long thin strips.

Mix 2–3 tablespoons of the mushroom juices into the sauce, discarding the rest. Spoon the mushrooms and aubergines into the sauce and toss well together. Serve warm.

STIR-FRIED WATERCRESS WITH CROÛTONS

This very original, tasty way of preparing watercress is a revelation. It is perfect for a quick simple meal for two, along with a pasta dish such as the Linguine with Roasted Peppers and Pine-nuts on page 130.

SERVES 2

V

2 bunches watercress, washed and dried
2 tablespoons olive oil
1 clove garlic, peeled and finely chopped
½ teaspoon finely grated fresh root ginger

1 tablespoon dark sesame oil
freshly ground black pepper
croûtons, to sprinkle (see page 218)

Roughly chop the watercress, stems and all. Heat the oil in a wok or large pan and when hot put in the garlic and ginger. Stir fry for a few seconds, then add the watercress. Stir-fry for a further minute until the watercress softens, and then add the sesame oil and black pepper. Heat through for a few seconds and serve immediately, sprinkled with the croûtons.

ROSTI OF POTATO, CELERIAC & CARROT

Homely substantial food that is easy on the budget yet full of goodness and flavour. Serve with a salad of your choice (see pages 187–198), and some warm crusty bread.

SERVES 4

V

500g (1lb) potatoes, scrubbed
250g (8oz) carrots, scrubbed
250g (8oz) celeriac, peeled

sea salt and freshly ground black pepper
50g (2oz) butter or margarine

Grate the cleaned vegetables coarsely and mix together. Season with sea salt and freshly ground pepper.
   Heat the butter or margarine in a large frying pan until it begins to bubble, then pack the grated vegetables into the pan. Turn the heat down, and press down firmly with a spatula. Cover with a lid and cook very slowly for 45 minutes until the bottom is well-browned and the vegetables tender.
   Invert onto a large warmed plate and serve cut into wedges.

PURÉE OF BRUSSELS SPROUTS

Purées of vegetables are very simple to make and are an excellent way to ring the changes with seasonal vegetables. Their flavour is brought out fully, their smooth texture mouthwatering, and the effect satisfying. A little goes a long way so purées are economical food.

SERVES 4

V

500g (1lb) Brussels sprouts, trimmed
25g (1oz) butter or margarine
90ml (3fl oz) skimmed or soya milk, or
   single cream

grated nutmeg
freshly ground black pepper

Cook the sprouts in boiling water for 20–25 minutes, so that they are very soft. Drain, and blend with the butter or margarine, and the milk or cream. Season to taste with nutmeg and pepper. ◆
   Heat through in an ovenproof dish at 180°C/350°F/gas mark 4 for 10 minutes, or warm through in a pan on top of the hob.

PARSNIP GRATIN

For those who love the sweet, slightly spicy taste of parsnips, this is a wonderful yet simple stand-by. It is great winter food, delicious with egg dishes or rice. Another superb way of cooking parsnips is oil-roasting them in the same way as the new potatoes on page 118.

SERVES 4

500g (1lb) small young parsnips
300ml (½ pint) béchamel sauce (see page 218)
1 tablespoon chopped tarragon

freshly ground black pepper
15g (½oz) Cheddar cheese, grated finely
50g (2oz) fresh granary breadcrumbs (see page 42)

Scrub the parsnips but don't peel them. Cut into rounds the thickness of a coin, cutting the big rounds in half across. Cover with water and simmer for 5–6 minutes, or until tender.

Meanwhile heat the béchamel sauce and stir in the tarragon. Leave to infuse over a very low heat for 5 minutes, then fold in the parsnips. Season to taste with black pepper. Put into an ovenproof dish. Mix the grated cheese with the breadcrumbs and sprinkle over the top.

Bake at 190°C/375°F/gas mark 5 for 15 minutes, or until light golden-brown and crisp on top.

TURNIPS IN CREAM WITH PARMESAN

A real treat: using young turnips for their delicate flavour, this is a delicious side vegetable. Serve it with a rice dish (see pages 143–151) and a tossed salad, and you have the perfect meal.

SERVES 3–4

1lb (500g) young turnips
300ml (½ pint) single cream
grated nutmeg, to taste

freshly ground black pepper
1 clove garlic, peeled
grated Parmesan cheese, to sprinkle

Scrub the turnips clean but leave the skins on. Slice them finely. Put into a bowl and pour over the cream. Season with nutmeg and pepper and mix.

Rub an ovenproof dish with a cut clove of garlic, then pour in the turnip mixture. Cover with foil and bake at 190°C/375°F/gas mark 5 for 45 minutes, or until the turnips are tender.

Sprinkle the top thickly with grated Parmesan, and brown lightly under a hot grill.

Vegetables: main courses

When there is an abundance of seasonal vegetables, I like to make the most of them, so many delicious and wholesome vegetable main courses appear in my household. A great number of them freeze very well, which means that we can eat truly seasonal vegetables out of season.

One of the great 'inventions' of recent cooking is the oil-roasted vegetable. We've known about potatoes and parsnips for ever, but now we find we can roast aubergines, broccoli, leeks, peppers, cauliflower and courgettes, too – you name it, you can roast it. And what a fantastic way of cooking: it requires minimum effort and for the three-quarters of an hour that the vegetables are roasting, you can more or less leave them to it – just the occasional turning is required. Oil-roasted vegetables are very versatile: they are delicious with pesto or fresh tomato sauce, served as a main course; you can produce them as a side vegetable; or you can use them in pasta dishes such as lasagne, toss them into fragrant jasmine rice, or serve them in sandwiches.

Here's a selection of recipes for main dishes from around the world – Italy, Greece, France, Russia and the United States – plus a few home-grown inventions! Use organic vegetables as frequently as you can – you will be rewarded with true flavour, plus the knowledge that you are not eating pesticides and fertilisers as well. Organic vegetables may be a little more expensive, but eat them in season you may find them considerably cheaper.

Organic produce

Non-organic fruits and vegetables are grown on land which has artificial fertilisers applied to it, and they are sprayed regularly with pesticides. Residues from both of these are found in the produce. Some fruits and vegetables are waxed or polished to make them look more attractive to the customer, or to give them longer shelf life. Organic fruit and vegetables are grown with only natural fertilisers and disease is kept at bay without the use of chemical sprays. They are therefore 'clean', and free of toxic chemicals.

Filo leeks with light tomato & basil sauce

A wonderfully easy way of using filo pastry, and an elegant way of serving leeks: they are simply rolled up in the pastry and baked until crisp and golden. Serve with lots of fresh tomato sauce. You can also wrap the leeks in puff pastry and make them in the same way.

Serves 4

V

6 long leeks, medium thick
200g (7oz) filo pastry
olive oil, to brush

full quantity Light Tomato and Basil Sauce
(see page 174)
1 teaspoon of sesame seeds, to sprinkle

Trim and wash the leeks, then cut them into 3 equal lengths. Steam until tender – about 10 minutes. Cool, and then dry on kitchen paper. ◆

Cut the filo sheets into strips as wide as the length of the leeks. Brushing the sheets with olive oil, roll the leeks up in one sheet each, leaving the ends open. Brush the tops with extra oil so that they brown well. Sprinkle with the sesame seeds.

Place on a greased baking sheet and bake at 200°C/400°F/gas mark 6 for 20–25 minutes, or until the filo pastry is golden and crisp. Meanwhile, make the tomato sauce (see page 174).

To serve, arrange the leek parcels on plates and spoon the tomato sauce over.

ROASTED VEGETABLES WITH PESTO

Roasting vegetables is beautifully simple and you can use them endlessly, varying the choice through the seasons. You can eat them either with pesto, as here, which is delicious with noodles, or with the Light Tomato and Basil Sauce on page 174 and some rice. I've put them into lasagnes and other pasta dishes, and served them as a side dish.

SERVES 4

V

1.25–1.5kg (2½–3lb) vegetables such as small potatoes, leeks, carrots, cauliflower, yellow peppers, squash, aubergines, broccoli etc., cut into bite-size pieces

3–4 tablespoons olive oil
4–5 tablespoons Pesto Trapanese (see page 169), or shop-bought pesto sauce
a little extra olive oil

Put the vegetables into a roasting pan and dribble the oil over them.

Roast at 190°C/350°F/gas mark 5 for 40–50 minutes, turning occasionally, until the vegetables are tender and browned.

Thin the pesto with a little olive oil until it is the desired consistency. Serve the vegetables on warm plates and spoon some pesto over each helping.

CAPONATA AU GRATIN

A southern Mediterranean dish with all the characteristic flavours of the sun – olives, herbs and tomatoes, plus the distinctive pungency of capers. These lively rustic tastes are excellent with the Grilled Polenta on page 140 – peasant food with a sophisticated edge!

SERVES 4

1 tablespoon olive oil
half an onion, chopped
300g (10oz) aubergine, chopped or diced
250g (8oz) courgettes, sliced
175g (6oz) fennel, sliced
1 x 400g (14oz) can tomatoes, drained
1 tablespoon tomato purée

1 teaspoon dried mixed herbs
18 black olives, halved and pitted
1 tablespoon capers, rinsed
150ml (¼ pint) vegetable stock (see page 218)
50g (2oz) Mozzarella cheese
2 teaspoons grated Parmesan cheese

Heat the oil in a pan, add the onion, cover with a lid and soften over a gentle heat for 10 minutes, stirring occasionally.

Add the aubergine, courgette and fennel and sauté for 3–4 minutes. Stir in the remaining ingredients apart from the cheeses and simmer gently for about 15 minutes.

Pour into a gratin dish, sprinkle with the cheeses and set under the grill for a few minutes, or until the cheese bubbles.

ITALIAN AUBERGINE & CHEESE BAKE

This rich dish from sunny Italy is best eaten with a tossed salad and either plain pasta or fresh bread. It goes down well with a glass of red wine.

SERVES 4–6

1kg (2lb) aubergines, sliced thickly
salt
olive oil, to brush
300ml (½ pint) Light Tomato and Basil
   Sauce (see page 174)
250g (8oz) Mozzarella cheese, sliced
150g (5oz) Ricotta cheese
a handful of fresh basil leaves
freshly ground black pepper
finely grated Parmesan cheese, to sprinkle

Sprinkle the aubergine slices with salt and leave to 'sweat' for half an hour, then wipe dry on kitchen paper. Now brush lightly with olive oil and place on a baking tray in a single layer.

Bake at 220°C/425°F/gas mark 7 for 12 minutes, or until golden-brown and soft. Cool. ◆

Layer up the aubergines with the tomato sauce, Mozzarella and Ricotta in a lightly oiled casserole dish, sprinkling each layer with a few fresh basil leaves and seasoning with freshly ground pepper. Finish with a layer of Mozzarella, then sprinkle with the finely grated Parmesan.

Bake at 180°C/350°F/gas mark 4 for 40 minutes. Serve hot.

MUSHROOM STROGANOFF

As far as I am concerned, this is THE best recipe for this famous dish. Friends in Moscow made it for me over an evening of laughter made memorable by their typically warm, spontaneous Russian hospitality. This has become a favourite dish, and I make it with as many different varieties of mushrooms as I can get hold of.

SERVES 2–3

50g (2oz) butter or margarine
2 onions, chopped
500g (1lb) mixed mushrooms such as flat,
   oyster, chestnut, chanterelles, cèpes, shiitake,
   etc., sliced
150ml (¼ pint) red wine
1 tablespoon soy sauce
3 teaspoons paprika
¼ teaspoon grated nutmeg
½ teaspoon ground cinnamon
salt and pepper
300ml (½ pint) soured cream
chopped tarragon, to garnish

Melt the butter or margarine in a frying pan, add the onions and soften over a low heat, covered with a lid, for 10 minutes. Turn up the heat a little, add the sliced mushrooms and toss thoroughly. Cook for 5 minutes, still covered with a lid, or until the juices are released.

Now stir in the red wine, soy sauce, paprika, nutmeg and cinnamon. Season with salt and pepper. Simmer, uncovered, until the liquid reduces by half – about 5 minutes.

Remove from the heat and stir in the soured cream. Sprinkle with a little chopped tarragon and serve with rice.

CAULIFLOWER & MUSHROOMS IN BLACK BEAN SAUCE WITH CASHEW NUTS

A fabulous stir-fry for a quick tasty meal, this is delicious with either rice or noodles. Yellow bean sauce is easily obtainable from supermarkets and ethnic grocers, and is an invaluable stand-by on the larder shelf for this kind of food.

SERVES 2–3
V

1 tablespoon groundnut oil
350g (12oz) cauliflower, cut into small florets
350g (12oz) small button mushrooms, cut in half
2 cloves garlic, peeled and sliced
50g (2oz) cashew nuts (unroasted)
2 tablespoons black bean sauce
2 tablespoons dark sesame oil
a handful of fresh coriander leaves, to garnish

Heat the oil until it smokes in a wok, then put in the cauliflower and mushrooms and stir-fry briskly until they are coated in the oil – about 1 minute. Then add the garlic and cashew nuts and sauté over a lower heat. Add 2 tablespoons water, cover with a lid and steam until the cauliflower is tender – about 4–5 minutes.

Now stir in the black bean sauce and mix in well. Cover with a lid, and warm through over a very low heat for a few minutes more.

Toss in the dark sesame oil just before serving, and garnish with a few fresh coriander leaves.

BUCKWHEAT WITH ROASTED VEGETABLES

One of my favourite dishes and a regular stand by. It's hard to beat the earthy, full flavour of buckwheat. Here it is combined with a selection of vegetables seasoned with thyme and garlic to make a scrumptious dish. You can vary the vegetables according to the season.

SERVES 4
V

250g (8oz) aubergine
250g (8oz) broccoli (calabrese or purple sprouting)
250g (8oz) squash or courgette
250g (8oz) tomatoes
175g (6oz) new potatoes
5 tablespoons olive oil
2 teaspoons fresh thyme
250g (8oz) roasted buckwheat (see page 18)
2 cloves garlic, peeled and crushed
salt and pepper

Cut all the vegetables into small bite-size pieces and put into a roasting pan. Drizzle with 4 tablespoons of the olive oil, and roast at 190°C/375°F/gas mark 5 for 25–35 minutes, turning from time to time.

Add the thyme, mix in well and return to the oven for a further 15 minutes, or until the vegetables are tender and brown.

Meanwhile heat the rest of the oil in a saucepan and when hot stir in the buckwheat. Toss thoroughly to coat in the oil. When hot, pour over enough water to cover – it will come to the boil immediately – turn the heat down low and cover with a lid. Simmer for 6–8 minutes, or until the buckwheat is tender, but do not allow it to go mushy. Drain, mix in the crushed garlic, then combine with the roasted vegetables.

Season with salt and pepper and serve.

CREAMY GRATIN DAUPHINOIS WITH LEEKS

A variation on a great French dish, this mixture of potatoes, leeks and cream baked slowly in a low oven makes heavenly winter food – satisfying and wholesome. Wonderful on its own, or with a salad as a simple meal, it can also be served as a side dish for a party.

SERVES 6

875g (1¾lb) potatoes, peeled
500g (1lb) leeks, washed and trimmed
butter or margarine
salt and pepper
1–2 cloves garlic, peeled and sliced finely (optional)
300ml (½ pint) single cream
300ml (½ pint) skimmed or soya milk

Slice the potatoes very thinly, on the side of the grater or in the food processor. Soak in cold water for a few minutes, then drain and pat dry on a tea-towel.

Slice the leeks thinly. Make layers with the 2 vegetables in a shallow, well-buttered dish, seasoning with salt, pepper and garlic as you go. Pour the cream over the top, then the milk.

Bake at 170°C/325°F/gas mark 3 for 1½ hours, turning the heat up to 190°C/375°F/gas mark 5 for the last 10 minutes just to brown the top.

STUFFED SQUASH

You can use any of the big squashes for this recipe. Marrows work really well too, so this is a useful way to cope with the high summer glut. Squash is utterly delicious cooked in this way, by slow baking with a tasty filling. Serve it with the Winter Slaw on page 198 and you have a wonderful meal for a wintry evening.

SERVES 4
V

2 tablespoons olive oil
100g (4oz) roasted buckwheat (see page 18)
4 spring onions, chopped finely
2 medium carrots, grated
100g (4oz) spinach, washed and cooked in its own liquid until tender
2–3 teaspoons soy sauce
2 tablespoons fresh chopped mint
lots of freshly ground black pepper
1 large butternut squash
Tabasco sauce

Heat 1 tablespoon of the oil in a medium saucepan and sauté the buckwheat in it, tossing over a brisk heat so that it brings out the aroma. Add water to cover and simmer for 10–12 minutes until the buckwheat is tender but not mushy.

Meanwhile, sauté the spring onions in the rest of the oil, add the grated carrots and toss until slightly softened.

Chop the spinach and add to the cooked buckwheat with the mint. Season to taste with soy sauce and freshly ground black pepper.

Cut the squash in half lengthways and remove the seeds to make a hollow in the centre. Spoon the filling into each half and press the halves together. Wrap securely in foil and bake at 180°C/350°F/gas mark 4 for 2 hours until completely soft.

Unwrap and serve cut in thick slices. Hand Tabasco around for those who like to spice up their food.

AUBERGINES & GREEN BEANS IN COCONUT MILK, WITH LEMON GRASS & CHILLI

You can buy lemon grass from some supermarkets, and from oriental grocers. It has a delicate and distinctive flavour – aromatic and lemony – which works blissfully in this mixture. Coconut milk is simple to make now that you can buy it in powdered form.

SERVES 4–6

V

COCONUT MILK

You can make coconut milk very easily from a powdered form that comes in sachets from ethnic grocers and some supermarkets. Mix it with water according to the instructions on the packet – they offer a thick and creamy milk, or a thinner version.

60g (2½oz) coconut milk powder
450ml (¾ pint) water
500g (1lb) aubergines, cut into small dice
250g (8oz) green beans, topped and tailed
   and cut into 1cm (½in) lengths
half a Chinese cabbage, shredded finely
5 shallots, sliced finely
4 cloves garlic, peeled and sliced finely
6 waterchestnuts, sliced finely

2 teaspoons cayenne pepper
1 scant tablespoon ground coriander
the juice and grated rind of half a lime
1 teaspoon salt
3–4 stalks lemon grass, bruised
1–2 small green chillies, chopped finely
50g (2oz) dry-roasted peanuts, ground
   coarsely
sprig of coriander, to garnish

Mix the coconut powder with the water and stir to a smooth cream.

Put the prepared vegetables, spices, lime rind and juice, salt, lemon grass and chillies into a casserole and cover with the coconut milk. Simmer very gently for 20–25 minutes, or until the vegetables are tender.

Leave to stand for about 20 minutes for all the flavours to infuse, then sprinkle with ground peanuts, garnish with coriander and serve with noodles or jasmine rice.

ORIENTAL STIR-FRY OF GREEN BEANS & COURGETTES WITH GINGER & GARLIC

This classic stir-fry from the Far East is the perfect answer when you have neither time, energy nor inclination to cook, yet you want something both tasty and nutritious to eat. Once you master the basics of stir-frying, there is no end to the improvisations you can make – and it's a wonderful way to eat.

SERVES 2–3

V

1 tablespoon groundnut oil
250g (8oz) French beans
500g (1lb) courgettes
75g (3oz) bamboo shoots, sliced finely
2cm (¾in) piece fresh root ginger, peeled and
   grated finely

3 cloves garlic, peeled and sliced very finely
3 spring onions, sliced finely
2 tablespoons black bean sauce

In a wok heat the oil until smoking, then stir in the vegetables and stir-fry them briskly over this high heat for 1–2 minutes. Turn the heat down, add 2–3 tablespoons water and cover with a lid. Steam until the vegetables are tender but still crisp – about 3–4 minutes.

Add the ginger, garlic and spring onion, and stir-fry over a lower heat for a further 2 minutes. Pour over the black bean sauce and cook for 1 minute. Serve immediately with basmati or jasmine rice.

SPECIAL VEGETABLES SATAY

*I*nspired by a recipe given to me by an Indonesian friend, this dish is very easy to make now that you can get hold of the ingredients so easily. Powdered coconut milk is a great innovation; and satay sauce is available from supermarkets, although the brands vary and you will find that some are far better than others. This is a wonderful meal served with thin egg noodles.

SERVES 6

V

60g (2¹/₂oz) coconut milk powder
450ml (³/₄ pint) water
2 x 7.5cm (3in) pieces lemon grass
2.5cm (1in) piece fresh root ginger, grated coarsely
1 small green chilli
4 lime leaves, torn, or the pared rind of half a lime
100g (4oz) satay sauce (see page 34)

1.5kg (3¹/₂lb) mixed vegetables such as Chinese cabbage, bamboo shoots, sweet potato, cauliflower, mushrooms, beansprouts, French beans, broccoli, courgettes, mangetout, baby sweetcorn, etc., all cut very small and steamed until tender (see page 30)
a handful of fresh coriander leaves, to garnish

Mix the coconut powder into the water and stir to a smooth cream. Add the lemon grass, ginger, chilli and lime and put into a saucepan. Infuse over a very gentle heat, covered with a lid, for 30 minutes. Strain.

Add a little at a time to the satay sauce, mixing thoroughly until smooth.
Pour over the prepared vegetables and mix well together. Garnish with a scattering of fresh coriander leaves.

QUICK SAUTÉ OF CAULIFLOWER & CASHEW NUTS WITH SPINACH

*T*his original idea came from a Chinese friend who has adapted his style to a western way of cooking. A crunchy stir-fry of cauliflower, tomato and cashew nuts beautifully spiced with ginger, garlic and spring onion is heaped onto a bed of cooked spinach. It is memorable.

SERVES 4

V

1 tablespoon groundnut oil
1 medium cauliflower, cut into small florets
750g (1¹/₂lb) leaf spinach
1 clove garlic, peeled and sliced finely
¹/₂ teaspoon finely grated fresh root ginger
2 ripe tomatoes, skinned (see page 30)

6 spring onions, sliced thinly
50g (2oz) waterchestnuts, sliced finely
75g (3oz) cashew nuts
1–2 tablespoons soy sauce
sea salt and freshly ground black pepper

Heat the oil in a wok or large frying pan, add the cauliflower and stir-fry over a high heat for 5–6 minutes.

Wash the spinach and cook in its own water; drain, then chop roughly.

Add 2–3 tablespoons water to the cauliflower, cover with a lid and simmer over a low heat for a further 3–4 minutes. Turn up the heat a little and stir in the garlic and ginger. Chop and add the tomatoes, spring onions and waterchestnuts and cook for a further 2 minutes, then add the cashew nuts. Stir in soy sauce, to taste.

Drain the spinach thoroughly, chop finely and season to taste with sea salt and pepper. Divide the spinach between 4 small dishes. Heap the stir-fried vegetables over the top and it is ready to serve with basmati or jasmine rice.

PERSIAN AUBERGINES

This very original way of cooking aubergines – with a crisp, crunchy topping tasting of herbs and spices – comes from the Middle East. It is delicious with a potato dish of your choice, and the Light Tomato and Pecorino sauce on page 179. You could also serve it as a starter for a special meal.

SERVES 4

3 medium aubergines
salt
250g (8oz) Greek yoghurt
6 spring onions, chopped finely
2 cloves garlic, peeled and crushed
50g (2oz) crunchy peanut butter

the grated rind of 1 lemon
2 tablespoons chopped coriander
2 teaspoons ground cumin
a pinch of cayenne
a little olive oil, to brush

Cut the aubergines lengthways into thin strips, sprinkle them with salt and leave to one side to 'sweat' for about 30 minutes.

Mix together all the other ingredients except the oil.

Pat the aubergines dry on kitchen paper, and place them on a large, flat baking sheet greased with olive oil. Cover with the spicy peanut butter topping and bake at 180°C/350°F/gas mark 4 for 25–30 minutes, or until the aubergines are soft and the topping lightly browned. Serve hot or warm.

SAUTÉED VEGETABLES WITH MELTED CHEESE

A very simple idea, this is surprisingly delicious – a tasty and succulent dish that is definitely more-ish. It takes only minutes to prepare, so it is ideal when you are short of time – and very rewarding to make.

SERVES 3–4

2 tablespoons olive oil
250g (8oz) broccoli, cut into small florets
250g (8oz) mushrooms, sliced
150g (5oz) French beans, trimmed and cut in half
250g (8oz) squash, peeled and diced

250g (8oz) leeks, shredded finely
1–2 teaspoons soy sauce
1–2 cloves garlic (optional)
100g (4oz) Cheddar cheese (low-fat if preferred), grated

Pour the oil into the wok, coating the sides well. Heat until very hot, add the prepared vegetables and stir-fry in the hot oil, tossing until well coated and beginning to brown.

Turn the heat down and season to taste with soy sauce and garlic (if using). Stir well and cover with a lid. Leave to steam for 7–8 minutes, or until the vegetables are tender but still crisp.

Sprinkle the grated cheese over the top, cover again, and leave to stand for a minute or two off the heat until the cheese melts.

Serve from the wok, with plain noodles or rice, and a tossed green salad.

VEGETABLE STIR-FRY WITH YELLOW BEAN SAUCE & CHILLI

It is so easy to obtain ingredients like yellow bean sauce from oriental grocers (see page 28), that it is well worth trying your hand with them. This combination, simplified as it is for western tastes, is gorgeous to look at, and the beautiful spices certainly gets the taste buds tingling.

SERVES 3–4

V

1 tablespoon olive oil
2 shallots, sliced finely
1cm (½in) piece fresh root ginger, peeled and grated
1 clove garlic, peeled and crushed
1 small red chilli, sliced very finely
2 tablespoons yellow bean sauce

2 tablespoons groundnut oil
250g (8oz) courgettes, trimmed
100g (4oz) mangetout, topped and tailed
175g (6oz) cauliflower florets
350g (12oz) broccoli
175 g (6oz) sweet potato or yama
handful of fresh coriander leaves, to garnish

Heat the olive oil in a pan, add the shallots, cover with a lid and soften over a very low heat for 5–8 minutes. Add the ginger, garlic and chilli and simmer for a few minutes longer. Pour over the yellow bean sauce.

Heat the groundnut oil in a wok until very hot, then toss in all the prepared vegetables and stir-fry briskly over a high heat for 3–4 minutes. When heated through, add 2–3 tablespoons of water, cover with a lid and turn the heat down. Cook gently until the vegetables are 'al dente' – about 6–7 minutes.

Stir in the sauce, toss well together and heat through for a minute. Serve with noodles or jasmine rice. Garnish with fresh coriander leaves.

FENNEL WITH BLUE CHEESE

A sensational dish with rich flavours, this goes really well with baby new potatoes and a green salad. You can use leeks instead of fennel – both taste delicious.

SERVES 4

2 fennel bulbs, each weighing about 500g (1lb)
100g (4oz) low-fat cottage cheese
50g (2oz) blue cheese such as Danish Blue, Gorgonzola, Roquefort, etc.

freshly ground black pepper
50g (2oz) breadcrumbs
1 tablespoon olive oil
full quantity Light Tomato and Basil Sauce (see page 174)

Cook the fennel in boiling water for 8–10 minutes, or until tender; drain and cool. Separate the layers carefully, leaving the bulb intact.

Blend the cottage cheese with the blue cheese in the food processor and season to taste with black pepper. In another bowl, mix the breadcrumbs with the olive oil. ◆

Stuff the cheese mixture into the layers of the fennel bulbs and place in an ovenproof dish. Spoon the tomato sauce over the top and sprinkle with the breadcrumb mixture.

Bake at 180°C/350°F/gas mark 4 for 20 minutes, or until the breadcrumbs are golden. Serve hot, straight from the oven.

THE VERSATILE POTATO

A hugely popular vegetable, the potato is an integral part of our culture. Chips with everything. But being the versatile vegetable that it is, there are countless inspired ways of cooking it. There are many varieties of potato, too, and you will find from experimenting which are your favourites. Some are floury, some waxy: the former are better for mashing or in soups, the latter are excellent in salads.

This valuable staple is cheap food, and full of goodness – particularly if you don't peel them, since much of the goodness is in the skin. If you want to make sure you are not taking in toxic agricultural chemicals, buy organic potatoes. There is hardly any difference in price, and there is all the difference in the world in flavour. It is a different beast.

CRISPY POTATO SKINS WITH SALSA

The skins of baked potatoes are irresistible crisped in the oven with a little olive oil. They are delicious with Quick Salsa, or with Satay Sauce.

SERVES 3–4

4 large baking potatoes

3 tablespoons olive oil

half-quantity Quick Salsa (see page 84), to serve

Prick the potatoes with a skewer and bake them at 220°C/425°F/gas mark 7 for 1 hour. Cut in half, scoop out the flesh and discard. (You can use it for mashed potatoes or for the Potato and Spinach Ring on page 119.) Cut the skins into 3 strips, dip into olive oil and return to the oven to crisp up for 10 minutes. Serve hot with the Quick Salsa.

Crispy Potato Skins; Potatoes with Eggs & Capers (page 113); Potato Salad with Sun-dried Tomatoes (page 116)

POTATOES HONGROISE

A peasant dish from Hungary in which potatoes are cooked very slowly – casserole style – with onions, paprika and tomatoes. Spicy, warming food for cold weather.

SERVES 3–4

V

2 tablespoons olive oil
1 medium onion, chopped finely
1–2 teaspoons paprika
2 large tomatoes, peeled and chopped roughly
500g (1lb) small potatoes, cut into thick, round slices

about 350ml (12fl oz) vegetable stock (see page 218)
sea salt and freshly ground black pepper
chopped parsley, to garnish

Heat the oil in a casserole and soften the onion in it for 4–5 minutes, covered with a lid. Season to taste with paprika, then stir in the tomatoes and potato rounds. Pour over enough stock to cover.

Bake at 180°C/350°F/gas mark 4, covered with foil, for 45 minutes, or until the potatoes are soft.

Check the seasoning, and serve sprinkled with chopped parsley.

POTATOES LYONNAISE

Lyons is famous for its gastronomy and this potato recipe has the authentic flavour of genuine French country cooking. It brings out the best in the potatoes, which are pan-fried slowly with sweet onions.

SERVES 4

V

750g (1½lb) potatoes
2 tablespoons olive oil
50g (2oz) butter or margarine
2 onions, sliced finely

sea salt, freshly ground black pepper and a pinch of mace
chopped parsley, to garnish

Peel the potatoes if they have thick skins. Otherwise, just scrub them and slice fairly thinly. In a heavy frying pan, heat the olive oil with just over half of the butter or margarine. Toss the potatoes in this mixture until well-coated and beginning to warm through.

Turn the heat down and cover with a lid. Cook gently, turning occasionally, for 30 minutes or until the potatoes are cooked through but not mushy.

Meanwhile, sweat the onions in the rest of the butter or margarine over a gentle heat. Stir until they are coated in the fat, then cover with a tightly-fitting lid and cook over a very low heat for 10–15 minutes, stirring occasionally, until they are soft and sweet.

Mix into the potatoes. Season to taste with sea salt, pepper and mace. Serve sprinkled with chopped parsley, either straight from the pan or on a warm serving dish.

SPICY POTATOES WITH BROCCOLI

This simple Indian-style mixture is delightfully spiced. It makes a delicious dish for cold weather, served with naan bread and rice.

SERVES 4–6

V

750g (1½ lb) potatoes, scrubbed and cut into cubes
2 teaspoons turmeric
2 teaspoons salt
3 tablespoons sunflower oil
2 medium onions, sliced
3 teaspoons cumin seeds

3 cloves garlic, peeled and sliced
1 teaspoon chilli powder
2–3 teaspoons ground ginger
2–3 teaspoons ground coriander
3 large tomatoes, chopped
750g (1½ lb) broccoli, cut into small florets (include the stalk)

Cover the potatoes with water in a saucepan and add the turmeric and salt. Bring to the boil and simmer for 8–10 minutes, or until the potatoes are tender. Drain, reserving the liquid.

Heat the oil in a separate pan, add the onion and stir-fry over a medium heat for 5 minutes. Stir in the cumin seeds and garlic and cook for a further minute or two, then add the ground spices. Stir in the tomatoes with their juices and sauté over a medium heat for 2 minutes. Finally, add the broccoli and toss well to coat with the mixture.

Add some of the potato water to the pan, stirring all the time to make a thick, creamy sauce. If necessary, add a little more tap water – but don't make the sauce too thin. Bring to the boil, cover with a lid and simmer gently for 6–8 minutes, or until the broccoli is tender. Finally, stir in the potatoes carefully and season to taste with a little sea salt.

POTATOES WITH EGGS & PEPPERS

A wonderful supper dish – tasty, yet easy to make. It is especially good if you use organic potatoes – the difference in flavour is immeasurable.

SERVES 2–3

500g (1lb) new potatoes
1 tablespoon olive oil
1 yellow pepper, deseeded and cut into strips

sea salt and freshly ground black pepper
1 tablespoon sunflower oil
3 fresh eggs

Scrub the potatoes and slice them fairly thin. Heat the olive oil in a non-stick frying pan and toss in the potatoes and peppers. Turn the heat down, sprinkle with salt and pepper and cover with a lid. Leave to steam very gently over a low to medium heat for about 30 minutes, or until the potatoes are tender.

Just before the end of the cooking time, fry the eggs. Heat the sunflower oil in another pan, break in the eggs and cook gently without disturbing them for a minute or two until they are lightly set. Carefully lift them out of the pan and place on top of the cooked potatoes.

Sprinkle with the salt and pepper and serve from the frying pan.

SPICED POTATOES, CAULIFLOWER & OKRA WITH GINGER & GARLIC

This simple dish was given to me in Hyderabad by the Indian family I was staying with, and I loved it. The vegetables are appetisingly spiced with ginger, garlic, cumin and coriander. They go beautifully with basmati rice and naan bread, to make an ideal family supper.

SERVES 3–4

V

350g (12oz) small potatoes, scrubbed
350g (12oz) cauliflower
175g (6oz) okra
2 small onions, sliced
25g (1oz) fresh root ginger, peeled and sliced
2 cloves garlic, peeled and chopped
2 teaspoons cumin seeds
2 teaspoons coriander seeds
2 tablespoons olive oil
salt

First prepare the vegetables. Cook the potatoes in boiling water for 5–6 minutes; drain, reserving the cooking liquid, and cut into quarters. Steam the cauliflower and okra until tender, then cut into bite-size pieces.

Put the onions, ginger, garlic and spices into a blender with 4 tablespoons of the potato water and blend to a paste.

Heat the oil in a pan, stir in the paste and leave to sizzle for a few seconds. Then turn down the heat, cover with a lid and soften over a medium heat for 5–8 minutes. (You may need to add about 150ml (¼ pint) of the potato water if the paste begins to stick to the pan.)

When the paste is soft, stir in the prepared vegetables, tossing them thoroughly in the mixture, and heat through. Season with a little salt, if desired, and serve immediately.

SUMMER POTATO SALAD WITH DILL

Simplicity itself – perfect on a warm summer's day al-fresco, with the Mustard and Cauliflower Flan on page 157 and a leafy green salad.

SERVES 2–3

2–3 tablespoons mayonnaise (see page 206)
2 teaspoons balsamic vinegar
4 spring onions, chopped finely
a large bunch of fresh dill, chopped
sea salt and pepper
350g (12oz) small, new organic potatoes, scrubbed
a sprig of fresh dill, to garnish

Mix the mayonnaise with the vinegar, then stir in the chopped spring onions and the dill. Season to taste with salt and pepper. ◆

Boil the potatoes so that they are still slightly crisp in the centre; drain and cool, then cut in half. Place in a serving dish, spoon over the dill mayonnaise and mix well together. Serve garnished with a sprig of fresh dill.

POTATO SALAD WITH SUN-DRIED TOMATOES

A wonderful version of potato salad, with interesting flavours. This makes a very good summer starter, or a fabulous lunch dish with a tossed green salad.

SERVES 2–3

V

FOR THE SALAD
50g (2oz) sun-dried tomatoes in oil
1 yellow pepper, deseeded and grilled (see page 30)
250g (8oz) new potatoes
half a red onion, chopped finely
mustard vinaigrette (see page 204)
salt

TO SERVE
mixed lettuce leaves
a little chopped tarragon, to garnish

First prepare the vegetables. Boil the potatoes 'al dente'; drain and cool, then cut in half or quarters depending on their size. Slice the sun-dried tomatoes into strips, quite wide. Cut the pepper into strips and then into squares. ◆

Mix the potatoes, tomatoes and pepper with the chopped red onion and dress with the mustard vinaigrette. Season to taste with a little sea salt, and toss thoroughly. Serve piled high on a bed of mixed lettuce leaves, sprinkled with a little chopped tarragon.

POTATO & LEEK CRUNCH

An irresistibly delicious supper dish for winter: leeks and potatoes simmered with aromatic rosemary, added to tomatoes and baked with a crunchy sunflower seed topping. Warming, tasty family food.

SERVES 2–3

300g (10oz) potatoes, scrubbed
150g (5oz) leeks, washed
a sprig of rosemary
1 x 400g (14oz) can chopped tomatoes, drained
a pinch of chilli powder

300ml (½ pint) cheese sauce (see page 218)
75g (3oz) breadcrumbs
25g (1oz) butter or margarine, melted
50g (2oz) sunflower seeds, browned under the grill (see page 134)
1 scant tablespoon chopped, raw onion

Cut the potatoes and leeks into small dice. Cover with water, add the rosemary and simmer for 8–10 minutes, or until the vegetables are tender but still slightly crisp. Drain thoroughly, removing the rosemary.

Mix the cooked vegetables with the drained tomatoes. Season to taste with a little chilli, then fold into the cheese sauce. Pour into an ovenproof dish. ◆

For the topping, mix the breadcrumbs with the melted butter or margarine and fold in the sunflower seeds and raw onion. Mix thoroughly. ◆

Spread the topping over the vegetables. Bake at 180°C/350°F/gas mark 4 for 25–30 minutes, or until golden-brown and crisp on top.

SPICY SWEET POTATOES

Sweet potato or yam is a very cheap and nutritious vegetable which makes warming food for winter. This simple sauté of spiced yam is a delicious side dish to go with the Pilaff on page 146 and a salad.

SERVES 2–3

2 tablespoons olive oil
500g (1lb) sweet potato (yam), peeled and sliced thinly
2 cloves garlic, peeled and sliced
1 teaspoon ground cumin

1 heaped teaspoon curry powder
150ml (¼ pint) water
salt
chopped coriander, to garnish

Heat the olive oil in a frying pan and toss in the sliced sweet potato and garlic. Stir-fry over a medium heat until the slices are well-coated and beginning to absorb the oil.

Sprinkle over the spices and mix well. Add the water, turn the heat down to low and cover with a lid. Leave to steam for 5–6 minutes, or until cooked through but still slightly crisp – if you overcook them they will go mushy and disintegrate. Season to taste with a little sea salt, and sprinkle with chopped coriander just before serving.

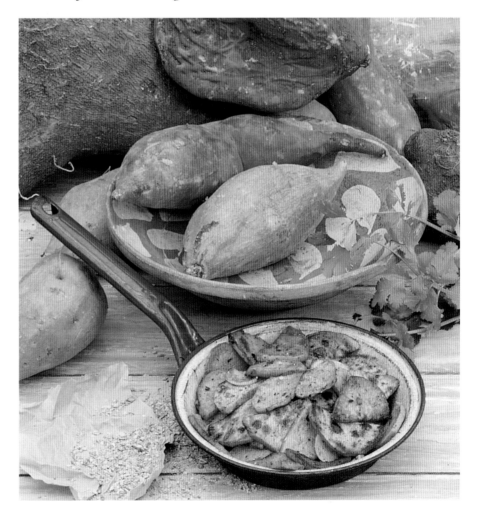

TUSCANY POTATOES

This traditional recipe from northern Italy has been handed down through the generations. Cubes of potato are simmered with aromatic herbs, garlic and olive oil to make a lovely light meal in their own right, or a side dish to go with the Pumpkin Soufflé on page 59.

SERVES 2–3

V

500g (1lb) small potatoes (preferably new)
a small bunch each of fresh rosemary and sage, chopped
3 cloves garlic, peeled and sliced

60ml (2fl oz) olive oil
300ml (½ pint) water or stock
sea salt

Scrub and slice the potatoes, then mix with the herbs, garlic and oil. Leave to marinate for as long as possible – up to an hour.

Place in a saucepan with the water or stock and a little sea salt. Bring to the boil, then simmer gently for 10 minutes – or until the water has all but evaporated and the potatoes are tender. Take care that they do not go mushy.

Serve with a tossed salad (see page 190).

OIL-ROASTED NEW POTATOES

These are utterly delicious – the easiest and best way I know of serving new potatoes.

SERVES 4

V

750g (1½lb) small new potatoes, washed
olive oil, to drizzle

finely chopped thyme or rosemary (optional)
sea salt

Wash the potatoes clean and cut them in half. Put into a metal baking dish and drizzle a little olive oil over the top.

Roast at 200°C/400°F/gas mark 6 for 35–40 minutes, or until crisp on the outside and tender inside. Add the herbs (if using) 15 minutes before the end of the cooking time.

Put into a serving dish, sprinkle with sea salt, and serve.

NEW POTATOES WITH CAPERS

The strong flavour of the capers balances the delicacy of the organic new potatoes, to give a fresh and unusual dish. This makes an excellent side dish.

SERVES 4

750g (1½lb) small new potatoes, scrubbed
25g (1oz) butter or margarine
25g (1oz) low-fat cream cheese

50g (2oz) capers
chopped parsley, to garnish

Boil the potatoes in their skins for 8–10 minutes, or until tender but still waxy, then drain.

Mash the butter or margarine with the cream cheese and capers and smooth over the potatoes. Spoon into a serving dish and sprinkle with the parsley.

Serve at once while the potatoes are still hot and the sauce thick.

POTATO & CELERIAC PURÉE

For all its simplicity, this is an exquisite dish since the 2 flavours combine perfectly. I love to serve it with a simple omelette and the Winter Slaw on page 198.

SERVES 4

V

500g (1lb) potatoes
350g (12oz) celeriac
1 small onion

2 tablespoons single cream, or skimmed or soya milk
sea salt and freshly ground black pepper

Scrub the potatoes and peel the celeriac. Chop them into rough cubes. Slice the onions. Put them all into a saucepan, cover with water and bring to the boil. Simmer for 20–30 minutes, or until very soft. Leave to cool a little in the water. Drain, reserving some of the water.

Liquidise the vegetables in the blender with enough of the cooking water to bring to the desired consistency. Thin out with the cream or milk and season to taste with salt and pepper.

Heat through in an ovenproof dish for 10–15 minutes at 180°C/350°F/gas mark 4, or reheat in a pan on top of the hob.

POTATO & SPINACH RING

This classic dish is an old favourite of mine, which makes a tasty and nourishing supper dish for all the family in cold weather. Serve it with the Winter Slaw on page 198, or a simple tossed green salad.

SERVES 3–4

750g (1½lb) potatoes, scrubbed
15g (½oz) butter or margarine
a little skimmed or soya milk
500g (1lb) spinach, washed
300ml (½ pint) béchamel sauce (see page 218)

a little single cream (optional)
grated nutmeg, mace and freshly ground black pepper

Cover the potatoes with water, bring to the boil and simmer for 20–25 minutes, or until completely soft. Drain, then return to the pan and mash with the butter and enough milk to bring to a creamy but firm consistency.

Spoon around the edge of a baking dish, leaving a hole in the centre for the spinach. Press down with the back of a fork.

Cook the spinach in its own water for 4–5 minutes, then drain thoroughly, and chop. Fold into the béchamel sauce with the cream (if using). Season to taste with nutmeg and mace and lots of freshly ground black pepper.

Pour into the centre of the potato ring. Bake at 190°C/375°F/gas mark 5 for 30 minutes, or until the potatoes are golden-brown on top.

EATING ON A BUDGET

Eating well on a budget is no problem once you focus on the delicious possibilities of using the basic, cheap staples with imaginative touches of herbs and spices. Rice and polenta dishes, pasta or pulses are excellent vehicles for garlic or chilli, Eastern spices or pesto, onions or cheese. You can make superb soups from root vegetables, and the potato – especially the organic potato – is a wonderful vegetable. Do as much of your shopping from street markets or in outlets for local produce as you can, and you will notice the difference to the bank balance.

PURELY PASTA

Pasta comes in many guises. It is usually made from refined durum wheat, a hard grain which gives a firm, nutty quality to the finished product. Sometimes egg is added to the dough, or pasta can be made with wholewheat. The shapes into which this dough is moulded are numerous – bows, tubes, ribbons, wheels and shells as well as the familiar spaghetti. It comes tomato-flavoured, mushroom-flavoured, spinach-flavoured, and made with herbs. Given the variety of ways you can serve pasta, you could probably eat pasta every day and never eat the same meal twice.

SPAGHETTI ALLA NORMA

I ate this on the first evening I ever spent in Sicily, in a little trattoria in the enchanting alleyways of Ortygia. The rustic, honest food went down in my notebook as having the authenticity of classic Italian food.

SERVES 3–4

250g (8oz) aubergines, sliced
250g (8oz) spaghetti
175g (6oz) plum tomatoes (fresh or canned), chopped
1 whole canned pimento, sliced finely
1 mild chilli (fresh), chopped very finely

2 tablespoons olive oil
100g (4oz) Ricotta cheese
a small bunch of basil, chopped
freshly grated Parmesan cheese, to sprinkle

Grill the aubergine slices for 5 minutes on each side, then cool. Chop into dice. Meanwhile, set the pasta on to boil (see page 122).

Soften the tomatoes, pimento and chilli in the oil for 5–6 minutes, then add the aubergines and cook gently for a further 5 minutes.

Stir in the Ricotta until it melts, then add the basil. ◆

Add the mixture to the hot, drained spaghetti and serve with grated Parmesan to hand around.

SPINACH & RICOTTA CANNELLONI

*Y*ou can buy dried cannelloni tubes
for stuffing from supermarkets.
However, this filling also works extremely
well with the savoury Buckwheat Crêpes
on page 88. Simply fill the pancakes with
the spinach and Ricotta mixture and roll
up into tubes, tucking in the ends. Spoon
over the tomato sauce and bake in the
same way.

SERVES 4

350g (12oz) cooked spinach (1¹/₂ lb fresh,
cooked or 1 x 400g (14oz) can)
250g (8oz) Ricotta cheese
3 medium spring onions, chopped finely
sea salt and freshly ground black pepper
¹/₂ teaspoon ground nutmeg

a squeeze of lemon juice
16 cannelloni tubes
300ml (¹/₂ pint) Light Tomato and Basil
Sauce (see page 174)
50g (2oz) Cheddar cheese, grated finely
50g (2oz) fresh breadcrumbs (see page 42)

Drain the spinach thoroughly, chop finely and squeeze dry. Mix with the
Ricotta and spring onions, then season to taste with salt, pepper, nutmeg and a
squeeze of lemon juice.

Stuff the cannelloni tubes with the mixture (I use the thin end of a teaspoon
to push it down). Put into an ovenproof dish and spoon the tomato sauce over
the top.

Mix the grated cheese with the breadcrumbs and sprinkle over the top. Bake
at 190°C/375°F/gas mark 5 for 20–25 minutes, or until bubbling and golden-
brown on top.

PECORINO

This is used in much the same way as
Parmesan, but it is a sheep's cheese –
made from ewe's milk. Sheep are farmed
using fewer hormones and other chemical
treatments than cattle, so I prefer to use
their cheese. Pecorino has a mild, sharp
flavour and similar texture to Parmesan.

Both taste infinitely better grated fresh
from the block, rather than ready-grated.

PARMESAN

This fine, hard cheese – made from
unpasteurised, skimmed cow's milk – is
matured for 2–3 years before using. There is
a brand of 'vegetarian' Parmesan which is
made without using rennet (an enzyme
obtained from the stomach lining of a newly
killed calf).

TO COOK PASTA

This is my personal version of cooking pasta, which I swear by. It works every time and avoids the
ghastly mess of water boiling out all over the stove. Once you've used this method, you will never
use another. Allow 2 litres (3¹/₂ pints) of water per 250g (8oz) pasta.

1. Bring the water to the boil in a large pan and add a generous pinch of sea salt.

2. Put the pasta into the water, bring back to the boil, then draw off the heat. Add 1 tablespoon olive
oil (to prevent the pasta sticking together), stir and cover with a lid.

3. Leave to stand for anything between 5 and 10 minutes, depending on the kind of pasta you are
using. Chinese noodles, for example – which are made from soft wheat – will take only 4–5 minutes,
whereas penne may take up to 9 or 10.

Stir from time to time, and when the pasta is soft but still firm and slightly nutty in texture ('al
dente'), drain it. Shake well in the colander to remove all excess water. Toss immediately in its sauce
and serve as soon as possible.

BUCKWHEAT PASTA WITH BEURRE NOISETTE & MUSHROOMS

The earthy quality of buckwheat goes superbly well with the nutty flavour of beurre noisette. I use as many varieties of mushrooms as I can find for this recipe – if you can find chanterelles or cèpes in autumn you will be well-rewarded.

SERVES 2–3

V

Pasta stores for long periods in the kitchen cupboard so it is always to hand, and doesn't take long to prepare. It is an excellent stand-by for busy people, who also find that, because it releases energy into the body relatively slowly, it keeps them going for a long time. Athletes use it for this reason. And children love it – even the fussiest child will be found eating spaghetti.

3 tablespoons olive oil
350g (12oz) leeks, washed and sliced finely
175g (6oz) mushrooms such as chestnut, flat, cèpes, chanterelles, etc., sliced finely
2 cloves garlic, peeled and sliced finely
1 small dried chilli, sliced finely
sea salt and freshly ground black pepper
175g (6oz) buckwheat pasta
50g (2oz) butter or margarine

Heat 1½ tablespoons olive oil in a heavy-based pan and toss in the thinly sliced leeks. When they are well-coated with the oil, cover with a lid and sweat over a medium heat for 10 minutes, or until completely soft.

Meanwhile, heat the remaining oil in a sauté pan until quite hot, toss in the mushrooms, garlic and chilli and stir-fry over a medium heat until the mushrooms are cooked but still crisp – just a few minutes. Add to the softened leeks, and season to taste with salt and pepper.

Put the pasta into a pan of boiling, salted water and bring back to the boil. Draw off the heat and leave to stand for 4–8 minutes, according to which type you use. The instructions will be on the packet, and the time allowed for standing is the same as that given for boiling. Strain through a colander.

Put the butter or margarine into a small pan and heat over a medium to hot flame until it froths, then turns brown and sizzles. Pour immediately over the well-drained pasta, fold in the mushroom mixture and serve immediately.

FRESH EGG PASTA WITH TOMATOES, TARRAGON & CRÈME FRAÎCHE

The light fresh flavours of this recipe are highlighted by the special pungency of tarragon. This dish is quick and easy to prepare, and delicious with the Mixed Summer Leaf Salad on page 187.

SERVES 3–4

V

400ml (14fl oz) crème fraîche or single cream (or soya cream for vegans)
2 large shallots, sliced finely
1 x 200g (7oz) can tomatoes, drained and chopped
a bunch of tarragon, chopped
a bunch of parsley, chopped
salt and pepper
350g (12oz) fresh egg pasta such as tagliatelle
a few fresh tarragon leaves, to garnish
freshly grated Pecorino or Parmesan, to hand around

Heat the crème fraîche or cream with the shallots and simmer for 3 minutes. Then add the tomatoes and herbs and simmer until reduced – about 10 minutes. Season to taste with salt and pepper. Leave to infuse while you cook the pasta. ◈

Cook the pasta in boiling water until 'al dente' (see page 122). Drain and toss in the sauce immediately. Serve on warm plates, scattering each helping with a few tarragon leaves, and hand around freshly grated cheese.

PASTA RIBBONS WITH PEPERONCINI, AGLIO E OLIO

Use the very finest olive oil for this recipe – the pronounced flavour really comes across in this simple dish, where it is mixed with chillies, shredded leek and garlic. A truly sensational dish, wonderful with fresh crusty granary bread and a seasonal mixed tossed salad.

SERVES 6

V

3 cloves garlic, peeled and crushed
150ml (¼ pint) extra virgin olive oil
2 very small fresh red chillies, chopped very finely
625g (1¼lb) any pasta ribbons, such as tagliolini

1 very small, young leek, shredded finely
sea salt
freshly grated Parmesan cheese, to sprinkle

Crush the garlic into the oil and add the finely chopped chillies . Leave to infuse while you cook the pasta. ◆

Cook the pasta 'al dente' (see page 122), adding the leek for the last 2 minutes of cooking. Drain thoroughly, then toss in the oil and season to taste with salt, if necessary. Serve immediately, with grated Parmesan to pass around.

TAGLIATELLE WITH MANGETOUT & CREAMY SAFFRON SAUCE

This is one of the best pasta dishes ever. The delicate flavour of the saffron is balanced by the chervil and shallots in a creamy sauce – it is a winner! Serve it with warm ciabatta bread and a mixed, garlicky salad.

SERVES 4

V

350g (12oz) mangetout, topped and tailed
6–8 saffron threads for preference (or 1 teaspoon turmeric)
200ml (7fl oz) crème fraîche or single cream (or soya cream for vegans)
500g (1lb) fresh tagliatelle
25g (1oz) unsalted butter or margarine

3 shallots, sliced very finely
2 strips lemon peel, slivered
salt and pepper
a bunch of chervil, chopped finely
grated Parmesan or Pecorino cheese, to sprinkle

> ### TAGLIATELLE
> These are flat strips of pasta, made with egg. They are available dried or fresh (from the cold counter) and can be green (made with spinach) white, red (made with tomato) or black (made with mushrooms).

Steam the mangetout for 2–3 minutes only, so that they are still crisp. Cut into 1cm (½in) lengths.

Mix the saffron threads or turmeric into 3 tablespoons of the crème fraîche or single cream. Heat gently to bring out the flavour of the saffron, then leave to cool.

Set the pasta on to boil at this point (see page 122).

Meanwhile, melt the butter or margarine in a pan, add the shallots, cover with a lid and leave to soften over a very low heat for 6–7 minutes. When soft, stir in the saffron cream and lemon peel and bring to a simmer.

Stir in the mangetout and the rest of the cream and season to taste with salt and pepper. Mix in the chervil. ◆

Toss the cooked, drained pasta with the sauce and serve immediately with freshly grated Parmesan or Pecorino to hand around.

TAGLIARINI WITH BABY COURGETTES & GARDEN HERBS

This dish is best made in the early summer when herbs in the garden are at their best: still young, full of essential flavour, and tender. Wonderful food for a fine summer evening, served with the salad on page 187.

SERVES 4

V

TAGLIARINI

This is a smaller version of tagliatelle (see page 124), made without egg and therefore suitable for vegans.

---

a large bunch of fresh garden herbs such as lemon balm, chives, tansy, rosemary, tarragon, fennel, thyme, etc., all chopped very finely

200ml (7fl oz) crème fraîche or single cream (or soya cream for vegans)

100g (4oz) mangetout, trimmed

500g (1lb) fresh tagliarini

3 shallots, chopped finely

3 tablespoons olive oil

salt and freshly ground black pepper

1 teaspoon cayenne pepper

625g (1¼lb) baby courgettes, steamed lightly and diced

grated Parmesan or Pecorino cheese, to hand around

Mix the chopped herbs into the crème fraîche or cream and leave to infuse for an hour or so.

Meanwhile, blanch the mangetout in boiling water for one minute; drain and refresh under cold running water. Put the pasta on to boil.

Soften the shallots in the olive oil over a gentle heat, then add the crème fraîche mixture. Season to taste with salt, pepper and cayenne, then toss in the diced courgettes.

Toss together with the hot, drained pasta and serve with Parmesan or Pecorino cheese to sprinkle over the top.

A HEALTHY DIET

It is generally accepted that a healthy diet is one that is relatively low in saturated fats, high in fibre and carbohydrates, low in refined sugar and rich in vitamins and minerals. If you are eating lots of vegetables and fruit, cereals, pulses and a judicious amount of dairy products, your diet will be a varied, healthy and nutritious one. Just watch that you don't overdo the butter, cream, cheese and eggs. Avoid cakes and biscuits, sugary jams and preserves. So long as you make sure that you get the correct requirements of protein, vitamins and minerals (see pages 219–220), you will be eating a balanced diet.

Recent medical research has shown that people who don't eat meat live healthier lives than carnivores, and have less chance of getting certain cancers or of suffering heart conditions. Obesity and high blood pressure are far less common, so are various forms of diabetes. Anecdotally, vegetarians say that they FEEL very healthy and full of energy, and that they feel the effects of ageing less.

BUTTERFLY PASTA WITH SQUASH & SPICY LEMON SAUCE

A fabulous dish for when you want stylish yet simple food. A tang of lemon and the spiciness of garam masala flavour a creamy sauce which is memorable and mouthwatering.

SERVES 4–6

V

500g (1lb) squash such as butternut, little gem, turban, etc.
500g (1lb) butterfly pasta
2 tablespoons olive oil
the juice of 1 lemon

the finely grated rind of half a lemon
200ml (7fl oz) crème fraîche (or soya creem for vegans)
2–3 teaspoons green garam masala paste

First prepare the squash: peel, remove the seeds and cut the flesh into small dice. Steam for 3–4 minutes until tender but not mushy, then cool a little. ◆

Put the pasta on to boil at this point (see page 122).

Mix the oil with the lemon juice and rind, then beat in the crème fraîche a little at a time until smooth. Heat gently, then stir in the garam masala paste. Mix into the cooked squash.

Toss all together with the hot, drained pasta and serve.

PARISIAN PENNE WITH LIGHT ROQUEFORT SAUCE

My great Parisian friend made this dish for a supper party when I visited her once, and I watched her make it. I was bowled over by the simple sophistication of the sauce. My notebook was to hand, so here is her recipe.

SERVES 4

> **PENNE**
> These short tubes of dried pasta can be bought plain or ribbed.

half an onion, chopped very finely
3 tablespoons olive oil
350g (12oz) penne
150g (5oz) Roquefort cheese, crumbled

150ml (¼ pint) skimmed or soya milk
whole nutmeg, grated
40g (1½oz) walnuts, ground coarsely, to garnish

Heat the oil in a small saucepan, add the onion, cover with a lid and soften over a very low heat for about 10 minutes. Meanwhile, set the pasta on to boil (see page 122).

Add the crumbled cheese to the onion and stir. Heat gently until it melts. Then pour in the milk, a little at a time, and mix to smooth sauce. Season generously with freshly grated nutmeg.

Toss the well-drained penne in the sauce, sprinkle with the ground walnuts, and it is ready to serve. Hand the pepper mill around for a twist of black pepper to go over each helping.

MUSHROOM & CHÈVRE LASAGNE

I love the simplicity of this lasagne, partly because I am so partial to mushrooms and there are lots of them in this dish. Cooked with a little white wine, and layered with goat's cheese, this makes great family food.

SERVES 6–8

2 tablespoons olive oil

1 onion, chopped finely

2 medium carrots, sliced finely

2 sticks celery, sliced finely

a large bunch of herbs such as thyme, marjoram, parsley, tarragon, chives etc., chopped

3 cloves garlic, peeled and chopped

750g (1½lb) mixed mushrooms such as shiitake, chestnut, flat, chanterelles, cèpes, etc., sliced fairly thickly

4 tablespoons tomato purée

5 tablespoons white wine

sea salt and pepper

900ml (1½ pints) béchamel sauce made with 300ml (½ pint) single cream (see page 218)

350g (12oz) lasagne strips

300g (10oz) good quality goat's cheese, sliced

50g (2oz) Cheddar cheese, grated

a little grated Pecorino cheese, to sprinkle

Heat the oil gently in a wok. Cook the onion, carrot, celery and herbs in it for 3–4 minutes until they begin to soften, then add the garlic and the mushrooms and cook for 5–6 minutes longer, stirring, until soft.

Stir in the tomato purée and white wine and simmer for a few minutes. Season to taste with salt and pepper. ◆

In a large casserole dish make layers using half of the béchamel, the lasagne, mushroom mixture and goat's cheese, until all the ingredients are used up.

Heat the rest of the béchamel gently and stir in the grated cheese. When it has melted, pour over the top of the lasagne and sprinkle with grated Pecorino.

Bake for 1 hour at 190°C/375°F/gas mark 5 until golden and sizzling.

SPICY NOODLES WITH BEANSPROUTS

A great stand-by: I can't count how many times I've made this dish, either with beansprouts or with other vegetables like mangetout, courgettes, or – in particular – broccoli. I keep the black bean sauce, dark sesame oil and chilli sauce in constant supply in the kitchen cupboard: they make food taste exotic so painlessly!

SERVES 3–4

V

FOR THE SAUCE

2 tablespoons black bean sauce

3 tablespoons dark sesame oil

3 cloves garlic, peeled and crushed

2–3 teaspoons chilli sauce (to taste – strength varies according to the make)

2 teaspoons soy sauce

FOR THE NOODLES

250g (8oz) beansprouts, steamed for 2–3 minutes

175g (6oz) Chinese noodles, egg or plain

100g (4oz) mangetout, trimmed and sliced thinly

a sprig of fresh coriander, to garnish

Mix all the sauce ingredients together. ◆

Cook the noodles in boiling water until tender – about 3 minutes – adding the mangetout for the final minute; drain.

Toss immediately in the sauce, add the drained beansprouts and toss again. Serve immediately, garnished with a sprig of coriander.

PENNE WITH SPINACH, PETITS POIS & CHÈVRE

An exquisite recipe: I have served this dish at dinner parties and everyone loves the elegant combination of green vegetables with the distinctive flavour of goat's cheese.

SERVES 6

500g (1lb) penne
125ml (4fl oz) olive oil
100g (4oz) mangetout, trimmed
250g (8oz) leaf spinach, shredded
250g (8oz) petits pois, cooked
400g (14oz) good-quality goat's cheese, crumbled

salt and pepper
thinly pared Parmesan or Pecorino cheese, to sprinkle
1–2 tablespoons finely chopped parsley, to garnish

Cook the penne 'al dente' (see page 122), and drain thoroughly. Toss in 2 tablespoons of the olive oil. Keep the pan covered while you prepare the rest.

Heat the remaining oil and soften the mangetout in it, stir-frying for about 2 minutes. Then add the shredded spinach and stir-fry for a minute longer, then add the petits pois.

Stir into the hot pasta, add the goat's cheese and mix thoroughly. Season to taste with salt and pepper and toss again.

Serve garnished with flakes of thinly pared Parmesan and finely chopped fresh parsley.

LINGUINE WITH ROASTED PEPPERS & HAZELNUTS

The inimitable flavour of roasted peppers is a perfect foil for fresh pasta in this cold sauce. A touch of garlic and chilli, the crunch of toasted hazelnuts, and a sprinkle of fresh coriander add their contribution to the fabulous flavours of this dish.

SERVES 4
V

LINGUINE
This narrow, flat pasta is made without egg – making it ideal for vegans.

---

2 large peppers, red and yellow
a little olive oil, to drizzle
3 tablespoons balsamic vinegar
4 tablespoons olive oil
3 cloves garlic, peeled and crushed
1 mild chilli, chopped very finely

500g (1lb) fresh linguine
sea salt
50g (2oz) hazelnuts, chopped and browned under the grill (see page 134)
a bunch of coriander, chopped
grated Pecorino cheese, to sprinkle

Cut the peppers into quarters and deseed. Slice thinly. Put into a roasting pan and drizzle a little olive oil over the top. Roast at 200°C/400°F/gas mark 6 for 30 minutes, or until the skins blister. Cool.

Mix the vinegar, olive oil, garlic and chilli together and marinate the peppers in it for an hour or two. ◆

Cook the linguine 'al dente' (see page 122), then drain and toss in the cold sauce. Season with salt, toss in the hazelnuts and the chopped coriander and mix well together. Transfer to a warm serving dish, sprinkle with Pecorino and serve immediately.

TORTELLINI 'IVY'

*A*rtichoke hearts are a delicacy – food for the gods. In this recipe, they are combined with sun-dried tomatoes and dill to make a superb foil for the cheesy tortellini. A memorable party dish.

SERVES 6

2 x 400g (14oz) cans artichoke hearts
2 teaspoons dried thyme
olive oil, to drizzle
500g (1lb) tortellini, filled with Ricotta or
   4-cheeses
3 cloves garlic, peeled and sliced finely
1–2 tablespoons olive oil

100g (4oz) sun-dried tomatoes in oil, drained
   and chopped
a small bunch of dill, chopped finely
sea salt
grated Parmesan, to sprinkle
a sprig of fresh dill, to garnish

Drain the artichoke hearts and rinse under the cold tap. Dry on paper towels. Put into a roasting pan with the dried thyme and drizzle olive oil over the top. Roast at 220°C/425°F/gas mark 7 for 40–45 minutes, or until well-browned. ◆

Set the tortellini on to boil now (see page 122).

Sauté the garlic in the oil until soft. Add the sun-dried tomatoes, then mix in the artichoke hearts and dill. Season to taste with sea salt.

Toss with the cooked tortellini and serve sprinkled with Parmesan and garnished with a sprig of dill.

TORTELLINI
These are little pasta envelopes, made with various fillings. They are available fresh or dried from most supermarkets.

NOODLES WITH QUICK-STEAMED VEGETABLES 'SWEET & SOUR'

*T*he speed and simplicity with which this is prepared takes some beating. Stir-frying vegetables brings out the best in their flavour and texture, and the sweet and sour sauce – obtainable from ethnic grocers or the larger supermarkets – makes them irresistible.

SERVES 3–4

V

2 tablespoons groundnut oil
4 spring onions, sliced finely
350g (12oz) broccoli florets, sliced
250g (8oz) courgettes, sliced thinly
100g (4oz) mangetout, topped and tailed

175g (6oz) baby carrots, sliced thinly
175g (6oz) noodles, cooked and drained well
300ml (½ pint) sweet and sour sauce
2 tablespoons chopped peanuts
a sprig of fresh coriander, to garnish

Heat the oil in a wok or large frying pan and toss in the prepared vegetables. Stir-fry for 4 minutes, then turn the heat down, add 2–3 tablespoons of water, cover with a lid and steam for 8–10 minutes, or until the vegetables are tender. Mix in the noodles and the sweet and sour sauce, and mix thoroughly. Serve immediately, sprinkled with chopped peanuts and garnished with a sprig of fresh coriander.

CHILLI COLD NOODLES

This truly wonderful dish goes really well with the Stir-fried Cauliflower on page 36. With its nutty flavour of dark sesame oil, and the hit of chilli on the palate, it makes a sensational centrepiece for a buffet table and everyone loves its distinctive flavours. You can use grated courgettes, instead of carrots, if you prefer.

SERVES 4
V

FOR THE NOODLES
250g (8oz) thin noodles, egg or plain
250g (8oz) beansprouts
2 medium carrots, grated finely
6 spring onions, sliced finely
half a bunch of coriander, chopped

FOR THE SAUCE
4 tablespoons dark sesame oil
1 tablespoon black bean sauce
2 teaspoons chilli sauce
2 cloves garlic, peeled and crushed
1 scant teaspoon balsamic vinegar
chopped roasted peanuts, to garnish

Cook the noodles in boiling water until soft – about 2 minutes – adding the beansprouts for the last 20–30 seconds. Drain and refresh under cold water. Drain thoroughly.

Combine the ingredients for the sauce and add to the noodles and beansprouts. Toss with the grated carrot, spring onion and coriander. Transfer to a serving dish and sprinkle with the chopped peanuts.

PASTA SALAD WITH ROASTED SQUASH & MINT

Cold pasta salads are invaluable – both for parties and for when you have to prepare meals ahead of time. They are cheap and easy to make, yet elegant and rewarding food. The mint in this one brings it to life – a great combination with the roasted squash.

SERVES 4–6
V

350g (12oz) pasta shapes, cooked 'al dente'
2 tablespoons tomato purée
1 tablespoon balsamic vinegar
4 tablespoons olive oil
4 cloves garlic, peeled

500g (1lb) squash, peeled and diced
2 tablespoons chopped mint
20 black olives, pitted
sea salt and freshly ground black pepper

Drain the pasta and rinse it thoroughly under the cold tap. Shake dry in the colander. Mix together the tomato purée, vinegar and 2 tablespoons of the olive oil. Toss into the cooled pasta and leave to marinate. ◆

Blanch the peeled garlic cloves in boiling water for 5 minutes, then drain and pat dry. Put into a roasting pan with the squash. Drizzle the remaining olive oil over the top and bake at 230°C/450°F/gas mark 8 for 30–35 minutes, or until the squash is slightly golden, turning from time to time.

Stir the roasted vegetables, with the pan juices, into the pasta and scatter with the mint and olives. Toss well, season to taste, and keep cool until ready to eat.

GARLICKY FETTUCCINE WITH PINE-NUTS

This is what I call weekend food – the garlic is so strong that only your nearest and dearest will tolerate you the next day. But it's uplifting food – not only garlic, but chilli too!

SERVES 3–4

V

FETTUCCINE
These long, flat strips of pasta are made with egg and look very similar to tagliatelle.

150ml (¼ pint) olive oil
¼ teaspoon chilli powder
4 cloves garlic, peeled and crushed
350g (12oz) fettuccine
75g (3oz) pine-nuts, browned under the grill
   (see below)

3 tablespoons chopped fresh basil
freshly grated Parmesan or Pecorino, to
   sprinkle

Heat the oil in a pan and mix in the chilli powder. Draw aside to cool, then stir in the crushed garlic. Cook the pasta 'al dente' (see page 122), drain thoroughly and toss in the oil mixture. Sprinkle with the nuts and basil and the dish is ready to serve.

Pass around freshly grated Parmesan to sprinkle over the top.

BROWNING NUTS
Browning nuts under the grill is a delicate operation because they can burn very suddenly.
   Put the nuts into a metal tray and place under a preheated grill. Shake from time to time to allow them to brown evenly all over, keeping a sharp eye on them in case they start to scorch. Pine-nuts are particularly easy to ruin, and don't need much time at all before they turn golden-brown.

BASIL TAGLIATELLE WITH QUATTRO FORMAGGIO

An unusual way of baking pasta with the famous four cheeses, plus a crunchy layer on top. This is brilliant – the delicate taste and aroma of basil comes through the mouthwatering cheesiness.

SERVES 3–4

40g (1½oz) each of Provolone, Fontina, Bel Paese and Parmesan (or Pecorino) cheese
250g (8oz) tagliatelle, cooked 'al dente' (see page 122)

1 tablespoon good olive oil
a handful of fresh basil leaves, shredded
grated Parmesan or Pecorino, to sprinkle

Grate all the cheeses. Toss the cooked, drained pasta in the oil, then sprinkle with the basil.

In a buttered baking dish make layers of half the pasta, half the cheese, half the pasta and the rest of the cheese.

Sprinkle with a little extra Parmesan or Pecorino and bake at 180°C/350°F/gas mark 4 for 20 minutes, or until golden-brown on top.

RICOTTA

This is an Italian cheese made from ewe's milk whey, left over from producing other cheeses. It is soft and smooth in texture, creamy-white in colour and fragrant, and used in its unripened state. It is unsalted and can be used for both savoury and sweet dishes.

PROVOLONE

Also made from unpasteurised cow's milk, Provolone is moulded by hand into its various shapes and is used in cooking as well as eaten straight. It has a soft, smooth texture and pale yellow colour, and a flavour which varies from strong to mild, depending on its maturity.

FONTINA

One of Italy's great cheeses, Fontina comes from the Aosta Valley in north-west Italy. It is made from unpasteurised cow's milk and is dark yellow with a brown rind. It has a mild flavour and is similar in texture to Gruyère, being soft and rubbery with lots of small holes.

BEL PAESE

A rich, creamy cheese with a delicate flavour, Bel Paese is made in various parts of Italy. It is yellow with an orange waxy rind.

PARMESAN AND PECORINO

See page 122.

PULSES, RICE & POLENTA

Rice is one of the cook's great stand-bys – many of the great dishes of the world are based around it, and you can quite confidently bring these into your kitchen to make classic family food.

THAI RICE NOODLES WITH CHILLI & PEANUT SAUCE

A taste of the exotic East: lemon grass, chilli, peanuts and coconut milk all conjure up the magic of Thai cuisine.

SERVES 4

V

100g (4oz) peanuts
2 tablespoons olive oil
3 tiny red chillies, sliced finely
6 large spring onions, sliced
1 tablespoon chopped chives
300ml (½ pint) coconut milk
   (see page 104)
1 lemon grass stalk, bruised
350g (12oz) cauliflower florets
   steamed 'al dente'

250g (8oz) beansprouts steamed
   for 2 minutes
lemon juice
salt
a bunch of fresh coriander,
   chopped
250–300g (8–10oz) rice
   noodles, soaked in hot water
   for 10 minutes

Grind the peanuts roughly in the food processor.

Heat the olive oil and sauté the chillies and spring onions in it over a low heat for 4–5 minutes, or until soft. Add the chives, then pour over the coconut milk and heat through. Stir in the lemon grass and peanuts and simmer for 5 minutes. ◆

Toss the cauliflower and beansprouts into the sauce, season with lemon juice and salt, then fold in the chopped oriander.

Drain the rice noodles. Make a 'nest' with them in a large serving dish and pile the Thai vegetables in the centre. Serve as soon as possible.

HUMMUS

Here are 2 versions of this deservedly famous Middle Eastern-speciality. One uses dried chickpeas, which is a more arduous process but you will see the point when you taste it! The other is for when you are in a hurry — it's still good. Whichever way you choose, it's worth making a lot because hummus freezes really well and is a useful thing to have in store.

SERVES 8

TAHINA

Tahina (or tahini) is an oily paste made from sesame seeds. These are sometimes roasted first to give the paste a strong nutty flavour. Dark tahina is made from the unhusked seeds. Both dark and light tahina can be found in health food shops or ethnic grocers. It keeps indefinitely in the refrigerator, and is a valuable source of zinc and calcium. The paste is a classic ingredient of the famous humus.

USING DRIED CHICKPEAS

250g (8oz) dried chickpeas
juice of 1 lemon
1 heaped teaspoon ground cumin
3 tablespoons natural yoghurt
1–2 tablespoons tahina paste (optional)
2 cloves garlic, peeled
sea salt

Soak the chickpeas in water for 5–6 hours. Drain, cover with cold water in a saucepan and bring to the boil. Simmer for 1 hour, cover, then leave to cool.

Strain, reserving some of the cooking liquid. Put the chickpeas into the blender with the lemon juice, cumin, yoghurt, tahina and garlic and blend until smooth. Add enough of the cooking water to bring to the desired consistency, and season to taste with salt.

USING CANNED CHICKPEAS

1 x 400g (14oz) can chickpeas, drained
juice of half a lemon
1/2 teaspoon ground cumin
2 tablespoons natural yoghurt
a little tahina paste, to taste (optional)
1–2 cloves garlic, peeled and crushed
sea salt
a little olive oil

Put the chickpeas, lemon juice, cumin and yoghurt in the food processor and whizz to a smooth purée. Season to taste with tahina paste (if using), garlic and sea salt and blend again. Thin out with a little olive oil, if necessary.

SPICY MIXED BEANS

This is a fairly 'instant' dish, but highly nutritious and satisfying. It is lovely with the Lemony Brown Rice on page 144. You should be able to find most of the ingredients in your store–cupboard.

SERVES 4
V

2 tablespoons sunflower oil
1 large onion, chopped
2 cloves garlic, peeled and crushed,
1–2 teaspoons chilli powder
1 x 400g (14oz) can chopped tomatoes
2 tablespoons tomato purée
1 tablespoon dried mixed herbs
100g (4oz) canned green beans
1 x 400g (14oz) can cannellini beans
1 x 400g (14oz) can kidney beans, drained

Heat the oil in a large saucepan and stir in the onion. Stir-fry for a minute or two, then turn the heat down and cover tightly with a lid. Let the onion soften for about 10 minutes.

Now add the garlic and the chilli and sauté for a few minutes. Stir in the tomatoes with their juices and the tomato purée, bring to the boil and simmer gently, covered, for 5 minutes.

Finally, stir in the drained canned beans and heat through. Check the seasoning and it is ready to serve.

EMANUELE'S POLENTA

My friend Emanuele gave me this dish for supper one blustery night in England and I loved its rustic simplicity. She made it using coarse polenta, which she brought back from her village in Southern France. Although it is difficult to obtain here, it gives the dish a wonderful texture so it is well worth hunting down. Failing that, you can make it with ordinary fine maize meal. The result is a scrumptious supper dish, which is cheap, easy to make and nutritious.

SERVES 4

175g (6oz) maize meal or polenta
1 litre (1¾ pints) vegetable stock (see page 218)
1oz (50g) butter or margarine
cayenne pepper, ground chilli and mace
1 tablespoon sunflower oil
1 large onion

250g (8oz) mushrooms, sliced
1 tablespoon dried mixed 'herbes de Provence'
1 x 400g (14oz) can chopped tomatoes, drained
50g (2oz) raisins
75g (3oz) Cheddar cheese (low-fat if preferred), grated

POLENTA

Polenta is wonderful and not, as some might imagine it to be, a heavy, bland cornmeal porridge. The polenta recipes here will convert even the most suspicious! They are inspired by eating out in San Francisco where Italy has its little kingdom and the cooks know what they are doing.

Place the polenta and stock in a large saucepan and bring slowly to the boil, stirring all the time to keep the mixture smooth and to prevent it going lumpy. When it comes to the boil, turn the heat down low and cook at a slow simmer for 10–12 minutes, stirring occasionally.

Once the polenta is tender, beat in the butter or margarine until well-amalgamated. Season to taste with the spices, then spoon into a shallow, buttered ovenproof dish and smooth the top. Leave to cool. (If you are making this ahead of time, place in the refrigerator.) ◆

Heat the oil in a pan, add the onion, cover with a lid and soften over a very low heat for 6–8 minutes. When soft, toss in the mushrooms and the herbs, cover and steam gently for 5 minutes, stirring occasionally.

Add the tomatoes, stir well and heat through. Simmer gently for 5 minutes, then add the raisins. ◆

Sprinkle the polenta with the grated cheese, then spoon the vegetables over the top. Bake in the oven at 180°C/350°F/gas mark 4 for 30 minutes.

THE PROTEIN QUESTION

It would be difficult to design a comprehensive meatless diet short on protein. Most plant foods contain it, and dairy produce is a good source. However, excess protein in the body can cause diseases such as osteoporosis and poor kidney function, and even certain forms of cancer. It is claimed that a meat–free diet has the advantage over a meat-based one, in that its protein content is adequate but not excessive. A well-balanced vegetarian diet will meet daily protein requirements.

The soya bean is a high-quality protein and all soya products such as soya milk and tofu are extremely good sources. Chick peas and lentils have a high protein content, so do baked beans and muesli, nuts and seeds. Eggs are reasonably high in protein, so are peanuts, bread and hard cheese. You will get smaller amounts of protein from brown rice, porridge, potatoes, broccoli and spinach.

For more details, see the Nutrition Chart on page 219.

GRILLED POLENTA WITH CHEESE, MUSHROOOMS & ROASTED GARLIC

I first fell in love with polenta in San Francisco, in a café where they served it hot with roasted garlic and sage – along with an inimitable leaf salad. Since then I've explored how to make polenta really light and tasty – a far cry from the awful 'porridge' I had thought it was – and I use it a lot. It's cheap, easy to make, and really delicious.

MAKES 4 SQUARES

FOR THE POLENTA
75g (3oz) maize meal
600ml (1 pint) vegetable stock (see page 218)
1 teaspoon cayenne pepper (or you can try a mixture of other spices and herbs: 1 large clove garlic, peeled and crushed; 1/2 teaspoon chilli; and 1 teaspoon ground cumin spice it up beautifully)
sea salt
25g (1oz) butter or margarine
50g (2oz) Cheddar cheese (low-fat if preferred), cut into thin slivers

FOR THE ROASTED GARLIC
1 whole head garlic (large cloves), skins on
olive oil, to brush
dried thyme and rosemary, to sprinkle
salt and pepper

FOR THE MUSHROOM GARNISH
225g (8oz) large flat mushrooms, sliced
olive oil, to brush

First cook the polenta. Put the maize meal into a saucepan and pour on the stock, stirring until it becomes smooth. Bring to the boil and simmer very gently for 10 minutes, stirring frequently until cooked.

Add the spices and garlic (if using), season to taste with salt and beat in the butter or margarine. Pour into a small rectangular dish, smooth down the top and leave to cool. You can leave this overnight if you wish.◆

Meanwhile roast the garlic. Cut off the pointed ends, but leave the skins on. Brush with olive oil and place in a shallow baking dish. Sprinkle with the herbs, salt and pepper. Bake for 40 minutes at 180°C/350°F/gas mark 4, or until soft. Leave to cool slightly, then squeeze out of the skins.

Now grill the mushrooms. Brush them liberally with olive oil and set under a hot grill for a few minutes until cooked on both sides.

Cover the cold polenta with the slivers of cheese and cut into 4 squares. Lift them out of the dish and set under the pre-heated grill for a few minutes, or until the cheese melts and the polenta is hot. Alternatively, microwave on full power for 1 minute.

Garnish the cheesy polenta squares with the roasted garlic and serve surrounded by the grilled mushrooms.

CHILLI BEANS WITH A CORNBREAD CRUST

Perfect family food for winter weather, this is scrumptious served with the Light Tomato and Basil Sauce on page 174 and plain, steamed broccoli.

SERVES 4–6

To cook pulses from scratch takes time and planning, since they have to be soaked for a long time ahead of cooking. When you are in a hurry you can use canned ones – I resort to them frequently and find them very good. They are wholesome food, full of goodness, with earthy colours and flavours. Perfect for cold-weather meals, as well as in salads for any season.

FOR THE BEANS

1 tablespoon olive oil

1 large onion, chopped

2 cloves garlic, peeled and chopped

½–1 teaspoon chilli powder, to taste

1 x 400g (14oz) can chopped tomatoes, drained

1 whole canned pimento, chopped

2 sticks celery, sliced

1 x 400g (14oz) can kidney beans, drained

FOR THE CORNBREAD CRUST

100g (4oz) cornmeal (maize meal)

25g (1oz) plain flour

salt and pepper

2 teaspoons baking powder

1 egg, beaten

125ml (4fl oz) skimmed or soya milk

2 tablespoons chopped dill

50g (2oz) Cheddar cheese (low-fat if preferred), grated

Heat the oil in a pan, add the onion, cover with a lid and soften over a low heat for 10 minutes.

Add the garlic and the chilli and stir-fry for 1 minute. Stir in the tomatoes, pimento and celery and cook for a further 5 minutes, stirring occasionally. Stir in the kidney beans and put into a baking dish. ◆

To make the cornmeal crust, mix the dry ingredients for the topping together in a bowl, and make a well in the centre.

In a separate bowl, beat the egg with the milk and chopped dill. Pour into the well in the dry ingredients and mix to a smooth batter.

Spread the topping over the chilli mixture and bake at 200°C/400°F/gas mark 6 for 25 minutes, or until risen and golden-brown.

GRADES AND VARIETIES OF RICE

Many of the great dishes of the world are based on rice: paella, pilau, risotto and the fried rice made famous by the Chinese – to name but a few. It is important to use the right type of rice for each dish.

Brown rice

This is the best rice in nutritional terms. It consists of the whole natural grain – without its edible husk removed – which means that it is high in dietary fibre, minerals and vitamins. It has a delicious flavour and a nutty texture. Brown rice needs a little more water and longer cooking than white rice – about 15–20 minutes.

Jasmine rice

Imported from Thailand and also known as Thai Fragrant rice, this delicate fragrant rice lends itself well to all East-Asian dishes. It is a long-grain rice, which is delicious cooked in coconut milk (see page 104).

Short-grain rice

Often used for risottos and puddings, this is usually eaten white – with the husk removed. Brown short-grain rice is delicious for risottos. It has a slightly crunchier texture and a higher fibre content than ordinary white rice.

Basmati rice

This narrow, long-grain rice from India or Italy has a delicate and distinctive flavour and is excellent with Indian food. Both brown or white are available.

Arborio rice

A quality rice from Italy, this has a good flavour and makes excellent risottos. It is plumper than long-grain rice, comes brown or white and is available from delicatessens.

Patna rice

This long-grain rice is the most versatile and popular of all the varieties. It comes white or brown, and is suitable for savoury dishes.

Pudding rice

This short-grain, polished rice goes soft and mushy when cooked, due to its high starch content. Excellent for a creamy rice pudding.

Wild rice

This is not a true rice at all, but the seed of a water-grass. It is long grained, grey-brown and nutty in flavour. Wild rice requires long cooking – 30–40 minutes – but it is nice to mix into rice dishes for variety.

Rice flour

A good thickening agent in sauces and stews, this can also be used in baking. It is successfully interchangeable with wheat flour and invaluable for people with an allergy to gluten.

Rice flakes

These are grains which have been flaked by processing to make them very quick to cook. You can use them to thicken soups or stews, or use them in milk puddings.

LEMONY BROWN RICE

A simple, unusual way of cooking rice, which forms a refreshing and lovely side dish.

175g (6oz) brown rice
the grated rind and juice of 1 lemon
2 tablespoons olive oil

2 tablespoons chopped parsley
salt

SERVES 3–4
V

Cover the rice with water and add the lemon juice and rind. Bring to the boil, cover tightly and turn the heat down very low. Cook gently for 30–35 minutes, or until the rice is tender.

Remove from the heat and allow to stand for 5 minutes, then season to taste with olive oil, parsley and salt. Toss gently with a fork before serving.

AROMATIC DHAL

This dhal – the famous Indian dish of lentils – is excellent as a side dish with a curry meal, or lovely on its own for a simple meal just with rice and a salad.

175g (6oz) green lentils
50g (2oz) fresh root ginger, peeled and
   sliced thickly
3 cloves garlic, peeled and left whole

2 teaspoons turmeric powder
2 jalapeno chillies, sliced in half lengthways
salt
100ml (4fl oz) crème fraîche (optional)

SERVES 4–5
V
●

Soak the lentils for 3–4 hours, then drain and rinse them. Put into a saucepan, cover with water and add the ginger, garlic, turmeric and chillies. Bring to the boil and simmer until the lentils are soft – about 1½ hours. Cool, remove the spices and drain, reserving the liquid. Blend to a purée, thinning out with enough of the cooking liquid to bring to the desired consistency – which should be quite thin. Season to taste with salt, then finish with the optional crème fraîche.

COOKING RICE

The simplest formula for cooking rice is to allow one measure of rice to two of water. Weigh the amount of rice required and put it into a measuring jug. You will need twice this measure of water to cook the rice.

To boil rice

Always rinse rice thoroughly before you use it, to wash off any grit and natural dust. Put into a saucepan and pour the water over. Bring to the boil, stir, then turn the heat down low and cover with a lid. Leave to simmer gently – resisting the temptation to lift the lid while it is cooking – so that the steaming process is not disturbed. The rice will absorb all the water in about 8–10 minutes, depending on the type of rice you are using. Brown rice takes up to 20 minutes.

Season with a little salt, fluff the rice and it is ready to eat.

To microwave rice

Put 250g (8oz) rice into a microwave container and cover with 450 ml (¾ pint) boiling water. Stir and cover. Cook on full power for 5 minutes.

Stir again, re-cover and cook for a further 6 minutes on defrost. Allow to stand for 3 minutes, then fluff up with a fork, and serve.

PUMPKIN OR SQUASH RISOTTO WITH PECORINO

You can use either pumpkin or squash for this recipe – these wonderful vegetables are often underrated and yet they are fabulous. Cooked up into this Epicurean risotto which melts in the mouth, they give the dish delicacy and succulence. Its elegance makes you forget how economical it is! You can also try this recipe using leeks instead of squash.

SERVES 4

(omit cheese) **V**

1 tablespoon olive oil
4 shallots, chopped finely
250g (8oz) risotto rice (see page 143)
500g (1lb) pumpkin or squash, peeled and seeded
1 teaspoon powdered saffron
90ml (3fl oz) dry white wine

750ml (1¼ pints) vegetable stock (see page 218)
1 tablespoon dried oregano
50g (2oz) Pecorino cheese, finely grated
salt and freshly ground black pepper
a sprig of parsley, to garnish

Heat the oil in a casserole pan and gently fry the shallots until soft but not browned, stirring occasionally. Turn the heat up and add the rice, stirring until coated with the oil.

Grate the pumpkin coarsely (use the food processor for this, if you have one – it will save you hours!). Add to the pan and stir-fry for 3–4 minutes, or until heated through.

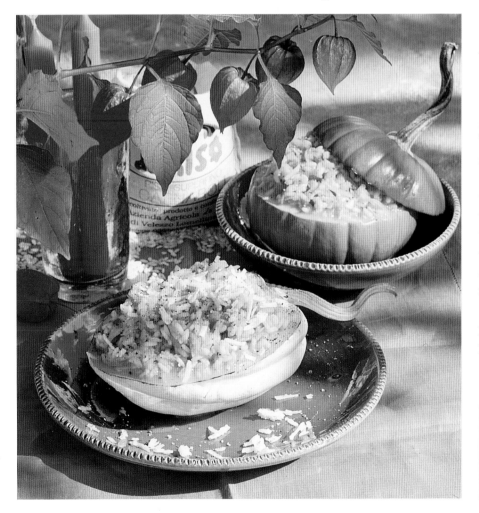

Sprinkle the saffron into the wine, turn the heat up and pour into the casserole pan. Stir until the liquid has absorbed, then start to add the stock: turn the heat down to medium and add to the pan a little at a time, making sure that each addition has been absorbed before you add any more. Keep stirring all the time.

Half way through the cooking time, add the oregano and continue to cook until the rice is tender and the pumpkin very soft. Remove from the heat, fold in the grated cheese and leave to stand for about 10 minutes to allow the rice to swell.

Season to taste with salt and pepper, garnish with a sprig of parsley and serve on hot plates.

LEFTOVER RICE DISHES
Re-heating leftover rice works very well – either in the microwave or a steamer (see page 30), covered with a plate or lid.

SOUTH INDIAN MUSHROOM RICE

A sublime dish of authentically spiced mushrooms cooked in coconut milk, served on top of a layer of rice which soaks up the delicious juices. This recipe comes from the south of India, from a friend of mine in beautiful Kerala.

SERVES 3

V

1–2 small green chillies, sliced finely
1 teaspoon ground coriander
1 teaspoon ground cumin
4 cloves garlic, peeled
1 small onion, peeled and sliced
60g (2¹/₂oz) coconut milk powder

450ml (³/₄ pint) water
500g (1lb) small button mushrooms (chestnut for preference)
salt
(250g) 8oz basmati rice

Put the chillies, spices, garlic and onion into the small bowl of the blender and work to a paste.

Mix the coconut milk powder with the water and stir to a smooth cream. Put into a pan with the paste and bring to the boil.

Add the mushrooms, turn down to a simmer, and cook uncovered for 20 minutes so that the sauce thickens and the mushrooms are tender. Season to taste with salt, then leave to cool for 15 minutes so that the sauce evaporates further. ◆

Cook the rice and place it in the bottom of a serving dish. Spoon the mushrooms over the top, then pour the sauce over the rice. Serve warm.

SPICY PILAFF WITH ORANGE & RAISINS

Exotic, with a flavour of Persian cooking, this pilaff has the sweet flavours of orange and raisins to give it something very different and distinctive. It is lovely with the oil-roasted vegetables on page 100, and the Light Tomato and Basil Sauce on page 174.

SERVES 4

V

the rind of quarter of an orange, peeled thinly
2 tablespoons vegetable oil
250g (8oz) basmati rice
1 teaspoon ground turmeric
4 spring onions, sliced

75g (3oz) raisins or sultanas
¹/₂ teaspoon allspice
600ml (1 pint) water
salt

Cut the orange rind into very thin strips about 1cm (¹/₂in) long.

Heat the oil in a heavy-bottomed pan and when hot stir in the rice, orange rind, turmeric, spring onions, raisins and allspice. Stir over a medium heat for a few minutes so that everything is well mixed, then pour over the water. Bring to the boil.

Cover tightly and leave to simmer over a very low heat for 25–30 minutes, or until the rice is tender. Season to taste with salt and leave to stand off the heat for 25–30 minutes before serving to allow the rice to swell.

MUSHROOM RISOTTO WITH SWEET RED PEPPERS

An ongoing favourite, this risotto is amazingly tasty, and very simple and economical to make. For minimum effort you get maximum reward, with the rich flavour of mushrooms and the tang of red peppers. Serve with grated Pecorino to hand around, and a tossed green salad.

SERVES 4

V

2 tablespoons sunflower oil
5 spring onions, sliced
250g (8oz) chestnut mushrooms, quartered
½ fresno or jalapeno chilli, sliced finely
1 whole canned pimento, sliced

300g (10oz) basmati rice
450ml (¾ pint) vegetable stock (see page 218)
salt

Heat the oil in a pan, add the spring onions, cover with a lid and soften over a very low heat for about 10 minutes, stirring occasionally.

Add the mushrooms, chilli and red pepper and stir until well-coated in the oil. Put in the rice and cook over a medium heat for 3–4 minutes, stirring. Pour in the stock and bring to the boil.

Cover tightly, turn the heat down low and cook very gently for 25 minutes until the rice is tender and all the liquid is absorbed. Season to taste with salt.

Fork through before serving, and serve with grated Pecorino to pass around.

RICE WITH YELLOW SPLIT PEAS & GARLIC

I enjoyed a dish similar to this one in a simple hotel in Udaipur in Northern India, and have never forgotten its comforting, warming qualities. This aromatic food has spices that linger on the palate.

SERVES 4

V

●

250g (8oz) yellow split peas
1 tablespoon sunflower oil
2.5cm (1in) stick cinnamon
1 green chilli, chopped finely
2 cloves
3 cloves garlic, peeled and chopped finely

1 small onion, sliced very finely
175g (6oz) basmati rice, rinsed under the cold tap
1 teaspoon salt
600ml (1 pint) water

Rinse the split peas under the cold tap, then soak them in cold water for an hour.

Heat the oil in a pan and sizzle the cinnamon, chilli and cloves in it. Stir in the garlic and onion and stir-fry until they begin to brown.

Add the rice, split peas and salt, and sauté over a medium heat for a couple of minutes. Add the water and bring to the boil. Cover tightly and simmer gently over a very low heat for 35–40 minutes.

Remove the whole spices before serving.

COUSCOUS À LA MAROCAINE

*W*hen I had couscous in Morocco I felt I was eating it for the first time. The dish was light and ethereal – flavoured with exotic spices and served alongside slow-cooked vegetables. It bore no resemblance to the gluey, heavy, solid pudding that many of us are familiar with. Aided by the now much improved couscous on the supermarket shelves, this dish is as close a version as I can get to the one that we ate under the stars in the desert.

SERVES 4

V

FOR THE VEGETABLES

2 onions

2 large leeks

350g (12oz) aubergine

4 large ripe tomatoes

3 large courgettes

2 large carrots

300ml (½ pint) water

a little sea salt

2 tablespoons mixed spices such as saffron, chilli, cumin, coriander, etc.

Tabasco sauce (optional)

FOR THE COUSCOUS

600ml (1 pint) water

250g (8oz) couscous

2 tablespoons olive oil or 1 large knob butter or margarine

First prepare the vegetables. Trim and wash them, then cut into rough chunks. Put into a casserole dish with the water and a little salt. Cover with foil and a tight-fitting lid, then set in the oven at 150°C/300°F/gas mark 2 for 2 hours 40 minutes.

Remove from the oven, stir in the spices and return to the oven for a final 20 minutes.

Meanwhile, cook the couscous. Bring the water to the boil in a large pan, then pour in the couscous in a gradual stream, stirring all the time as the water returns to the boil. Remove from the heat, cover with a lid and leave to stand for 10 minutes. Fluff up with a fork and toss lightly in butter, margarine or olive oil.

When the vegetables are cooked, check the seasoning – you can add a dash of Tabasco to heat it up a little if you have a taste for that – and dish up with the couscous.

Couscous

Couscous is a passion. I have been converted from its old image of sticky, tasteless lumps. I discover it to be light and fluffy, delicate and satisfying – and incredibly easy to prepare. Couscous now has pride of place in my everyday cooking.

Of Berber origin, couscous is a staple food in North-African countries. It is produced by moistening grains of semolina and forming them into tiny pellets which are then coated with fine wheat flour. Thus it is rich in starch and protein.

Traditionally couscous is steamed over the stew which it accompanies. However, pre-cooked couscous is now widely available which is the simplest thing in the world to cook (see above).

You can serve couscous with vegetable stews and stir-fries, or fry it up in a sauté of mixed vegetables. It is often served cold in a composite salad.

RICE NOODLES WITH BROCCOLI, GINGER, GARLIC & BLACK BEAN SAUCE

A simple way of bringing authentic East-Asian flavours into your home. Always keep a jar of black bean sauce in the store cupboard for dishes like this one and store root ginger in the freezer. This mouthwatering dish has become a regular for suppertime in my household.

SERVES 6

V

FOR THE SAUCE

4 spring onions, sliced very finely

2.5cm (1in) piece fresh root ginger, grated very finely

2–3 cloves garlic, peeled and crushed

3 tablespoons black bean sauce

1 tablespoon soy sauce

90ml (3 fl oz) dark sesame oil

FOR THE NOODLES

1.25kg (2½lb) broccoli

500g (1lb) rice vermicelli

Mix all the ingredients for the sauce together and leave to infuse while you cook the rest. ◆

Steam the broccoli whole, then cut into small florets.

Cover the rice vermicelli with cold water in a large saucepan, bring to the boil and leave to stand off the heat for 3–4 minutes. Drain thoroughly and toss with the broccoli florets and the prepared sauce. Serve warm.

RISO VERDE

A pretty dish of green and white layers which makes a great side dish to go with the Plait of Roasted Peppers on page 158. Or you can eat it as a simple supper on its own, just with a tossed salad.

SERVES 4–6

V

500g (1lb) spinach, washed and cooked in its own water

ground nutmeg, salt and pepper

175g (6oz) basmati rice, cooked (see page 143)

40g (1½oz) butter or margarine

500g (1lb) frozen peas, cooked

2–3 tablespoons single cream (or soya cream for vegans)

2 tablespoons chopped mint

175g (6oz) pistachios, shelled and chopped finely

Drain the spinach thoroughly and chop. Season with nutmeg, salt and pepper. Make a layer in the bottom of an ovenproof dish. ◆

Drain the rice and mix with the butter or margarine until melted. Season with salt and pepper and make a second layer on top of the spinach.

Drain the cooked peas and purée them with the cream. Mix in the mint, then pour over the rice. Sprinkle with the chopped pistachio nuts and bake at 180°C/350°F/gas mark 4 for 25 minutes.

VIETNAMESE RICE NOODLES WITH STEAMED VEGETABLES & MINT

I ate this dish in a Vietnamese café in San Francisco's Chinatown. Simple and unpretentious like so much Vietnamese food, this has fabulous flavours which linger in the memory. A jar of chilli and garlic sauce is a must for the larder shelf; it can be found in ethnic grocers.

SERVES 4

V

FOR THE STEAMED VEGETABLES
1kg (2lb) vegetables such as broccoli, carrots, sweetcorn, mushrooms, bamboo shoots, courgettes, mangetout and beansprouts

FOR THE SAUCE
3 tablespoons black bean sauce
2 teaspoons grated fresh root ginger
1 clove garlic, peeled and crushed
2 tablespoons sesame oil

FOR THE NOODLES
250g (8oz) rice vermicelli
1 tablespoon hot chilli and garlic sauce
3 tablespoons olive oil

TO SERVE
1 small soft green lettuce, shredded
a small bunch of fresh mint, chopped finely

First prepare the vegetables: cut them into bite-size pieces and steam until tender but still slightly crisp. Cool a little.

Combine the ingredients for the sauce, pour over the warm vegetables and toss well together.

Cover the rice noodles with water in a pan, bring to the boil, then remove from the heat and leave to stand for 3–4 minutes, or until tender; drain.

Mix the chilli and garlic sauce with the oil, pour over the noodles and toss well together.

To serve, combine the mint with the shredded lettuce and arrange on a large serving dish. Cover with the noodles and top with the steamed vegetables in their sauce.

SAVOURY PIES & PASTRIES
SPRING ROLLS

I love spring rolls – I never tire of them. These home-made ones are wrapped around a tasty mixture of finely cut vegetables and rice vermicelli, and seasoned with an oriental sauce. Serve them as a starter for a special meal, or as a supper dish accompanied by jasmine rice and a favourite salad – along with some of the dipping sauces on page 34.

MAKES 12 ROLLS
V

2 tablespoons sunflower oil

500g (1lb) mixed vegetables such as mangetout, French beans, broccoli, courgettes, waterchestnuts and asparagus, all cut very small

5cm (2in) piece fresh root ginger

3 cloves garlic, peeled

4 spring onions, chopped finely

1 tablespoon fresh coriander, chopped finely

half a fresh chilli, chopped very finely (or a scant 1/4 teaspoon chilli powder)

1 tablespoon black bean or yellow bean sauce

50g (2oz) rice vermicelli, soaked in hot water for 10 minutes, then drained and chopped

24 sheets filo pastry, 30 x 15cm (12 x 6in)

sunflower oil for deep-frying

Heat the oil in a wok or frying pan, add the vegetables and stir-fry over a high heat with the grated ginger, finely chopped garlic and spring onion, until just cooked. Stir in the coriander and chilli, then add the bean sauce and the vermicelli and leave to stand, covered with a lid but off the heat, for several minutes. ◆

Lay a tablespoon or two of the mixture onto a single sheet of filo pastry and roll it up, tucking in the ends to make a closed parcel. Immediately roll this roll in another sheet of pastry. Repeat with all the other spring rolls so that you have 12 filled rolls in all.

Heat 2cm (1in) oil in deep-fryer or wok to 190°C/375°F. Deep-fry the rolls in batches, turning until they are crisp and golden-brown. Drain on kitchen paper and keep warm. Serve as soon as possible.

To reheat from frozen, bake at 190°C/375°F/gas mark 5 for 20 minutes.

SPINACH & BLUE CHEESE PASTIES

You can vary the fillings for these delectably light pastry triangles throughout the seasons – broccoli, courgettes, peas, leeks and mushrooms all make tasty fillings. They are wonderfully easy to make, and a firm favourite whenever they appear in my household.

MAKES 6 PASTIES

500g (1lb) spinach, cooked, drained and chopped
300ml (½ pint) thick béchamel sauce (see page 218)

40g (1½oz) blue cheese, crumbled
500g (1lb) puff pastry, defrosted, or Blender Shortcrust Pastry (see page 218)
1 egg yolk, beaten

First make the filling. Stir the prepared spinach into the béchamel sauce, then add the crumbled cheese and mix thoroughly. ◈

Roll out the pastry fairly thinly and cut it into six 15cm (6in) squares. Moisten the edges with water.

Place one-sixth of the filling in the centre of each square. Take one corner of the pastry square and fold it over to the opposite corner to form a triangle. Dampen the inside edges of the pastry and press together with a fork, so that they are well-sealed.

Brush with beaten egg yolk and place on a well-greased baking tray. Bake at 220°C/425°F/gas mark 7 for 20–25 minutes, or until risen and golden.

BROCCOLI & PECORINO PASTIES

These turnovers can be made with puff pastry or your own home-made Blender Shortcrust (see page 218). They are filled with a cheesy broccoli filling, topped with a pesto crust and baked in the oven until golden-brown. They make a perfect supper dish to go with new potatoes and a tossed salad.

MAKES 6 PASTIES

1 tablespoon olive oil
3 large spring onions, chopped finely
250g (8oz) tomatoes, peeled (see page 30) and chopped finely
half a fresh chilli, chopped very finely (or ¼ teaspoon chilli powder)
500g (1lb) broccoli (calabrese or purple sprouting), steamed until tender

50g (2oz) pine-nuts, browned under the grill (see page 134)
100g (4oz) Ricotta cheese
25g (1oz) Pecorino cheese, finely grated
salt
1lb (500g) puff pastry, defrosted, or Blender Shortcrust Pastry (see page 218)
2 tablespoons pesto sauce

Heat the oil, add the spring onions, cover with a lid and soften over a very low heat. When soft, stir in the tomatoes and chilli and cook until the juices have evaporated – about 5 minutes.

Stir in the broccoli and toss over a medium heat until well-amalgamated. Off the heat, stir in the pine-nuts, Ricotta and Pecorino and season to taste. ◈

Roll out the pastry thinly enough to cut into 6 x 18cm (7in) rounds. Place one sixth of the mixture in the centre of each and fold over to make a semi-circle. Moisten the edges of the pastry with water and crimp edges with fingers to seal. Brush the tops with pesto.

Bake at 200°C/400°F/gas mark 6 for 30 minutes, or until well-risen and golden-brown. Serve hot.

TIROPITTA WITH MINT

A classic Greek dish that originates from Turkey, I first ate this on the shores of the Aegean overlooking the harbour at Nafplion. Blue skies and retsina are obviously the best accompaniments for this delicious pie, but failing that make yourself a Cretan Village Salad to go with it (see page 194), and get out the photographs...

SERVES 6

350g (12oz) Feta cheese
350g (12oz) low-fat cottage cheese
2 tablespoons chopped mint
2 spring onions, sliced finely

freshly ground black pepper and nutmeg
3 eggs, beaten thoroughly
olive oil, to brush
1 x 400g (14oz) packet filo pastry

Mash the cheeses together and mix in the mint and spring onions. Season liberally with pepper and nutmeg – the mixture doesn't need salt because of the saltiness of the Feta. Fold in the beaten eggs. ◆

Brush a 22cm (8½in) square baking tray with olive oil. Cut the filo pastry to fit the pan. Make a stack of 4 or 5 layers of pastry, brushing each one with olive oil. Spread the cheese mixture evenly over the top, then cover with a further 7–8 layers of the pastry, brushing each one with olive oil. Oil the top layer more liberally so that you get a crisp, brown top.

Bake at 190°C/375°F/gas mark 5 for 40–45 minutes, or until golden-brown. Allow to settle for 5 minutes or so before you cut it into 6 squares with a sharp knife.

MUSTARD CAULIFLOWER FLAN

Ideal family fare, this tart is a firm favourite. The tang of mustard is a delicious foil for the delicacy of cauliflower, the red onion is sweet, and the textures irresistible. It is as good warm or cold as it is hot.

SERVES 4–6
●

250g (8oz) shortcrust pastry or oil crust (see page 218)
1 large cauliflower, trimmed and divided into small florets
1 tablespoon olive oil
1 red onion, sliced finely

2 tablespoons Dijon mustard
2 tablespoons plain flour
2 eggs, lightly beaten
175ml (6fl oz) skimmed or soya milk
salt and pepper
paprika, to dust

Roll out the pastry to line a 23cm (9in) flan tin, line with foil, fill with baking beans and bake 'blind' (see page 30). ◆

Steam the cauliflower until tender but still crisp – about 5 minutes.

Heat the oil in a large saucepan and soften the sliced onion in it over a low heat for 6–8 minutes. Add the cauliflower and stir together thoroughly. Cook for another 2–3 minutes, then spoon into the flan case.

Mix the mustard with the flour to form a smooth paste. Gradually whisk in the eggs until the mixture is smooth, and then gradually stir in the milk. Season with salt and pepper. Pour over the top of the cauliflower mixture and bake at 180°C/350°F/gas mark 4 for 35–40 minutes, or until the filling is lightly set. Serve hot or cold, sprinkled with paprika.

ONION TARTE TATIN

This perennial favourite, based on a classic French recipe, is SO good. The combination of light puff pastry and red onions cooked slowly until caramelised, so they are slightly sweet, is exquisite. The tart is flipped upside down to serve so that the pastry crust which was on top during the cooking now forms the base. Brilliant with new potatoes and salad.

SERVES 2–3

25g (1oz) butter or margarine
1kg (2lb) red onions, peeled and sliced thickly
2 heaped tablespoons sugar
salt and pepper
cold water

olive oil
50g (2oz) sun-dried tomatoes in oil, drained and chopped coarsely
250g (8oz) frozen puff pastry, defrosted
beaten egg yolk, to glaze

Melt the butter or margarine in a very large saucepan and toss the onion slices in it for a minute or two. Sprinkle half the sugar over them, season with salt and pepper and add cold water to just cover.

Bring to the boil and simmer, uncovered, until the water evaporates – about 35–40 minutes. Stir towards the end of cooking to prevent burning. ◆

Oil a 23cm (9in) flan case and sprinkle with the remaining sugar. Scatter the chopped sun-dried tomatoes on top and then cover with the onions.

Roll out the pastry to make a circle the size of the flan case and cut into a round. Lay over the top of the onions and tuck the edges in. Brush with beaten egg yolk and bake at 220°C/425°F/gas mark 7 for 25–30 minutes, or until the top is risen and golden-brown.

To serve, flip upside down onto a warm plate and cut into wedges.

PUFF PASTRY PLAIT OF ROASTED PEPPERS & MUSHROOMS

This pastry plait looks most impressive, but is actually deceptively easy to make. It is delicious – a party piece – the perfect answer to a special dinner à deux. You can even cook it ahead of time and re-heat it in a medium oven for 10 minutes, making it appear completely effortless.

SERVES 2–3

2 medium peppers, all one colour or varied
1 Spanish onion, sliced into thin rings
3 tablespoons olive oil
250g (8oz) medium mushrooms, sliced
2 teaspoons dried mixed herbs

1 clove garlic, peeled and crushed
salt and pepper
250g (8oz) puff pastry, defrosted
1 egg, beaten
sesame seeds, to sprinkle

Grill or microwave the peppers (see page 30). Leave to cool slightly, then remove the stems, seeds and skins, and slice into long strips.

Sauté the onion in 1 tablespoon of the oil for several minutes until soft, then add the rest of the oil and toss in the mushrooms. Stir while they cook, over a hot flame, and then turn the heat down a little, add the herbs and garlic and cook until they are soft – about 5 minutes. Add the peppers, then season to taste. ◆

Roll the puff pastry out thinly to a large rectangle 40 x 28cm (16 x 11in). Spoon the filling in a pile along the middle. Cut the 4 edges of pastry into diagonal strips about 2cm (¾in) thick, and fold them over the filling alternately in a 'plait'. Brush with beaten egg and sprinkle with sesame seeds.

Bake at 220°C/425°F/gas mark 7 for 15 minutes, then lower the heat to 190°C/375°F/gas mark 5 for 10 minutes. Allow to cool for several minutes before cutting. Serve hot.

AUTUMN SQUASH PIE

*T*his excellent pie is simple to make, with wonderful flavours. The squash and leeks are mixed with a little Feta cheese and the pie is seasoned with ground mace to give it a zing. Serve it with baked potatoes and a salad, and you have a memorable meal.

SERVES 4

500g (1lb) squash such as little gem, butternut, etc., peeled and deseeded, then cut into bite-size pieces
500g (1lb) leeks, sliced
300ml (½ pint) béchamel sauce (see page 218)
100g (4oz) Feta cheese, crumbled

freshly ground black pepper
1–2 teaspoons ground mace
250g (8oz) puff pastry, defrosted, or Blender Shortcrust Pastry (see page 218)
1–2 tablespoons pesto sauce
a little olive oil

Steam the squash for 4–5 minutes and the leeks for about 8 minutes; drain thoroughly and leave to cool. Mix into the béchamel sauce and stir in the crumbled cheese. Season to taste with pepper and mace. Put into a pie dish.

Roll out the pastry to fit the pie dish. Moisten the rim of the dish with cold water and place a thin strip of pastry around the edge. Cut a circle from the rest of the pastry to overlap the dish by about 1cm (½in). Place carefully over the top of the pie and press down the edges with a fork to seal.

Mix the pesto with a little olive oil to bring to a thinner consistency, then use to brush over the top of the pastry.

Bake at 190°C/375°F/gas mark 5 if shortcrust, or 200°C/400°F/gas mark 6 if puff, for 20–25 minutes – or until well-risen and golden-brown.

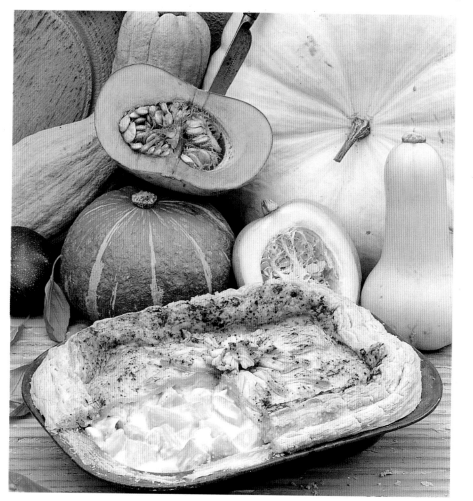

Puff Pastry Pizzas

These melt in the mouth, and are amazingly quick and easy to prepare. A wonderful recipe that you can use over and over again, varying the toppings to your heart's content.

Serves 2 as a main course,
4 as a snack

250g (8oz) frozen puff pastry, defrosted
3 ripe tomatoes, sliced
a small bunch of fresh basil
a little olive oil, to drizzle

6–8 black olives (optional)
75g (3oz) Mozzarella cheese, sliced
50g (2oz) Cheddar cheese, grated finely

Roll out the puff pastry to the size of a swiss roll tin (23 x 33cm/9 x 13in). Grease the tin and place the pastry inside

Arrange the sliced tomatoes over the top, scatter the basil leaves over them and drizzle with a little olive oil. Dot with olives if you are using them. Put slices of Mozzarella over the top in an even pattern, then sprinkle with the grated cheese.

Bake at 200°C/400°F/gas mark 6 for 25–30 minutes, and eat immediately.

Alternative toppings

Aubergine, Pepper and Mushroom
1 small aubergine, sliced and grilled
1 red pepper, grilled and cut into strips (see page 30)
100g (4oz) mushrooms, steamed in the microwave until tender
75g (3oz) Mozzarella cheese, sliced
50g (2oz) Cheddar cheese, grated finely

Tomato, Broccoli and Olives
3 ripe tomatoes, sliced
250g (8oz) broccoli (or leeks), steamed and sliced
6–8 black olives, pitted
75g (3oz) Mozzarella cheese, sliced
50g (2oz) Cheddar cheese, grated finely

CLASSIC ITALIAN PIZZA

A home-made pizza is one of the best things in the world. This one has a thin, crisp base and you can put whatever you like onto it (see below). This basic topping is hard to beat, though.

SERVES 2

FOR THE BASE

1 tablespoon dried easy-blend yeast

2 tablespoons warm skimmed or soya milk, or water

1 teaspoon sugar

100g (4oz) plain flour

1 teaspoon salt

1 whole egg

2 tablespoons olive oil, plus a little extra to brush

FOR THE TOPPING

1/2 red onion, sliced into thin rings

350g (12oz) ripe plum tomatoes, sliced thinly

2 cloves garlic, peeled and sliced very finely

250g (8oz) Mozzarella cheese, cut into matchsticks

salt and freshly ground black pepper

dried mixed herbs, to sprinkle

6–8 olives

olive oil, to drizzle

a handful of fresh basil leaves, to garnish

First make the base. Blend the dried yeast with the warm water or milk, and the sugar. Leave for 10 minutes to dissolve completely.

Sift the flour and salt into a large mixing bowl. Make a well in the centre and pour in the yeast mixture with the egg and the olive oil. Mix well together, then knead to a smooth, light dough – for about 10 minutes.

Put into a bowl and brush with olive oil. Cover with a towel and leave to rise in a warm place (an airing cupboard or radiator is ideal) for 1½ hours.

Now knead again, and press out into a greased 30cm (12in) baking tin with your knuckles. It will be very thin.

Scatter the onion rings over the pizza base and cover with layers of sliced tomato. Sprinkle with the slivers of garlic, then season with salt, pepper and the dried mixed herbs. Scatter the Mozzarella matchsticks over the top, then arrange the olives in a pattern and drizzle all over with olive oil. Bake at 230°C/450°F/gas mark 8 for 15–20 minutes, or until the top is browned and the base crisp. Garnish with a scattering of basil leaves and serve immediately.

ALTERNATIVE TOPPINGS

caramelised red onion, blue cheese and rosemary

grilled aubergine and pesto

leeks, tomatoes and goat's cheese

roasted aubergine and Mozzarella

multicolour peppers, tomatoes and Mozzarella

wild mushrooms, garlic and herbs

artichoke hearts, onions and cheese

sun-dried tomatoes and cheese

ENTERTAINING: STARTERS

GRILLED MARINATED SHIITAKE MUSHROOMS 'BEURRE ROUGE'

*T*hese delectable mushrooms are a wonderful opener for a dinner party. Aromatic with herbs, they are served with a circle of light puff pastry and one of French cuisine's great sauces.

SERVES 4

FOR THE MUSHROOMS
5 tablespoons balsamic vinegar
150ml (¼ pint) olive oil
4 sprigs fresh thyme
4 cloves garlic, peeled and sliced
sea salt and freshly ground back pepper
20 shiitake or oyster mushrooms

FOR THE PUFF PASTRY CIRCLES
250g (8oz) puff pastry
beaten egg yolk, to glaze

FOR THE BEURRE ROUGE
(see page 164)

Combine the vinegar, oil, thyme, garlic and seasonings in a bowl and leave to infuse overnight.

Place the mushrooms in a deep platter and pour the marinade over them. Toss well until thoroughly coated, then leave to marinate for 3–4 hours.

Roll out the puff pastry fairly thick – about 0.5cm (¼ in) – and cut into 4 circles with a cutter. Brush with beaten egg yolk, set on a baking tray and bake at 220°C/425°F/gas mark 7 for 10–12 minutes, or until risen and golden-brown. Keep warm in a low oven.

Make the sauce at this point (see page 164) and leave to infuse while you grill the mushrooms.

Set the mushrooms on a grill tray, discarding the marinade, and place under a hot grill for about 30 seconds on each side.

Arrange in a circle on 4 separate plates with the puff pastry in the centre. Spoon the beurre rouge over the mushrooms and serve immediately.

BEURRE ROUGE

This fine sauce is a variant of 'Beurre Blanc', being made with red wine vinegar rather than with white.

2 shallots, chopped finely
1 tablespoon red wine vinegar
60–90ml (2–3 fl oz) red wine

100g (4oz) butter or margarine, cut into
  small cubes

Put the shallots into a small pan with the vinegar and wine. Set over a medium heat and boil rapidly until reduced to a scant tablespoon.

Turn the heat right down and whisk in the butter or margarine a few cubes at a time. The sauce will become thick and creamy as you work – be careful not to overheat it or it will curdle.

NUTTY GREEN SALAD WITH GRILLED GOAT'S CHEESE

Although this recipe requires thinking ahead, it is worth it for the wonderful flavours that come through the process of marinating. This elegant starter could also make a light lunch in its own right. You can store any leftover marinade oil in the refrigerator for 3–4 days and use it for subsequent salad dressings.

SERVES 4

2 cloves garlic, peeled and sliced
3 sprigs fresh rosemary
300ml (1/2 pint) olive oil
250g (8oz) goat's cheese (6.5cm/2 1/2 in log
  for preference)
175g (6oz) pecans (or walnuts if you prefer),
  chopped coarsely

4 tablespoons basic vinaigrette (see page 204)
Tabasco or chilli sauce (see page 34)
4 handfuls mixed leaves such as frisée,
  lollo rosso, arugula, sorrel, watercress,
  lambs' lettuce, etc.

Marinate the garlic and rosemary in the oil for several hours, then slice the goat's cheese into thick rounds and add to the oil. Marinate overnight. ◈

Toast the pecans under a medium grill until slightly crisp – be careful not to burn them – tossing them occasionally to make sure that they brown evenly. Put to one side.

Season the vinaigrette to taste with Tabasco or chilli sauce to give it a zing. Toss the salad leaves in the dressing and divide among 4 plates.

Lift the cheese rounds out of the olive oil and set them on a grill tray under a hot grill until slightly melted. Arrange on the leaves, top with the toasted nuts and serve immediately.

ARTICHOKE SOUP WITH HAZELNUTS

A sophisticated soup – creamy and delicate – which is served with toasted chopped hazelnuts sprinkled over the top. Serve it with the Basil and Garlic Bread on page 81.

SERVES 4–6

750g (1½lb) Jerusalem artichokes
40g (1½oz) butter or margarine
250g (8oz) onions, sliced
2 stalks celery, sliced

1.2 litres (2 pints) vegetable stock (see page 218)
salt and freshly ground black pepper
300ml (½ pint) single cream
75g (3oz) hazelnuts

Peel the artichokes roughly – it doesn't matter if some of the skins are left on, so long as they are clean. In fact, they add flavour and goodness to the soup.

Melt the butter or margarine in a large saucepan and toss in the onions and celery, coating them with the fat. Cover with a lid and steam gently over a very low heat for 10 minutes.

Now add the artichokes and stir until well-mixed. Pour in the stock and bring to the boil. Simmer, covered, for 40 minutes until the artichokes are completely soft.

Purée in the blender.

Return to a clean saucepan, season to taste with salt and pepper and stir in the cream. Reheat gently.

Grind the hazelnuts roughly in the small bowl of the food processor – or chop them finely with a knife and crush in a pestle and mortar. Brown under a medium grill, shaking them from time to time and being careful not to let them burn. Cool.

Pour the soup into bowls and serve sprinkled with the toasted hazelnuts.

RED & YELLOW SALAD WITH CRISP-FRIED BABY SWEETCORN

The colours of this hot and cold salad look beautiful on the table, and get a special meal off to a great start. Easy to make, original and stylish!

SERVES 4

4 medium red tomatoes
8 small yellow tomatoes
5 tablespoons toasted almond vinaigrette (see page 206)
lettuce leaves and alfalfa sprouts, to serve

8 whole canned baby sweetcorn, drained
maize meal
beaten egg
olive oil for shallow-frying
4 slices Mozzarella cheese

Slice or halve the tomatoes and dress them in the toasted almond vinaigrette. Divide among 4 plates, placing them inside a crisp lettuce leaf. Scatter some alfalfa over the top of each.

Roll each baby sweetcorn kernel in maize meal, then in beaten eggs, then once more in the maize meal. Heat the olive oil in a shallow frying pan and cook the corn until crisp all over. Cut each one in half and keep warm.

Grill the Mozzarella until bubbling, then arrange with the hot sweetcorn on top of the salad. Serve at once.

WARM BABY CORN 'BEURRE NOISETTE'

Simplicity itself. This takes only a matter of minutes to prepare, and is unbelievably good. A starter in a million!

SERVES 4

V

2 x 400g (14oz) cans baby sweetcorn, drained
75g (3oz) butter or margarine

2 tablespoons wine vinegar
4 sprigs of coriander

Put the sweetcorn into a dish, cover with clingfilm and heat through in the microwave for 1 minute – or cook in a steamer (see page 30) for 2 minutes. Put to one side, still covered to keep warm.

Heat the butter or margarine in a small pan over a medium heat until it starts to froth and foam, and then watch carefully for it to turn nut-brown – you don't want it to burn and blacken. Remove from the heat immediately it turns a nut-brown colour. Off the heat, stir in the vinegar – it will sizzle madly, so stand back.

Arrange the warm sweetcorn in a serving dish, pour over the beurre noisette and serve immediately, garnished with fresh coriander.

SALSIFY 'BEURRE NOISETTE'

Salsify is a truly gourmet vegetable with the most delicate of flavours. It's a bit of a fiddle to peel, as you have to be careful not to let it discolour, but it is worth all the trouble! Simply brilliant with nut-brown beurre-noisette, the juices mopped up with fresh bread.

SERVES 4

V

750g (1½lb) salsify
75g (3oz) butter or margarine

2 tablespoons wine vinegar
2–3 tablespoons chopped parsley, to garnish

Wash the salsify and peel it, dropping the peeled pieces into water with a touch of lemon juice or vinegar added in order to prevent discoloration.

Cut into 2.5cm (1in) lengths and cover with cold water in a saucepan. Bring to the boil and simmer for about 10 minutes, until the salsify is tender. Drain and keep warm.

Heat the butter or margarine in a small pan over a medium heat until it starts to froth and foam, watching carefully for it to turn nut-brown. Be careful not to let it burn. Remove from the heat immediately it turns colour.

Off the heat, stir in the vinegar – it will sizzle madly – then pour over the warm salsify and serve immediately, garnished with the parsley.

SALADE GOURMANDE WITH SUN-DRIED TOMATO AIOLI

A lovely composite salad in which the leaves are fragrant with a tarragon vinaigrette, and where you dip 'al dente' French beans and asparagus into an amazing mayonnaise. I had this in a San Francisco restaurant and have never forgotten it.

SERVES 4

(omit aioli) V

FOR THE TARRAGON VINAIGRETTE

1 tablespoon lemon juice

1 tablespoon sherry or wine vinegar

3 tablespoons olive oil

1 tablespoon chopped tarragon

sea salt

FOR THE SALAD

4 red leaf lettuce leaves

4 frisée leaves

300g (10oz) French beans, steamed 'al dente'

12 asparagus spears, steamed 'al dente'

4 oyster or wild mushrooms, sautéed in butter or margarine for 30 seconds on each side

Mix all the ingredients for the dressing together and stir thoroughly until smooth. Leave to infuse while you prepare the aioli (see below).

Dress the salad leaves in the tarragon vinaigrette and put into a decorative dish. Criss-cross the beans over the top. Arrange the asparagus spears around the edge and top with the mushrooms.

Serve with individual bowls of sun-dried tomato aioli for people to dip their vegetables into.

SUN-DRIED TOMATO AIOLI

2 egg yolks

2 cloves garlic

1/2 teaspoon salt

50g (2oz) sun-dried tomatoes in oil

150ml (1/4 pint) olive oil

lemon juice, to taste

Put all the ingredients apart from the oil and lemon juice into the small bowl of the blender. Run the machine for 2 minutes until the ingredients are a smooth purée. Start to add the oil very slowly – drop by drop – while the machine is still running. As the mayonnaise starts to thicken and go glossy, increase the flow of oil to a thin stream until it is all used up. Do not add too much at once or the mayonnaise will curdle. Finally, season to taste with lemon juice, which will also help to thin it out.

Divide into 4 little bowls and serve with the salad (above).

FILO BASKETS WITH ASPARAGUS 'PESTO TRAPANESE'

These are dainty morsels indeed: crisp wafery cups with a filling of asparagus, sprinkled with grated Pecorino and black pepper, served with a touch of a brilliant version of pesto made with almonds and tomato. Elegant and memorable! (Any leftover pesto can be frozen and used for pasta sauce.)

MAKES 6 BASKETS
(omit cheese) V

FOR THE BASKETS
6 x 15cm (6in) squares filo pastry
olive oil, to brush

FOR THE FILLING
24 stalks fresh asparagus, cooked (see page 13)
25g (1oz) fresh Pecorino cheese, grated finely
freshly ground black pepper

Cut the sheets of filo into 7.5cm (3in) squares. Brush a set of 6 deep muffin tins with oil and line each one with 3 squares of filo, brushing them with olive oil as you go along, and turning them half a turn each time to make a star shape. Bake at 190°C/375°F/gas mark 5 for 10 minutes. Cool in the tins, then remove carefully. ◆

Meanwhile, make the pesto sauce (see below).

Cut the asparagus into short lengths, reserving the bottom ends for soup. Place 4 of these pieces in each little pastry basket, and sprinkle with Pecorino and pepper. Top with a dollop of the pesto trapanese and serve.

PESTO TRAPANESE

1 small bunch basil leaves
1 clove garlic, peeled and crushed
50g (2oz) almonds, skinned

1 medium tomato, skinned
150ml (¼ pint) extra-virgin olive oil

Put the basil, garlic and almonds into the blender and work the machine until they are minced. Chop the tomato and add, running the machine again. Pour in the olive oil in a thin stream as the machine is running so that it works into a thick sauce.

GRILLED BRIE WITH APRICOTS

You can also make this recipe using little rounds of puff pastry, which are cooked in a hot oven until golden. Buy canned fruit in juice rather than in syrup — the latter is heavy with sugar, which masks the flavour of the fruit.

MAKES 4 CROÛTONS

FOR THE CROÛTONS

4 thin slices of granary bread or French Stick cut into diagonals
groundnut oil for deep-frying
2 teaspoons Dijon mustard
2 teaspoons runny honey
12 canned apricot halves in juice
175g (6oz) Brie, rind removed

TO SERVE

mixed salad leaves
lime vinaigrette (see page 205)

Cut each slice of bread into a 7.5cm (3in) round with a pastry cutter. Heat 1cm (½in) oil in a deep frying pan or wok. Add the croûtons and fry until crisp and golden on both sides. Drain on kitchen paper and keep warm in a low oven.

Combine the mustard with the honey and use to brush the cut surface of the apricot halves. Cut the Brie into slices and then into little squares.

Place the apricots on a baking sheet, arrange the slices of cheese on top and set under a hot grill for 3–4 minutes, or until the cheese puffs up and starts to turn golden-brown.

Toss the salad leaves in the lime vinaigrette and divide between 4 serving plates. Place 3 apricot halves on each croûton and arrange on top of the beds of salad. Eat as soon as possible.

MUSTARDS

English mustard is made from brown and white mustard seed, which are husked, then mixed with flour and turmeric to make them yellow. It is usually fine and smooth, and very strong.

There are some grainy versions of English mustards, made from ground whole seeds, white wine, allspice and black pepper. These are also hot and pungent.

French mustard is generally milder and more subtle in flavour than English. The most famous one is Dijon mustard, which is quite pale in colour since it contains no colourings. It has a wonderful flavour and works well in salad dressings and sauces.

Moutarde de Meaux is a wholegrain mustard with a coarse texture since it contains the husks of the mustard seeds.

German mustards come in many varieties of colour and flavour.
American mustard is sweeter and milder than many European mustards. Like English mustard, it is coloured with turmeric.

SAUTÉED GRATED COURGETTES WITH DRAGON SAUCE

Tarragon gets its name from a word meaning little dragon – hence the title of this sauce. Here, it is mixed with garlic, walnuts and olive oil, and thinned out with crème fraîche. Superb with this mouthwatering dish of courgettes, which is so quick, easy and cheap to make. Serve with warm French bread.

SERVES 4

V

4 medium courgettes
50g (2oz) butter or margarine

sea salt and pepper
4 tiny sprigs tarragon, to garnish

Start by making the dragon sauce (see below). Leave to infuse while you prepare the rest.

Grate the courgettes coarsely – or better still, if you have a julienne cutter, either manual or on your blender, use that.

Heat the butter or margarine in a large pan until hot and sizzling and sauté the courgettes in it for 2–3 minutes, turning all the time. When they are heated through and lightly cooked, but not mushy, remove from the heat and season with pepper.

Divide among 4 warmed plates and top with a couple of spoonfuls of the dragon sauce in the centre of each one. Serve at once, garnished with a sprig of tarragon.

DRAGON SAUCE

(use soya creem) V

1 large bunch of fresh tarragon, chopped
1 clove garlic, peeled and crushed
50g (2oz) walnuts
3 fl oz (90 ml) olive oil

lemon juice, to taste
freshly ground black pepper
2 tablespoons single cream or crème fraîche (or soya creem for vegans)

Blend the tarragon, garlic and walnuts in the blender and when well-minced, start to add the olive oil in a very fine stream until the sauce thickens and amalgamates. Season to taste with lemon juice and pepper, and finally stir in the cream or crème fraîche. ◈

CRISP-FRIED MOZZARELLA WITH FRESH CRANBERRY & ORANGE SAUCE

This more-ish dish makes a sizzling start to a party. The cheese is crisp on the outside and melting inside – its richness balanced by the freshness of the sauce. The cranberry and orange sauce was given to me by an American friend, an enthusiastic cook who produced this memorable version of the national sauce one Thanksgiving.

SERVES 4

250g (8oz) Mozzarella cheese
flour for dipping
2 eggs
1 tablespoon olive oil
salt and pepper
100g (4oz) fresh breadcrumbs (see page 42)
olive oil for shallow-frying
a handful of fresh basil leaves, to garnish

Start by baking the cranberry sauce (see below).

Cut the Mozzarella into strips about 10cm (4in) long and 1cm (½ in) thick. Dip in flour to coat them all over. Beat the eggs with the olive oil and season with salt and pepper.

Dip the floured strips of cheese in the egg mixture, then roll in breadcrumbs. Dip lightly into the egg mixture again, holding with toothpicks. Press the breadcrumbs into the cheese with your fingers to make them stick.

Heat enough olive oil in a large sauté pan to shallow-fry the slices. Dip them into the hot oil and cook until golden and crisp on both sides, and the cheese melts in the centre – about 1 minute on each side.

Drain and put on kitchen paper to soak up excess oil. Divide between 4 plates, place a large spoonful of fresh cranberry sauce on top and garnish with fresh basil leaves.

CRANBERRY & ORANGE SAUCE

500g (1lb) fresh cranberries, washed
150ml (¼ pint) fresh orange juice
100g (4oz) sugar
2 teaspoons grated orange rind

Put all the ingredients into the pan. Cover with water and cook gently for 6–8 minutes, or until the cranberry skins burst. Simmer for a further 4–5 minutes until the mixture turns into a sludge and the liquid has reduced. Press through a sieve to separate the skins from the juice, and stir well.

CRISPY FILO PARCELS

A wonderful start to a meal, these filo parcels melt in the mouth and look stunning when cut open – with melting cheese and a sweet onion mixture inside. Alternatively, you could use the mushroom filling for the Crostini on page 179. Serve with a few salad leaves tossed in the Tarragon Vinaigrette on page 189 and a sauce such as Light Tomato Sauce see below.

MAKES 4 PARCELS
(omit cheese) V

FOR THE FILLING
25g (1oz) butter or margarine
625g (1¼lb) red onions, peeled and sliced thickly
2 heaped tablespoons sugar
cold water

freshly ground black pepper
50g (2oz) Camembert or Brie

FOR THE PARCELS
40g (1½oz) butter or margarine
16 x 15cm (6in) square sheets of filo pastry

First prepare the filling. Melt the butter or margarine in a very large saucepan and toss the onion slices in it for a minute or two. Sprinkle the sugar over them and add cold water to just cover. Bring to the boil and simmer, uncovered and undisturbed, until all the liquid evaporates – about 35–40 minutes. It should be quite dry. At the end of cooking, stir from time to time to stop the onions burning. Season with freshly ground black pepper.

Drain through a sieve and leave to cool while you prepare the pastry. ◆

Melt the butter or margarine. Brush 4 squares of filo pastry with the melted butter. Stack the sheets one on top of the other, making a half turn each time to form a star shape. Repeat with the other sheets to make 4 pastry stars.

Now assemble the parcels. Place a slice or round of cheese in the centre of each pastry star, then top with 2 tablespoons or so of the onion mixture. Bring the edges of the filo over the top to make a parcel. Pinch together and brush with more butter or margarine.

Set on a greased baking sheet and bake at 190°C/375°F/gas mark 5 for 15–20 minutes, or until golden-brown and crisp.

LIGHT TOMATO & BASIL SAUCE

SERVES 4
V

2 tablespoons olive oil
4 cloves garlic, peeled and crushed
1 x 400g (14oz) can tomatoes in juice

a large bunch of fresh basil leaves, chopped
salt and pepper

Heat the oil in a pan, add the garlic and soften over a low heat without browning for about 5 minutes. Add the tomatoes and basil, bring to simmering point and simmer very gently for 5 minutes. Season with salt and pepper, then purée in a blender. ◆

Note: you can also make this sauce with dried mixed herbs, substituting 1 tablespoon 'herbes de Provence' for the basil.

STUFFED ZUCCHINI WITH SAFFRON MAYONNAISE

*E*legant food for summer parties, these courgettes have an aromatic mushroom filling and are served with a delicate, pale-golden saffron mayonnaise. The Warm Spinach Salad on page 198 goes exceptionally well with this dish.

4 large zucchini (courgettes), 15cm (6in) long and 2.5cm (1in) thick

250g (8oz) mushrooms, minced in the blender (see page 77) or chopped finely

75g (3oz) Pecorino cheese, grated finely

75g (3oz) fresh breadcrumbs (see page 42)

a medium bunch of basil, chopped

lots of freshly ground black pepper

2 egg yolks, beaten

olive oil, to grease

¹/₂ quantity Saffron Mayonnaise (see page 206)

SERVES 4

Simmer the zucchini in boiling water for 5 minutes (or steam them, see page 30). Plunge into a bowl of cold water and leave to cool.

When cold, cut in half lengthways and scoop out the flesh. Chop finely, then dry on kitchen paper. Wipe the insides of the 'boats' with kitchen paper, too. Put the chopped flesh into a bowl with the minced mushrooms, 50g (2oz) cheese, the breadcrumbs and the basil. Season to taste with pepper, then mix in the egg yolks. ◆

Lightly grease a baking sheet with olive oil. Fill the zucchini 'boats' with the stuffing, rounding it up. Sprinkle with the remaining cheese and bake at 200°C/400°F/gas mark 6 for 20 minutes.

Serve with the saffron mayonnaise.

FRESH TOMATO & HERB TARTS, CRÈME FRAÎCHE SAUCE WITH DILL

A wonderful dinner party coup: each person has a small individual tart, light as a feather and filled with the true flavour of ripe tomatoes and fresh herbs. They are SO delicious, and the dill sauce is the finishing touch to this dream.

SERVES 4
(omit egg yolk and sauce) V

500g (1lb) puff pastry
1 egg yolk
8 medium tomatoes (plum for preference), sliced fairly thin
1 tablespoon chopped marjoram

1 tablespoon fresh thyme (or 1 teaspoon 'herbes de Provence')
freshly ground black pepper
4 tablespoons olive oil

Grease 4 individual tartlet tins, 15cm (6in) in diameter. Roll out the pastry fairly thinly and cut into rounds 1cm (½in) larger in diameter than the tins. Place inside the tins and trim the edges. Brush the rims with beaten egg yolk.

Arrange the sliced tomatoes inside the pastry cases, overlapping them slightly and tilting them up around the edges. Sprinkle with the herbs and black pepper, then drizzle 1 tablespoon olive oil over each.

Bake at 220°C/425°F/gas mark 7 for 20–25 minutes, or until the pastry is well-risen and cooked through.

Meanwhile, make the sauce (see below).

Remove the tarts from the oven carefully turn out onto warm plates and spoon over a little of the dill sauce.

CRÈME FRAÎCHE SAUCE WITH DILL

200ml (7fl oz) crème fraîche
a large bunch of fresh dill, chopped

2 egg yolks

Heat the crème fraîche gently with the dill. Stir in the egg yolks and cook over a gentle heat, stirring all the time until the sauce begins to thicken like custard – do not overheat it, or the sauce will curdle. ◆

Note: If you make the sauce ahead of time and want to reheat it, stand it in a bowl of hot water over the lowest heat until it gently warms through.

ROASTED FENNEL & GRILLED POLENTA WITH PECAN PESTO TOPPING

This is a brilliant party piece, inspired by my love of polenta. The crusty pesto topping on creamy, slightly fragrant polenta makes it memorable. With the simplicity of roasted fennel, it is sublime. You can store any remaining pesto in a jar in the refrigerator for up to 3 weeks, or freeze it. It is superb on pasta.

SERVES 4

FOR THE POLENTA
600ml (1 pint) vegetable stock (page 218)
a sprig each of fresh thyme and rosemary, roughly chopped
100g (4oz) maize meal or polenta
freshly ground black pepper and a pinch of cayenne
25g (1oz) butter or margarine
2 cloves garlic, peeled and crushed

FOR THE FENNEL
2 large or 4 small bulbs of fennel, quartered or cut in half
2 tablespoons olive oil
Ground black pepper

First cook the polenta. Bring the stock to the boil with the herbs and maize meal, stirring all the time to keep the mixture smooth and prevent it going lumpy. When it comes to the boil, turn the heat down low and simmer gently for 10–12 minutes, stirring occasionally.

Once it is cooked, season to taste with cayenne and black pepper and beat in the butter or margarine until it melts. Stir in the crushed garlic. Spread into a buttered oven proof dish and smooth the top, then leave to cool while you prepare the rest. ◈

Put the fennel pieces into a baking tray. Trickle the olive oil over them and roast at 200°C/400°F/gas mark 6 for 30–40 minutes until browned and cooked, basting them with the oil from time to time. Season with pepper.

Meanwhile, prepare the pesto sauce (see below).

When the polenta is cold, spread the pesto thickly over the top, cut into 4 squares and transfer carefully to a greased grill tray. Set under a medium grill for 2–3 minutes, or until lightly browned on top. Serve alongside the hot roasted fennel.

PECAN PESTO

a large bunch of basil
2 cloves garlic, peeled and crushed
75g (3oz) pecan nuts

150ml (¼ pint) olive oil
50g (2oz) Pecorino cheese, grated
2 tablespoons crème fraîche

In the small bowl of the food processor, blend the basil, garlic and nuts until minced. Add the olive oil and cheese and run the machine again. Finish by stirring in the crème fraîche.

MUSHROOM CROSTINI WITH LIGHT TOMATO & PECORINO SAUCE

An exceptional filling of minced mushrooms cooked with vinegar and red onions makes a fine dish inside a crisp bread casing. Served with the aromatic tomato sauce tasting of the Italian Riviera, it makes a stylish dish.(Serve with the Light Tomato and Basil Sauce on page 174)

SERVES 4–6
V

25g (1oz) butter or margarine
1 red onion, chopped finely
350g (12oz) assorted mushrooms such as flat, chestnut, shiitake, chanterelles, etc., minced in the blender (see page 77)
2 cloves garlic, peeled and crushed
1 tablespoon sherry vinegar
1 large tomato, peeled and chopped

8 tarragon or marjoram leaves, chopped
salt and pepper
2 tablespoons single cream (or soya cream for vegans)
2–3 large bread rolls, cut in half and hollowed out
4 sprigs of tarragon or marjoram, to garnish

Heat the butter or margarine in a large sauté pan over a medium heat. Add the chopped onion, cover with a lid and cook slowly until soft – about 10 minutes.

Add the minced mushrooms and garlic and sauté for 3 minutes. Then add the vinegar, tomato and tarragon or marjoram and cook for 3 more minutes.

Season to taste with salt and pepper, then remove from the heat and drain off the juices: pull the mushroom mixture up to one end and set the pan at a slight tilt. Leave to drain like this for 3–4 minutes, then carefully remove the mushroom mixture from the pan. Spoon into a bowl, stir in the cream and divide between the hollowed-out bread rolls.

Set on a baking sheet and bake at 190°C/375°F/gas mark 5 for 15 minutes. Make the tomato sauce at this point (see below).

To serve, place the crostini in the centre of a plate, pour some sauce around each one and garnish with a sprig of tarragon or marjoram.

LIGHT TOMATO AND PECORINO SAUCE

2 tablespoons olive oil
1 onion, chopped finely
1 x 400g (14oz) can chopped tomatoes, with juice
2 tablespoons chopped basil leaves

2 tablespoons chopped parsley
25g (1oz) Pecorino cheese, grated
2 tablespoons single cream
pepper

Heat the oil in a medium saucepan and cook the onion gently, covered with a lid, for 10 minutes until soft.

Add the tomatoes and herbs and simmer gently together for 5 minutes.

Stir in the grated Pecorino and season with pepper. Finally, stir in the cream.

Liquidise in the blender to a smooth, fine sauce, and it is ready to serve.

Pastel terrine with fresh cranberry & orange sauce

You've got to be in the mood to cook this dish: it takes time and energy but it is definitely worth it. Not only is it a work of art, but it is also a gastronomic feast. It is wonderful with the Creamy Saffron Mayonnaise on page 61 or the Cranberry and Orange Sauce on page 173.

SERVES 6–8

FOR THE FIRST LAYER
15g (¹/₂oz) butter or margarine
1 onion, chopped
2 x 330g (11oz) can sweetcorn, drained
1 egg plus 1 egg yolk, beaten together
¹/₄ teaspoon chilli powder

FOR THE SECOND LAYER
25g (1oz) butter or margarine
2 onions, chopped
1 x 400g (14oz) can plum tomatoes, chopped and drained
2 tablespoons pesto sauce
1 egg plus 1 egg yolk, beaten together

FOR THE THIRD LAYER
625g (1¹/₄lb) leeks, steamed or boiled until tender
1–2 teaspoons curry paste
1 egg plus 1 egg yolk, beaten

175g (6oz) mushrooms, sliced

full-quantity Cranberry and Orange Sauce (see page 173)

Start by preparing the first layer. Melt the butter or margarine in a pan, toss in the chopped onion, cover with a lid and cook over a gentle heat for 10 minutes until soft. Stir in the sweetcorn, then spoon into the bowl of the blender and liquidise to a rough purée. Fold into the beaten eggs and season to taste with chilli powder.

Next prepare the second layer. Soften the onion in the butter or margarine, as above. Stir in the drained tomatoes and cook for 5 minutes over a medium heat until most of the liquid has evaporated. Stir in the pesto sauce, pour into the food processor and blend to a purée. Fold in the beaten eggs.

Now make the third layer. Purée the cooked leeks with the curry paste, then stir into the beaten eggs.

Assemble the terrine. Thoroughly grease a 1.5 litre (2¹/₂ pint) loaf tin. Place a third of the sliced mushrooms in the bottom of the tin and press down well. Cover with the sweetcorn mixture, then place a second layer of mushrooms on top. Spoon over the tomato sauce and cover with a third layer of mushrooms. Finally, top with the layer of leeks.

Put the loaf tin inside another, bigger tin. Fill the outer tin with boiling water, set on a baking tray and bake in the centre of the oven at 200°C/400°F/gas mark 6 for 1 hour 15 minutes, covering with foil for the last 30 minutes of cooking. It is ready when a sharp knife inserted in the centre comes out clean.

Set the tin on a wire rack and leave to cool for at least half an hour. Loosen the edges carefully with a sharp knife, and invert onto a large serving dish.

Serve sliced, warm or cold, with the cranberry and orange sauce.

COUSCOUS WITH ROASTED AUBERGINE & RED PEPPER SAUCE

The stunning flavour of roasted peppers in this beautiful red sauce is perfect with roasted aubergine. Creamy-white couscous makes up this good-looking trio.

SERVES 4

V

FOR THE AUBERGINES
2 medium aubergines
olive oil

FOR THE COUSCOUS
600ml (1 pint) water
250g (8oz) couscous

Start by roasting the peppers for the Red Pepper sauce (see below).

Next prepare the aubergines. Slice them into 9mm (³⁄₈in) rounds and brush both sides with olive oil. Spread on a greased baking sheet and roast at 230°C/450°F/gas mark 8 for 15–20 minutes, or until golden-brown in colour and soft inside.

Meanwhile, make the couscous. Bring the water to the boil in a large saucepan. Pour in the couscous in a thin stream, stirring all the time as the water returns to the boil, to avoid lumps. Remove from the heat and cover with a lid. Leave to stand for 10 minutes. Fluff up with a fork.

Put the couscous in a mound in the centre of a large platter. Surround with the sliced aubergine, and serve with the red pepper sauce to hand around.

RED PEPPER SAUCE

3 red peppers
200ml (7fl oz) vegetable stock (see page 218)

2–3 tablespoons single cream or crème fraîche
  (or soya creem for vegans)

Roast the peppers at 200°C/400°F/gas mark 6 for 30–40 minutes, until charred. You can microwave the peppers if you are in a hurry – give them 5–6 minutes on full power and allow to cool before peeling – but you miss out on the roasted flavour.

Cool, then skin them roughly (don't worry if some pieces of skin don't want to come off – they give texture to the sauce!).

Put into the blender with the stock and run the machine until the sauce is smooth. Put into a bowl, stir in the cream and keep warm.

FESTIVAL VOL-AU-VENTS

Light, crisp vol-au-vents with different fillings make a stunning main course. The 3 flavours here add a festive touch to a special meal. They are easy to make, and delectable.

MAKES 24 SMALL CASES

LEEK FILLING

ASPARAGUS FILLING

MUSHROOM FILLING

24 small vol-au-vent cases

Cook the vol-au-vent cases as instructed on the packet, and cool on a rack. Remove the lids and fill 8 with the leek filling, 8 with the asparagus filling and 8 with the mushroom filling (see below).

To reheat, bake at 190°C/375°F/gas mark 5 for 15 minutes.

40g (1½ oz) cheese (low-fat if preferred), finely grated

175g (6oz) cooked leeks, puréed in the blender

Mix the grated cheese into the puréed leeks. No seasoning is needed. ◆

250–300g (8–10oz) asparagus, cooked until tender but still slightly crisp
15g (½oz) butter or margarine
½ clove garlic, peeled and crushed
1 scant tablespoon flour

scant 150ml (¼ pint) single cream
1 tablespoon finely chopped fresh marjoram or thyme
salt and freshly ground black pepper

Chop the asparagus finely.

Melt the butter or margarine in a pan, add the crushed garlic and cook for 1 minute. Stir in the flour and gradually add the cream to make a thick sauce, stirring all the time.

Add the marjoram or thyme and simmer gently for 5 minutes. Fold in the asparagus and season to taste with salt and pepper. ◆

25g (1oz) butter or margarine
350g (12oz) chestnut mushrooms, minced in the blender (see page 77)

2 cloves garlic, peeled and crushed
a bunch of fresh thyme, chopped
salt and freshly ground black pepper

Melt the butter or margarine in a pan, add the mushrooms and cook gently until soft. Add the garlic and thyme and stand the pan at a tilt to allow the excess liquid to drain off. Season to taste. ◆

FILO PASTRY PARCELS WITH BABY VEGETABLES IN A LIGHT TARRAGON SAUCE

These filo parcels are fabulous – really delicate, mouthwatering and brilliant. They are best served with the mixed leaf salad on page 190 and some ciabatta bread, heated first in the oven for about 10 minutes. You can use asparagus, mangetout or petits pois for the filling – whichever are your favourites.

SERVES 4
(use Tomato Coulis, page 185, as sauce) V

FOR THE FILLING
175g (6oz) French beans
250g (8oz) baby sweetcorn
350g (12oz) broccoli

FOR THE SAUCE
50g (2oz) butter or margarine
2 tablespoons flour
300ml (½ pint) single cream
a good-size bunch of tarragon, chopped finely
25g (1oz) cheese (low-fat if preferred), finely
  grated
salt and pepper

FOR THE PARCELS
16 sheets of filo measuring 20cm (8in) square
olive oil, to brush

Chop all the vegetables small and steam them together for about 5 minutes until crisp. Leave to cool while you prepare the sauce.

To make the sauce, melt the butter or margarine in a pan and stir in the flour. Gradually add the cream, stirring all the time, until the sauce is thick and smooth. Add the tarragon and the cheese and cook gently for 5 minutes, stirring occasionally. Season to taste with salt and pepper.

Fold the cooked vegetables into the sauce and set to one side.

Now assemble the parcels. Brush 4 sheets of filo pastry with olive oil and layer up – one on top of the other. Repeat with the remaining pastry to create 4 stacks and place on a greased baking tray. Place one quarter of the vegetable mixture in the centre of each and fold the edges up to the centre. Pinch together to make a decorative shape, and brush with more oil.

Bake at 190°C/375°F/gas mark 5 for 30 minutes until golden. Eat as soon as possible, fresh from the oven. But they will also reheat well if you make them in advance.

CLASSIC TARTE AU FROMAGE WITH TOMATO COULIS

A simple but elegant main course for a special occasion or festive celebration – so long as you can cope with timing! This delicious tart, light and mouthwatering, is served with a simple fresh tomato coulis. Some new potatoes and a crisp salad are all that it requires to go with it.

SERVES 4

FOR THE TART

250g (8oz) frozen shortcrust pastry, defrosted, or the Crisp Oil Pastry on page 218
25g (1oz) butter or margarine
2 tablespoons plain flour
150ml (1/4 pint) warmed skimmed or soya milk

freshly ground black pepper
1/2 teaspoon cayenne pepper
a pinch of nutmeg
50g (2oz) Gruyère cheese, grated
15g (1/2oz) grated Pecorino cheese
2 eggs, separated

Roll out the pastry and use to line a 22cm (8½in) flan dish. Line with foil, fill with baking beans and bake 'blind' (see page 30). Cool on a rack.

Meanwhile, make the filling for the tart. Melt the butter or margarine and stir in the flour. Gradually add the warmed milk and stir until smooth. Simmer gently for 5 minutes, then season with black pepper, cayenne pepper and nutmeg. Stir in the grated cheeses. Thoroughly beat the egg yolks and stir them in. Cool a little.

In a separate bowl, whisk the egg whites until they are very stiff. Fold them into the cheese mixture. Pile into the pastry case and sprinkle with a little more grated Pecorino.

Bake at 200°C/400°F/gas mark 6 for 12–15 minutes, or until risen and golden-brown but still slightly creamy inside.

While it is in the oven, make the tomato sauce (see below) and keep warm.

Serve the tart at once, cut into wedges, with a spoonful or two of the tomato coulis on the plate beside it.

TOMATO COULIS

V

2 tablespoons olive oil
1 clove garlic, peeled and crushed
1 tablespoon fresh chopped basil (or dill or tarragon, if you prefer)

2 tablespoons fresh chopped parsley
750g (1½lb) canned plum tomatoes, drained and chopped
sea salt and freshly ground black pepper

Heat the oil in a large pan and gently cook the garlic and herbs for about 1 minute. Stir in the tomatoes and cook, uncovered, over a high heat for about 8 minutes or until the sauce starts to thicken. Season to taste with salt and pepper, and pass through a sieve or purée in the blender.

SPARKLING SALADS

The beauty of salads lies not only in their colour and freshness, but in the ease with which they can be made, and their vital health-giving properties. Vitamins and minerals abound in the colourful kaleidoscope of vegetables that you can use in salads – multicoloured peppers, dark green watercress, bright red tomatoes, delicate chicory and celery, and the fresh green of herbs. A wide variety of leaves both crispy and soft, crinkly and smooth, red and green form the basis of many salads. Equally, cooked vegetables can be used in salads, served cold. Among the best of these are beetroot, courgettes, potato and French beans. Mushrooms are a delight in salads, as are pulses as the days get colder. Salads are for all seasons of the year: healthy, easy, beautiful food.

MIXED SUMMER LEAVES WITH SLIVERED PECORINO & RASPBERRY VINAIGRETTE

A stylish salad with an elegant dressing to which sesame oil adds its dark, nutty flavour. I use raspberry vinegar a lot and recommend it highly (see page 188).

SERVES 4

FOR THE SALAD
6 large handfuls of salad leaves
    such as oak leaf, frisée, sorrel,
    lollo biondo, Webbs, radicchio,
    ruchetta, lambs' lettuce, etc.
75g (3oz) fresh Pecorino cheese,
    pared finely

FOR THE DRESSING
1–2 tablespoons soy sauce
3 tablespoons raspberry vinegar
3 tablespoons dark sesame oil
2 tablespoons olive oil

Trim and wash the salad leaves and spin them dry. Shave the Pecorino into paper-thin strips. Mix the dressing ingredients together and toss with the leaves. Cover with the cheese shavings and the salad is ready to serve.

SPROUTED SEED SALAD

This is one of those deliciously healthy salads that immediately makes you feel vital and alive. It is incredibly cheap to make, and you can dress it either with a vinaigrette – the Tarragon Vinaigrette on page 189 is wonderful – or with mayonnaise. Good food for slimmers!

SERVES 4

V

100g (4oz) mixed sprouted seeds (see page 9)

175g (6oz) canned flageolet beans, washed and drained

4 stalks of celery, sliced finely

75g (3oz) raw turnip, grated

75g (3oz) radicchio, shredded

a handful of alfalfa sprouts

4 tablespoons vinaigrette or mayonnaise (see pages 204 and 206)

Mix together all the prepared ingredients. Put into a pretty dish and toss thoroughly with the dressing.

MALAY-STYLE SALAD WITH SPICY PEANUT SAUCE

Great as a tasty starter, or as a dish to go on a buffet table, this is an interesting salad with its crunchy peanut texture and the spiciness of chilli sauce.

SERVES 4

V

FOR THE SAUCE

65g (2½oz) peanuts, ground finely in the blender

150ml (¼pint) orange juice

5 tablespoons dark sesame oil

3 tablespoons soy sauce

2 teaspoons chilli sauce (see page 34)

FOR THE SALAD

half a Chinese cabbage, shredded

8–10 young spinach leaves, torn

a handful of corn salad (lambs' lettuce)

2 medium tomatoes, sliced thinly

6–8 radishes, trimmed and sliced finely

4 waterchestnuts, sliced finely

6 medium button mushrooms, sliced thinly

1 hard-boiled egg, sliced thinly, to garnish

First make the sauce: mix all the ingredients together in a jar and shake vigorously until well-blended.

Mix the salad leaves, tomatoes, radishes, waterchestnuts and mushrooms in a large bowl and toss in the sauce. Leave to stand for about 20 minutes before serving. Garnish with slices of hard-boiled egg.

RASPBERRY VINEGAR

MAKES 3 LITRES (5 PINTS)

750g (1½ lb) raspberries, hulled cold water

1.2 litres (2 pints) malt vinegar

1kg (2lb) granulated sugar

Put the raspberries into a large pan and cover with cold water. Bring to the boil, lower the heat and simmer gently for 30 minutes. Strain off the juice – there will be about 1.2 litres (2 pints) – discarding the fruit. Put into a clean saucepan and pour in the vinegar and sugar. Slowly bring to the boil, stirring all the time so that the sugar dissolves. Simmer for abut 10 minutes, or until the mixture is syrupy and clings to the spoon.

Keep in clean wine bottles, corked, and store in a cool dark place.

SPICY MUSHROOM SALAD

This original salad has great textures and flavours – and it is so easy to make. It makes a delicious light lunch or supper dish in summer.

SERVES 4 AS A SIDE DISH OR 2 AS A MEAL

350g (12oz) small button mushrooms, cleaned
4 tablespoons mayonnaise
1–2 tablespoons curry paste or garam masala paste

1 small clove garlic, peeled and crushed
the finely grated rind of quarter of a lemon
sea salt
Iceberg lettuce and Melba toast or granary bread, to serve

Put the mushrooms into the food processor and work the machine until they are minced (see page 77).

Mix the mayonnaise with the curry paste and season to taste with garlic, lemon rind and sea salt. Mix into the minced mushrooms to coat well.

Serve inside the curve of a crisp lettuce leaf, with Melba toast or warm granary bread.

FRENCH BEAN & TOMATO SALAD WITH TARRAGON DRESSING & CROÛTONS

An elegant and sophisticated dish to serve at a special meal as a starter, or as a light lunch dish in its own right.

SERVES 4–6

V

If you want to use salads as part of a slimming regime, watch what you dress them with. In themselves they are excellent for dieting since they are full of nourishment – but the low calorie effect can be ruined by rich dressings. But get that right and you can eat as much as you can manage as often as you like – you'll never go hungry and the excess weight will melt away!

FOR THE SALAD
250g (8oz) French beans, cooked 'al dente'
6 tomatoes, skinned and sliced (see page 30)
1 shallot, sliced very thinly
2 slices bread, crusts removed
a cut clove of garlic
vegetable oil for shallow-frying
a handful of tarragon leaves, to garnish

FOR THE DRESSING:
2 tablespoons tarragon vinegar
1 tablespoon chopped tarragon
2 tablespoons olive oil
3 tablespoons crème fraîche (or soya creem for vegans)
salt and pepper

Place the beans and sliced tomatoes decoratively in a shallow bowl and arrange the shallot slices over the top.

Cut the bread into small cubes. Rub a frying pan with a cut clove of garlic, heat 1cm (½in) vegetable oil in the pan and toss the cubes of bread in it until crisp and golden all over. Drain on kitchen paper and leave to cool.

Mix all the dressing ingredients together and spoon over the top of the salad. Sprinkle with the croûtons and garnish with extra tarragon leaves. Toss all together just before serving.

BEETROOT WITH SOURED CREAM & GARLIC

*U*nlikely as it might sound I had this salad on the Trans-Siberian express and I have to say it was the only memorable dish to be served over the 5 day-trip. But it was superb – and here is my version, which I surround with radicchio leaves as much for the colour as for the freshness of flavour.

SERVES 4

625g (1¼lb) baby beetroot, washed
1 clove garlic, peeled and crushed
300ml (½ pint) soured cream

black pepper
radicchio leaves, to serve
a handful of chopped fresh dill, to garnish

Cook the beetroot in water to cover for 15–20 minutes, or until tender. Allow to cool a little in the water, then peel. Cut into tiny dice.

Meanwhile, mix the crushed garlic into the soured cream and season with freshly ground black pepper. Mix in the diced beetroot. Line an elegant dish with radicchio leaves, pile the beetroot salad into the centre and serve sprinkled with dill.

MIXED LEAF SALAD WITH CROÛTONS & TOMATO VINAIGRETTE

A variety of mixed leaves – with all their differing shapes and colours – makes a glorious yet simple salad. I picked up the recipe for the tomato vinaigrette from a friend's kitchen in Paris. It is fresh and light, and makes an original and elegant dressing for the salad.

SERVES 4

V

FOR THE SALAD
8 handfuls of assorted leaves such as lollo rosso, sorrel, chicory, radicchio, oak leaf, frisée, lollo biondo, little gem, butter-head, etc.
a handful of alfalfa sprouts
3 tablespoons croûtons (see page 218)

Wash the leaves thoroughly and spin them dry. Put into a large bowl with the alfalfa sprouts and dress with the tomato vinaigrette (see below). Sprinkle the croûtons over the top and toss again.

TOMATO VINAIGRETTE

1 large ripe tomato, skinned and quartered
 (see page 30)
3–4 tablespoons olive oil
1 tablespoon finely chopped parsley

2 cloves garlic, peeled and crushed
a squeeze of lemon juice
salt and pepper

Blend the tomato in the food processor and gradually trickle in the oil while the machine is running. When well-blended, put into a bowl and stir in the parsley and garlic. Season to taste with lemon juice, salt and pepper.

GRACE KELLY'S CAESAR SALAD

The classic Caesar salad is an honest dish – ever popular and a great stand-by. In its simplicity, it consists of crisp Cos lettuce, grated Parmesan cheese and croûtons, tossed in a dressing of your choice. In this case, it is Hollywood's choice – à la beautiful Grace Kelly.

SERVES 2

1 egg
2 cloves garlic, peeled and crushed
150ml (¼ pint) olive oil
juice of half a lemon
2 teaspoons soy sauce

sea salt and freshly ground pepper
1 head romaine or cos lettuce
home-made croûtons (see page 218), made from 2 slices bread
grated Parmesan or Pecorino cheese, to sprinkle

Coddle the egg by placing it in a cup and pouring boiling water over it. Leave for 5 minutes, then break into a salad bowl. Crush the garlic into the bowl, then beat in the olive oil a little at a time with a fork. Add the lemon juice and soy sauce and season to taste with salt and pepper.

Tear the lettuce into pieces and toss gently in the dressing. Top with croûtons and grated Parmesan.

Serve with warm French bread and a glass of wine.

FRENCH BEANS WITH WALNUT OIL

Simplicity itself. This salad is blissful – the nutty flavour of the oil matches the nuttiness of the 'al dente' beans. For panache, serve it in a nest of lightly dressed radicchio leaves.

SERVES 4

V

750g (1½ lb) French beans, topped and tailed
5 tablespoons walnut oil

radicchio leaves, tossed in a little vinaigrette (see page 204)
sea salt

Steam or boil the French beans in boiling water until 'al dente' – for about 4 minutes; cool. Dress with quality walnut oil, pile into a nest of dressed radicchio leaves, sprinkle with sea salt – and eat!

CUCUMBER & MINT SALAD

The freshness of mint combines beautifully with the distinctive delicacy of cucumber – particularly if you can obtain organically grown ones. This is a refreshing salad, lovely as part of a salady meal served with fresh granary bread.

SERVES 3–4

1 medium cucumber, peeled
a large bunch of fresh mint

150ml (¼ pint) mayonnaise (see page 206)
nasturtium flower, to garnish (optional)

Cut the cucumber into paper-thin slices. Dry them on kitchen paper. Trim the mint and chop it very finely. Mix into the mayonnaise, then toss in the cucumber slices.

Serve as soon as possible, since the cucumber will continue to give out water and make the mayonnaise runny.

If you are feeling artistic and summery, pile the salad into a glass bowl and garnish with a nasturtium flower!

POTATO & WATERCRESS SALAD FROM THE AUVERGNE

A traditional village salad from the Auvergne, this is a great dish – typically French in its attention to detail. It has become a firm favourite in my family.

SERVES 4

(omit cheese) V

FOR THE DRESSING
2 tablespoons wine vinegar
4 tablespoons walnut oil
1 teaspoon Dijon mustard
sea salt and freshly ground black pepper
2 shallots, chopped very finely
3 sprigs watercress

FOR THE SALAD
750g (1½lb) new potatoes, washed
1 large bunch watercress, washed
175g (6oz) hard cheese such as Gruyère,
   Cantal, etc.

Put all the ingredients for the dressing in the food processor and liquidise. Put on one side while you prepare the salad to allow the flavours to develop.

Boil the potatoes until tender, but still slightly crisp in the centre – about 4–5 minutes. Cool, then slice.

Trim the watercress of any extra-long stalks, chop the rest, then toss with the potatoes.

Cut the cheese into cubes and mix with the potatoes and watercress. Spoon into a serving dish, pour over the dressing and toss well together.

WARM SHIITAKE MUSHROOM SALAD

This is SO good – for a special occasion or just to treat yourself it is original and irresistible.

SERVES 4

2 large handfuls rocket (arugula), washed
150ml (¼pint) virgin olive oil
500g (1lb) shiitake mushrooms, cut in half
3 tablespoons fresh chopped tarragon
1 medium shallot, peeled and chopped very
   finely

2oz (50g) pine-nuts, browned under the grill
   (see page 134)
2–3 tablespoons fresh lemon juice
salt
½ teaspoon cayenne pepper

Divide the rocket leaves between 4 plates.

In a frying pan, heat the olive oil almost to smoking. Add the mushrooms and cook briefly for 2 minutes. Remove from the pan with a slotted spoon in order to drain them.

Put into a bowl with the tarragon, shallot, pine-nuts and lemon juice. Season to taste with salt and cayenne pepper, then spoon over a little of the warm olive oil. Pile on top of the rocket leaves and serve immediately.

CRETAN VILLAGE SALAD WITH FETA & OREGANO

I have a special regard for the Cretans, and this salad conjures up memories of sitting over a simple lunch in the shade, watching the noonday sun beat down on an olive grove, inhaling the inimitable fragrance of wild thyme that pervades the mountains.

SERVES 6–8

FOR THE SALAD
1 large Cos lettuce
500g (1lb) ripe plum tomatoes, cut into
    segments
1 cucumber, halved lengthways and sliced
1 green pepper, deseeded and sliced
250g (8oz) Feta cheese, cut into small cubes
1 tablespoon fresh chopped mint
1 tablespoon dried oregano
24 black olives
sea salt and pepper

FOR THE DRESSING
4 tablespoons lemon juice
6 tablespoons extra virgin olive oil

Wash the lettuce and spin it dry. Shred it roughly. Put in a large bowl with all the other prepared ingredients and season with salt and pepper. Mix together the lemon juice and olive oil for the dressing. Pour over the salad just before serving and toss well.

LEEKS WITH ROQUEFORT DRESSING

Rich and rustic food, this is for the hungry. Leeks and blue cheese are flavours that linger – and they go wonderfully well with a glass of red wine.

SERVES 4

1kg (2lb) leeks
75g (3oz) Roquefort cheese
6 tablespoons olive oil

2 tablespoons crème fraîche
4 teaspoons wine or sherry vinegar
freshly ground black pepper

Trim and wash the leeks. Cut into 15cm (6in) lengths and cook until tender – about 10–12 minutes; cool.

Blend the cheese with the rest of the ingredients to a smooth paste in the blender. Season to taste with lots of pepper.

Toss with the cooled leeks and serve with hot granary bread and butter.

GIANFRANCO'S PASTA SALAD

Gianfranco's pasta salad has never failed me. It comes out at parties over and over again – it is simply the best!

SERVES 10–12

V

SLIMMING

You can lose excess pounds by eating, exclusively, large amounts of fruit and vegetables – especially salads – as part of a planned strategy to lose weight. A fruit breakfast, a salad for lunch, a vegetable meal in the evening – all as much as you can eat – will satisfy the appetite and mean that you never go hungry between meals, or feel deprived. As with all diets, take good advice before you embark on one, and make sure that you are taking in the right balance of nutrients – including protein and carbohydrates – by checking the information on pages 219–220.

500g (1lb) penne or pasta shells, cooked 'al dente' (see page 122)
350g (12oz) French or runner beans, topped and tailed
1 head celery, trimmed and chopped finely
2 yellow peppers, deseeded and sliced finely
8 radishes, trimmed and sliced finely
1 small fresh cauliflower, cut into tiny florets

juice of 1 lemon
4–5 large cloves garlic, peeled and crushed
a large bunch of mixed fresh herbs such as fresh thyme, dill, tarragon, fennel, marjoram, etc.
150ml (¼ pint) olive oil
sea salt

Drain the pasta and run it under cold water in the colander.

Cook the French beans in boiling water for 3–4 minutes so that they are cooked, but still crisp. Cool, then cut into 2.5cm (1in) lengths.

Add the prepared vegetables to the pasta in a large bowl and mix well together. Toss in the lemon juice and mix thoroughly.

Stir the crushed garlic and chopped herbs into the olive oil. Add sea salt to taste. Toss the pasta salad with this mixture and keep cool until ready to serve.

CHICORY & SWEET PEPPER SALAD WITH CORIANDER

A simple salad that is lovely to look at with its pale green, cream and yellow colours. Use organic potatoes for the best flavour – and you have a treat in store!

SERVES 6

V

4 heads chicory, sliced finely
2 sweet yellow peppers, deseeded and sliced finely
4 new potatoes, cooked and sliced very finely

a handful of alfalfa sprouts
3 tablespoons fresh chopped coriander leaf
5 tablespoons Mustard Vinaigrette (see page 204)

Combine all the prepared vegetables in a salad bowl and toss in the vinaigrette. Leave for up to an hour before serving to allow the flavours to develop.

WARM RED PEPPER SALAD

*I had this salad for lunch in the
Boulevard St. Germain in
Paris, and was stunned by its simplicity.
Memorable colours and flavours – a
delicious dish.*

SERVES 4
V

3 ripe red peppers
4 tablespoons quality olive oil

freshly ground black pepper

Cut the peppers into quarters, remove the stalks and deseed them. Cut each quarter into 3 strips, place them skin-side up on a grill tray and set under a hot grill until the skin blisters. Put into a plastic bag for 15 minutes to cool, then peel: the skins will have loosened and will come off easily.

Spoon into a shallow ovenproof dish and drizzle with the olive oil. Sprinkle with freshly ground black pepper and bake at 190°C/375°F/gas mark 5 for 10 minutes. Serve warm, with good bread, as a starter or for a simple lunch.

WARM SPINACH SALAD WITH WALNUT OIL & CROÛTONS

One of my great favourites. I love raw baby spinach – it tastes so nutritious. A simple salad of strong flavours – this is wonderful.

SERVES 3–4

500g (1lb) baby spinach leaves
1–2 cloves garlic
50g (2oz) butter

2 slices of bread, cut into ¼in (5mm) cubes
3–4 tablespoons walnut oil
the juice of half a lemon

Wash the spinach leaves and spin them dry.

Rub a frying pan with one of the cut cloves of garlic. Crush the rest into the pan with the melted butter and slowly fry the cubes of bread until golden. Drain on kitchen paper.

Dress the spinach with the oil and lemon juice, then toss in the croûtons.

WINTER SLAW

The answer to winter salads is to forgo lettuce, which is long out of season, and concentrate on other raw vegetables, packing in the vitamins and minerals. This combination, which includes pulses for extra protein, is a great favourite. You can dress it in mayonnaise or in a vinaigrette of your choice.

SERVES 4–6

V

100g (4oz) flageolet beans, soaked for 6
  hours or overnight
1 tablespoon dried mixed herbs
100g (4oz) red cabbage, shredded finely
100g (4oz) white cabbage, shredded finely
100g (4oz) brussels sprouts, trimmed and
  sliced finely

75g (3oz) raw turnip, grated
100g (4oz) carrots, grated finely
6 stalks celery, sliced finely
3–4 radicchio leaves, shredded
½ red onion, chopped finely
75g (3oz) sultanas
a dressing of your choice (see pages 202–207)

Drain the soaked flageolets and cover with fresh cold water. Add the herbs, bring to the boil and simmer for 1–1¼ hours until tender. Drain and cool. Add to the prepared vegetables and mix thoroughly. Dress in 5 tablespoons of your chosen dressing and pile into a serving dish.

OILS & VINEGARS

The art of making salad dressings is greatly enhanced by making full use of a range of different oils and vinegars.

OLIVE OIL

This has a unique flavour and comes in 2 types: virgin and pure. Virgin olive oil is cold-pressed from the pulp of high-grade olives with no further processing techniques. It is green, with a rich flavour, and expensive. Pure olive oil is made by pressing fruit, stone and pith together, with heat applied. It is paler in colour and less rich in flavour. Either way, cold-pressed olive oil has a superior flavour, having not been subjected to heat in the extraction process which destroys some of the flavour and goodness.

SUNFLOWER OIL

This mild-flavoured oil has a light texture that lends itself to dressings – particularly mayonnaise. A reasonable substitute for olive oil, and far less expensive.

WALNUT OIL

Although this is expensive, it's a fine oil to have in your cupboard to use for special occasions. Its remarkable nutty flavour goes beautifully with cold leeks and other composite salads, and is delicious on pasta. Likewise, *HAZELNUT OIL* makes a dressing with a difference – similarly nutty, rich and distinctive.

DARK SESAME OIL

This deep amber-brown oil with its rich slightly burnt flavour is excellent on salads. For the best value, buy it from ethnic grocers – it is more expensive in regular supermarkets.

GROUNDNUT OIL

Oil extracted from the groundnut or peanut, this is ideal for stir-fries because it is tasteless – a clear palette for the spicing. It is also excellent for making mayonnaise which is not heavy in flavour. Groundnut oil is considerably cheaper than olive oil.

OTHERS

You may come across *POPPY SEED OIL*, made from the opium poppy, and one of my favourites is *PUMPKIN SEED OIL* which, like dark sesame oil, has a burnt, nutty flavour and is thick and rich. *GRAPESEED OIL* is great for dressings and good for mayonnaise.

VINEGARS

The subtle flavours of various vinegars add their nuances to salad dressings. Red and white wine are the most commonly used vinegars for salad dressings – either plain or laced with herbs, garlic or fruit. Herbs steeped in vinegar look lovely as well as giving out their fragrance: a French tarragon wine vinegar is a product to respect. I love to use raspberry vinegar (see page 188) for certain dressings, and balsamic vinegar (see page 39) has a constant place in my cupboard. Sherry vinegar gives an unusual edge to a salad dressing, and cider vinegar is credited with health-giving properties but is usually used in pickles and relishes.

You can also use fresh lemon juice as an alternative to vinegar in salad dressings. It is delicious and makes a refreshing change.

WHITE WINE VINEGAR

This is one of the most commonly used vinegars, which gives a subtle tang to the dressing. It is often infused with tarragon or other herbs – rosemary, sage, mint, garlic or mixed herbs with chilli.

RED WINE VINEGAR

Similar in flavour to white wine vinegar, this gives a denser, darker quality to the dressing.

RASPBERRY VINEGAR

This is becoming increasingly popular – along with other fruit vinegars – giving a full fruity flavour. (See page 188.)

SHERRY VINEGAR

This gives an unusual flavour to salad dressings.

BALSAMIC VINEGAR

A very fine vinegar from Italy, this is made from fermented grapes and aged in wood barrels. It is dark brown, thick, aromatic and full of flavour.

CIDER VINEGAR

Famous for its health-giving properties, this makes a distinctive dressing and is cheaper than wine vinegar.

LIME VINAIGRETTE

Lovely and fresh, this is a light, thin dressing – the summery tang of lime does wonders for leafy salads.

SERVES 4

V

the grated rind and juice of 2 limes
1 tablespoon wine vinegar
2–3 tablespoons chopped parsley
¼ teaspoon each ground cumin and cardamom

1 clove garlic, peeled and crushed
5–6 tablespoons olive oil
sea salt

Mix together the first 5 ingredients, then whisk in the olive oil. Season to taste with salt.

Store any unused vinaigrette in the refrigerator for 3–4 days.

ROQUEFORT VINAIGRETTE

A thick, strongly flavoured dressing which is delicious on steamed, cold vegetables such as broccoli or leeks.

SERVES 6

2 teaspoons Dijon mustard
2 tablespoons lemon juice
50g (2oz) Roquefort cheese, crumbled

125ml (4 fl oz) olive oil
freshly ground black pepper

Mix the mustard with the lemon juice, then stir into the crumbled cheese. When thoroughly blended, stir in the olive oil gradually until the dressing thickens. Season with pepper.

Use within 24 hours.

WALNUT VINAIGRETTE

A stunning dressing for a tomato salad, or for cold steamed vegetables. It is quite thick, with a crunchy texture.

SERVES 4

V

1 small shallot, chopped finely
the juice of 1 lemon
40g (1½oz) walnut pieces, ground or chopped very finely

sea salt and freshly ground black pepper
60ml (2 fl oz) walnut oil
5 tablespoons olive oil

Mix the shallot with the lemon juice and walnut pieces. Season to taste with sea salt and freshly ground black pepper. Whisk in the walnut oil and finally add the olive oil, stirring until amalgamated.

Store for 3–4 days in the refrigerator.

TOASTED ALMOND VINAIGRETTE

I had this on a visit to San Francisco and have never forgotten it. It is irresistible – the crunchy, roasted almond flavour is beautiful with salad leaves, or on a simple tomato salad.

SERVES 4

V

1 tablespoon sherry vinegar
1 teaspoon Dijon mustard
salt and pepper
5 tablespoons olive oil

1 small clove garlic, sliced very finely and chopped
1 tablespoon chopped chives
25g (1oz) lightly toasted slivered almonds, crushed

Whisk the vinegar with the mustard and salt and pepper. Beat in the oil and garlic and work until smooth. Finally, stir in the chives and crushed almonds. Use within 24 hours.

HOME-MADE MAYONNAISE

MAKES 300ML (½ PINT)

1 egg
1 teaspoon Dijon mustard
300ml (½ pint) olive or sunflower oil

sea salt and freshly ground black pepper
lemon juice, to taste

Break the egg into the bowl of the blender and add the mustard. Run the motor until they are well mixed, then start to add the oil drop by drop. As the mayonnaise starts to thicken, increase the flow to a thin stream – do not add too much at a time, or the mixture will curdle. When all the oil is used up, continue to run the machine for another minute until the mayonnaise thickens. Season to taste with salt, freshly ground pepper and lemon juice.
Store in the refrigerator for up to 5 days.

SAFFRON MAYONNAISE

This is lovely with minced raw mushrooms, or a tomato salad.

SERVES 6–8

12 strands saffron
1 tablespoon boiling water

2 tablespoons crème fraîche
230ml (8 fl oz) mayonnaise (see above)

Soak the saffron in the hot water for 10 minutes, then mix into the crème fraîche. Combine with the mayonnaise and mix well.
Use within 24 hours.
Note: For a cheaper version of the above, use ground turmeric or powdered saffron, allowing 1 teaspoon per 150ml (¼ pint) mayonnaise.

SPICY WALNUT MAYONNAISE

This is good with hard-boiled eggs, halved and spread on top. Try it on potato salad for a change, or with leeks.

SERVES 4

50g (2oz) walnuts
1 teaspoon garam masala paste

5 tablespoons mayonnaise
3 tablespoons walnut oil

Grind the walnuts in the food processor.

In a separate bowl, mix the garam masala with the mayonnaise, then stir in the nuts. Finally, beat in the walnut oil. The mayonnaise will be very thick, so if you want it thinner, stir in a couple of tablespoons of water until it is the consistency you desire.

Use within 24 hours.

GREEN PEPPERCORN MAYONNAISE

You can buy jars of soft green peppercorns in brine. They are a luxury – they have an exquisite flavour which does wonders for a mayonnaise. Just crush several in a pestle and mortar (or with the back of a spoon), and mix into the mayonnaise. Increase the amount according to taste.

GREEN HERB MAYONNAISE

A beautiful bright green dressing which you can also use as a dip.

MAKES 300ML (½ PINT)

a medium bunch each of basil and parsley (you can also use watercress)
300ml (½ pint) mayonnaise

2 cloves garlic, peeled and crushed
lemon or orange juice

Put the herbs, mayonnaise and garlic in the blender and run the machine until the mixture is smooth and bright green. Season to taste with the fruit juice.

Use within 24 hours.

RASPBERRY VINEGAR MAYONNAISE

Make a thick home-made mayonnaise as above, but without adding the lemon juice. Instead, add 1–2 tablespoons raspberry vinegar (for your own home-made version, see page 188) until it is the desired taste and consistency.

DELECTABLE DESSERTS

BLACKBERRY & APPLE TART

*A*s summer turns into autumn, one of the treats that the countryside offers is a harvest of blackberries. In this dish, the colour of their juices stains the apples rich purple, and the fruit smells wonderful as it is cooking. This simple pie is completely irresistible, and tastes sublime served with thick cream or yoghurt.

SERVES 4–6
(omit egg white) **V**

500g (1lb) cooking apples
  (preferably Bramleys), peeled
  and cored
fresh lemon juice
250g (8oz) blackberries, cleaned
  and hulled

caster sugar, to sprinkle
250g (8oz) sweetcrust pastry, or
  frozen shortcrust (see
  page 218)
1 egg white
caster sugar, to dust

Slice the apples, sprinkling them with lemon juice as you go, to keep them from discolouring. Mix them with the prepared blackberries and put into a pie dish, making a pile that rises a little in the centre. Sprinkle with sugar as you put the fruit in. ◆

Roll out the pastry to fit a 23cm (9in) pie dish. Moisten the rim of the dish with water and lay the rolled-out pastry on top. Crimp the edges with your fingers, trim, then brush with beaten egg white and sprinkle with caster sugar.

Bake at 200°C/400°F/gas mark 6 for an initial 45 minutes, then turn the heat down to 180°C/350°F/gas mark 4 for a further 25 minutes, or until the pastry is set and light golden-brown.

Cool for 10 minutes, then serve cut in wedges.

Blackberry & Apple Tart and Pear, Blackberry & Walnut Crisp (page 214)

WHITE CHOCOLATE MOUSSE

Creamy white, sprinkled with dark chocolate, this mousse is a dream. I love the flavour of white chocolate, and this recipe is so easy that I make it often – and never tire of eating it.

SERVES 4–6

175g (6oz) white chocolate
250ml (8fl oz) crème fraîche
50g (2oz) caster sugar

3 egg whites
1/2 teaspoon cream of tartar
grated dark chocolate, to garnish

Break up the white chocolate and put it into a bowl. Set over a saucepan of simmering water until it melts.

Beat the crème fraîche with the sugar. Pour in the melted chocolate and mix thoroughly.

Beat the egg whites with the cream of tartar until stiff, then fold into the chocolate mixture. Chill until set – for several hours.

Sprinkle grated dark chocolate over the top and it is ready to serve.

LIGHT ORANGE CHEESECAKE

This light, cooked cheesecake is deliciously orangy and smooth, and is topped with a thick layer of sweetened Greek yoghurt. It melts in the mouth.

SERVES 8–10

FOR THE BASE
175g (6oz) plain digestive biscuits
40g (1 1/2oz) melted margarine

FOR THE CHEESECAKE
750g (1 1/2lb) low-fat cream cheese
175g (6oz) caster sugar
the grated rind of 2 oranges
4 eggs, separated
300ml (1/2 pint) thick Greek yoghurt
25g (1oz) icing sugar, sifted
a little ground cinnamon, to decorate

Crumble the biscuits finely (you can use the blender or a pestle and mortar), and stir in the melted margarine. Mix thoroughly. Line a 22.5cm (10in) loose-bottomed cake tin with greaseproof paper and press the biscuit mixture into the base. ◈

Beat the cream cheese with the sugar, orange rind and the egg yolks.

In a separate bowl, whisk the egg whites with an electric whisk until they are very stiff, then carefully fold into the cream cheese mixture.

Pour over the prepared base and cook at 160°C/325°F/gas mark 3 for 1 hour and 15 minutes. It will still appear runny in the centre, but will set as it cools. Cover with a towel, and leave on a rack until cold.

Beat the Greek yoghurt with the icing sugar until smooth. Remove the cheesecake from the tin and cover with a thick layer of the sweetened yoghurt. Dust with a little cinnamon before serving.

If you want very light, simple desserts with no adornment it is the simplest thing in the world to create fresh fruit mixtures and toss in a little mint or lemon balm for extra elegance. Vegans and slimmers can have a field day.

CAPPUCCINO MERINGUE TRIFLE

This very simple version of trifle is flavoured with coffee. The topping is made of meringue pieces folded into crème fraîche. Elegant!

SERVES 4–6

8 trifle sponges
150ml (¼ pint) strong black coffee
a little sherry or brandy (optional)
500g (1lb) fresh peaches, peeled (see page 30) and stoned (or equivalent canned fruit)

8 meringues (see below)
300ml (½ pint) crème fraîche
2 squares dark chocolate, grated

Place the trifle sponges in a single layer over the bottom of a glass dish. Mix the coffee with a little sherry or brandy, if desired, and spoon over the top so that the sponges soak it up. Drain the peaches and arrange on top.

Break the meringues into pieces and fold into the crème fraîche. Pile over the top of the peaches.

Decorate with a sprinkling of dark chocolate and chill until ready to serve.

MERINGUES

MAKES 8

2 egg whites
a pinch of salt

100g (4oz) caster sugar

Whisk the egg whites and a pinch of salt using an electric whisk until they form soft peaks. Slowly whisk in the sugar, about 1 tablespoon at a time, beating until the mixture becomes thick and forms stiff peaks.

Lightly grease a sheet of greaseproof paper and place on a baking tray. Place spoonfuls of the meringue mixture on the paper.

Bake in the bottom of a preheated oven at 140°C/275°F/gas mark 1 for 1½ hours, then turn the heat off and leave in the oven until cold. ◈

BAKED ALASKA

Using chocolate-chip ice cream makes a Baked Alaska with a difference. This classic American dessert is a wonderful mixture of hot and cold, being ice cream smothered in meringue which is cooked in a very hot oven for a short time so that the ice cream is still cold and the meringue topping hot.

SERVES 4

6 sponge cakes
5 tablespoons each of brandy (or a chosen liqueur) and skimmed milk, mixed together

350g (12oz) chocolate-chip ice cream
4 egg whites
100g (4oz) caster sugar

Place the cakes in the bottom of a 22cm (8½in) soufflé dish. Sprinkle the liqueur mixture over the top and leave to stand for up to an hour. ◈

Spoon the ice cream into the middle of the dish. Beat the whites until stiff, then gradually beat in the sugar until they hold their shape in stiff peaks. Cover the ice cream with this meringue mixture.

Bake at 230°C/450°F/gas mark 8 for 7 minutes. Serve immediately.

WALNUT & WHITE CHOCOLATE TART

A tart with a difference, with the irresistible contrast of nuts and smooth white chocolate. There are never any leftovers.

SERVES 6–8

175g (6oz) sweetcrust pastry (see page 218)
75g (3oz) butter or margarine
150g (5oz) soft brown sugar
the grated rind of 1 orange
3 eggs

100g (4oz) white chocolate, broken into small pieces
2 teaspoons vanilla essence
100g (4oz) walnut pieces

Roll out the pastry thinly and use to line a 22cm (8in) tin. Line with foil, fill with baking beans and bake 'blind' (see page 30). ◆

Cream the butter and gradually beat in the sugar and orange rind until light and creamy.

In a separate bowl, beat the eggs with an electric whisk. Using a wooden spoon, beat into the creamed mixture a little at a time. Add the white chocolate and vanilla and beat until smooth.

Sprinkle the walnut pieces over the bottom of the cooked pastry case. Pour the mixture over the top.

Bake at 200°C/400°F/gas mark 6 for 20 minutes or until golden-brown and lightly set in the centre. Cool on a rack and serve cold.

APRICOT BRULÉE

An elegant dessert which belies its simplicity: apricots smothered in almond-flavoured fromage frais, then bruléed with a topping of crushed ratafias and sugar. Served chilled, this is exceptional.

SERVES 4–6

1 x 400g (14oz) can apricots in natural juice
a few drops of almond essence
500g (1lb) fromage frais

100g (4oz) ratafia biscuits, crushed
75g (3oz) soft light brown sugar

Drain the apricots and chop them. Put into the bottom of a heatproof dish.

Stir the almond essence into the fromage frais and spoon it over the fruit. Sprinkle the crushed ratafias over the top and cover with the sugar.

Place under a hot grill until the sugar melts and caramelises. Cool, then refrigerate until ready to eat.

PEAR, BLACKBERRY & WALNUT CRISP

This late summer dessert is superlative – an impeccable combination of flavours with a nutty, crisp topping. Serve it warm, with custard or Greek yoghurt.

SERVES 4–6

V

100g (4oz) walnuts
200g (7oz) plain flour
75g (3oz) soft light brown sugar
4 tablespoons granulated sugar

1 teaspoon ground cinnamon
75g (3oz) unsalted butter, softened
4 ripe pears, peeled
250g (8oz) blackberries

Toast the walnuts under a hot grill, shaking from time to time until they brown evenly. Cool, and chop finely.

Put the flour, sugars and cinnamon into a bowl and work in the softened butter with your fingertips until the mixture resembles fine breadcrumbs. Stir in the walnuts.

Core and slice the pears quite thinly and put into a 22cm (8½in) soufflé dish with the blackberries. Mix well. ◈

Level the fruit and cover evenly with the topping. Bake at 190°C/375°F/gas mark 5 for 40 minutes, or until the top is lightly browned.

BEST STRAWBERRY SHORTCAKE

A classic – and for good reason. Come summer, when strawberries are at their height, this is a real treat: layers of crisp shortbread sandwiching strawberries and cream. Who could resist?

SERVES 6

FOR THE SHORTBREAD
250g (8oz) plain flour
a pinch of salt
1 teaspoon baking powder
50g (2oz) caster sugar
100g (4oz) butter
2 tablespoons double cream or crème fraîche

FOR THE STRAWBERRY AND CREAM FILLING/TOPPING
1kg (2lb) strawberries, washed
300ml (½ pint) double cream or crème fraîche, whipped
caster sugar, to taste

Sift the flour with the salt and baking powder, then stir in the sugar. Cut the butter into small cubes and rub it in with your fingertips until the mixture resembles fine breadcrumbs. Moisten with the cream and knead lightly until smooth. Divide into 2 and roll out to make 2 x 20cm (8in) circles. Bake at 200°C/400°F/gas mark 6 for 12 minutes, or until light golden-brown. Cool on a rack. ◈ ●

Crush one quarter of the berries with a fork. Hull and slice the remaining strawberries and mix together. Sweeten to taste, with sugar.

Pile two-thirds of the strawberries on top of one shortcake biscuit and cover with two-thirds of the whipped cream.

Place the second shortcake on top and pile the remaining strawberries on top. Decorate with the rest of the cream. Keep chilled and serve as soon as possible – it goes mushy if assembled too long in advance.

VACHERIN AUX FRAISES

The palest of pinks, this strawberry mixture makes a sea on which to float clouds of meringue. One of summer's prettiest and most delicate desserts.

SERVES 4

350g (12oz) strawberries, washed
1 egg white
300ml (½ pint) crème fraîche

2–3 tablespoons caster sugar
8 meringues (see page 211)

Hull the strawberries and whizz them to a pulp in the blender, or pass them through a sieve. Whisk the egg white until stiff.

Whip the crème fraîche with the sugar, then fold in the stiffly beaten egg white. Fold into the strawberry purée. Arrange in a shallow glass bowl. Chill. When ready to serve, place the meringues on top or around the edge.

ANGE AUX FRAMBOISES

For special occasions – whether anniversaries, summer parties or Sunday lunch in the garden – this gâteau always hits the spot. It is light, creamy and slightly moist from the raspberries and their juices. It vanishes!

SERVES 8

FOR THE SPONGE
75g (3oz) plain flour
2 teaspoons cream of tartar
6 egg whites
¼ teaspoon salt
175g (6oz) caster sugar
1 tablespoon lemon juice
1 teaspoon vanilla essence

FOR THE FILLING
350g (12oz) raspberries
1–2 tablespoons caster sugar
250g (8oz) Mascarpone or cream cheese
250g (8oz) thick Greek yoghurt

TO DECORATE
300ml (½ pint) double cream, whipped

Sift the flour into a bowl with 1 teaspoon of the cream of tartar, then sift again.

Beat the egg whites with the remaining teaspoon of cream of tartar and the salt until they form soft peaks. Fold in 2 tablespoons of the sugar and continue beating, adding the remaining sugar 2 tablespoons at a time until the mixture forms stiff peaks. Beat in the lemon juice and vanilla.

Fold in the flour 2 tablespoons at a time until it is all used up.

Grease and flour a 25cm (10in) cake tin. Spoon the mixture into the tin, level the top and bake at 190°C/375°F/gas mark 5 for 20 minutes. Turn the heat down to 170°C/325°F/gas mark 3 and cook for a further 20 minutes.

Remove from the oven and leave to cool in the tin for 10 minutes before turning out onto a wire rack to cool completely. ◆ ●

Cut horizontally into 4 layers.

Now make the filling/topping. Toss the raspberries with the 1–2 tablespoons of the caster sugar so that the juices start to run.

Mash the Mascarpone or cream cheese with the yoghurt and sweeten to taste with the rest of the sugar. Divide between the 4 sponge layers, topping each with a quarter of the raspberries and stacking them up as you go along.

Decorate the top with whipped cream. Leave for 24 hours before eating so that the juices permeate the cake.

BEST LEMON MERINGUE PIE

*H*eavenly: this is the best lemon meringue pie you will ever have eaten. Deservedly a great classic of English cooking, its fresh lemon tang and the froth of meringue on top are truly wonderful.

SERVES 6

FOR THE PIE CRUST

250g (8oz) sweetcrust or shortcrust pastry, frozen or home-made (see page 218)

FOR THE LEMON FILLING

3 tablespoons cornflour
a pinch of salt
175g (6oz) caster sugar
150ml (¼ pint) boiling water
the juice of 1½ lemons
the grated rind of 1 lemon
15g (½oz) butter
4 egg yolks

FOR THE MERINGUE TOPPING

4 egg whites
a pinch of salt
75g (3oz) caster sugar

Line a 23cm (9in) flan dish with the pastry, line with foil, fill with baking beans and bake 'blind' (see page 30). Cool.

Meanwhile, make the lemon filling. Mix the cornflour, salt and sugar in a saucepan, blend in the water to create a smooth cream, then bring slowly to the boil, stirring all the time to prevent lumps. Simmer gently for 5 minutes in order to cook the flour. Stir in the lemon juice, rind and butter. Off the heat, beat in the egg yolks. Pour the lemon mixture into the pastry shell and bake at 180°C/350°F/gas mark 4 for 15 minutes.

While it is in the oven, make the meringue topping. Whisk the egg whites until stiff, then beat in a pinch of salt and start adding the sugar gradually until the mixture is stiff and glossy. Pile over the lemon filling and return to the oven at 150°C/300°F/gas mark 2 for a further 30 minutes. Switch off the heat and leave the pie to cool and set in the oven. Serve cold.

LEMON SNOW

*B*eautifully fresh and light, this is a great favourite and can be made in a matter of minutes. A delicious footnote to a good meal.

SERVES 3–4

150ml (¼ pint) soured cream or crème fraîche
40g (1½oz) caster sugar

the grated rind and juice of 1 lemon
2 egg whites, beaten until stiff

Beat the soured cream with the sugar until thick. Fold in the finely grated lemon rind with 2 tablespoons of the juice. Carefully fold in the stiffly beaten egg whites – as for a soufflé. Turn into a glass dish and chill for 2–3 hours. Eat the same day, because if left for longer it will separate.

BASIC RECIPES

GARLIC BUTTER

75g (3oz) butter or margarine   *2 cloves garlic, peeled and crushed*

Melt the butter or margarine in a small pan. Stir in the crushed garlic and leave to soften over the lowest heat for 5 minutes. Allow to cool and set slightly before using. Mash well with a fork before spreading since the garlic sinks to the bottom and separates out from the butter.

CHEESE SAUCE

Stir 50–75g (2–3oz) grated Cheddar cheese (low-fat if preferred) into the finished béchamel (above). Stir over a gentle heat with a wooden spoon until the cheese has melted.

BLENDER SHORTCRUST PASTRY

MAKES 300g (10oz)

75g (3oz) softened butter or   *3 tablespoons water*
margarine   *a large pinch of sea salt*
175g (6oz) plain flour

Put the ingredients into the blender and run the machine until they are well-blended. Knead lightly, and put into a bowl. Cover with clingfilm and chill for about an hour before using. Alternatively, place in the freezer and use as required.

CRISP OIL PASTRY

MAKES 300g (10oz)

175g (6oz) plain flour   *1½ tablespoons water*
5 tablespoons sunflower oil

Sift the flour with the salt into a bowl, stir in the oil and water and combine with a wooden spoon until the mixture comes together. Transfer to a floured board and knead briefly until smooth. Press into a greased 20cm (8in) flan case with your knuckles, and bake 'blind' (see page 30).

SWEET CRUST PASTRY

MAKES 525g (12oz)

350g (8oz) plain flour   *175g (4oz) margarine*
1 tablespoon granulated sugar   *3 tablespoons cold water*

Sift the flour into a large bowl and stir in the sugar. Rub in the margarine lightly until the mixture is like fine breadcrumbs. Add the water and mix to a dough. Kneed lightly on a floured board, then roll out to line a 28cm (11in) flan tin.

VEGETABLE STOCK

An excellent way of making full use of vegetable trimmings, and of having really tasty stock to hand.

Scraps of carrot, onion, leek, cabbage, tomato, Jerusalem artichoke, broccoli, cauliflower, etc. can all go into the pot – potato peelings are excellent too.

Put the trimmings into a large saucepan and cover with cold water. Add a little sea salt, some black peppercorns, a bay leaf and a teaspoon of mixed dried herbs. Bring to the boil and simmer, covered, for 45 minutes. Remove from the heat and leave to stand until cold.

Vegetable stock cubes are a perfectly acceptable alternative to home-made stock, and are a quick and easy substitute.

BÉCHAMEL SAUCE

MAKES 450 ml (¾ pint)

40g (1½oz) plain flour   *bay leaf (optional)*
40g (1½oz) butter or margarine   *salt and pepper*
450ml (¾ pint) skimmed milk (or
soya milk for vegans)

Put all the ingredients into a saucepan and whisk continuously with a wire whisk over a medium heat until the sauce comes to the boil and becomes smooth. Simmer for 5 minutes to allow the flour to cook thoroughly, stirring occasionally with a wooden spoon. Remove the bay leaf and season to taste with salt and pepper.

CROÛTONS

Day-old bread is best for making croûtons because being slightly dry it doesn't absorb much oil, which makes the croûtons light.

Cut the crusts off the bread (you can use these for breadcrumbs). Cut the bread slices into little cubes.

Pour sunflower oil into a large frying pan to about 5mm (¼ in) deep – the bread will absorb a lot of oil. Heat until a single croûton dropped into the oil sizzles and cooks quickly. Lower in the croûtons to fill the pan and cook until golden-brown and crisp, turning all the time. Turn off the heat and remove the croûtons with a slotted spoon. Put immediately onto kitchen paper to drain. Keep warm in a low oven, on clean kitchen paper so that any excess oil drains off.

GARLIC CHEESE CROÛTONS

Rub the frying pan with a cut clove of garlic before pouring in the oil. Fry the croûtons in oil, as above, then drain on kitchen paper and toss immediately in finely grated Parmesan or Pecorino cheese while still hot. Leave to cool before serving.

NUTRITION CHART

Balance is the secret of a good diet. No foods are 'good' or 'bad' – it is the overall picture that counts, as far as good health is concerned. It is important to eat a wide variety of foods in order to give you the nutrients that your body needs to maintain growth, to repair itself, to provide energy, and to supply enough vitamins and minerals. At least one balanced meal should be eaten every day, containing appropriate amounts of carbohydrate, protein, fat, dietary fibre, water, vitamins and minerals. Dietary needs vary according to age, activity and condition, and there are numerous books that give detailed information on this complex subject. But here are a few guidelines to ensure that you are getting a good nutritional balance in your daily diet.

ENERGY & WATER

Food is the fuel that gives the human body the energy to function, move and work, so correct amounts are essential. Certain foods provide more energy than others: some provide it quickly and others are released slowly into the system. Energy is used to perform muscular work and to maintain body temperature.

Water comprises two-thirds of our body weight and the human cannot survive for more than a few days without it. Many foods contain high levels, but it is also important to drink lots of water.

PROTEIN

Protein is essential to the body for growth and repair, and as protection against infection, but excess amounts cannot be stored. Many western diets contain far too much protein and this has been shown to cause diseases, including cancer. Yet many people still worry about not getting enough protein if they don't eat meat. However, research has shown that it is very difficult to find a meatless diet that is short of protein: beans and many other vegetables contain high amounts of it, so do nuts and seeds, eggs and dairy products such as milk and cheese.

Good sources of protein include: pulses, peanuts, pasta, cheese, flour, bread, frozen peas, chick peas, eggs, potatoes, seeds, rice, tofu, cereals, nuts, cauliflower, broccoli, garlic, spinach, sweetcorn, oats, TVP, soya milk, milk, yoghurt.

CARBOHYDRATES

Carbohydrates are the most important source of energy in the diet, and most of them are provided by plant foods. The indigestible part of carbohydrates is known as dietary fibre, which can prevent many digestive problems and protects against certain diseases, such as colon cancer and diverticular disease.

Good sources of carbohydrates include: sugar, pulses, potatoes, peas, peaches, bread, pasta, root vegetables, rice, nuts, chick peas, lentils, sweetcorn, dried apricots, bananas, pears, garlic, buckwheat.

Good source of dietary fibre include: pulses, beans, cabbage, carrots, most vegetables, apples, raisins, most fruit, peanuts, wholewheat bread, flour, oats, brown rice, pasta, wholemeal bread, potatoes, cereals.

FATS

Fats provide energy in a more concentrated form than carbohydrates and convert very easily into body fat. The average western diet contains too much fat, but the right amount is necessary to keep body tissue in good repair. People on a meatless diet have lower blood pressure and are at lower risk of heart disease than those who eat meat regularly.

Good sources of fats include: cream, cheese, yoghurt, eggs, nuts, seeds, avocados, olives, milk, margarine, vegetable oils, peanuts, oats, plant foods.

VITAMINS

The body cannot synthesise enough of its own vitamins and is dependent on food intake for maintaining healthy levels. Only small quantities are required and a well-balanced vegetable-based diet will contain good supplies of all the vitamins needed.

VITAMIN A is required for healthy skin, bone growth, resistance to infection and night vision. Sources include: carrots, margarine, eggs, milk, cheese, yoghurt, cream, basil, coriander, parsley, dried apricots, sweet potatoes, broccoli, leeks, lettuce, chillies, red peppers, spinach, tomatoes, watercress, pistachio nuts, sunflower seeds, leafy green vegetables, peaches.

VITAMIN B GROUP: B1 breaks down carbohydrates for energy; B2 helps convert proteins, fats and carbohydrates for the growth and repair of tissues and healthy skin; B3 is needed for energy, healthy skin and the nervous system; and B12 promotes red blood cell formation, growth, and a healthy nervous system. Sources of B vitamins include: eggs, cheese, pulses, spinach, cauliflower, dried apricots, wholemeal bread, cabbage, carrots, potatoes, brown rice, nuts, seeds, peas, milk, yeast, green vegetables, avocados.

Note: B12 is found only in dairy products and egg yolk. Therefore, vegans need to take a supplement.

VITAMIN C is required for healthy skin, teeth, bones and connective tissue. It also aids the absorption of iron into the body. Sources include: watercress, potatoes, broad beans, mangetout, broccoli, cabbage, cauliflower, chillies, red peppers, citrus fruits, coriander, fresh green vegetables, frozen peas, all fresh fruit, salad, vegetables, leafy green vegetables, potatoes.

VITAMIN D aids the absorption of calcium and phosphate, for healthy bones and teeth. Sources include: margarine, eggs, cereals, cream, yoghurt, cheese, milk.
Note: sunlight activates the metabolism of vitamin D in the body.

VITAMIN E protects vitamins A and C and other important substances in the body. Sources include: vegetable oil, nuts and nut oils, seeds, cream, Parmesan and Cheddar cheese, parsley, avocados, olives, chick peas, carrots, parsnips, red peppers, spinach, tomatoes, watercress, sweetcorn, wholegrain cereals, soya, lettuce.

VITAMIN K is effective for blood clotting. Sources include: fresh vegetables, cereals, most foods.
Note: vitamin K deficiency is rare.

MINERALS

Minerals perform a variety of important functions in the human body. The right balance of intake is important for long-term good health. Excess of any can be as dangerous as too little.

CALCIUM is a vital component of healthy bones and teeth and is the most abundant mineral in the human body. Lack of it can cause osteoporosis, a brittle bone syndrome most common among menopausal women. Research has shown that vegetarian women are less at risk of osteoporosis than omnivorous women. Calcium is also important for muscle contraction and blood clotting. Sources include: milk, cheese, bread, carrots, nuts, seeds, pulses, yoghurt, tofu, sesame seeds, dried apricots and other fruits, lemons, oranges, olives, beetroot, broccoli, celeriac, parsnips, garlic, onions, leafy green vegetables.
Note: vitamin D helps the absorption of calcium.

MAGNESIUM is required for strong bones and to promote enzymes in energy production. Sources include: cream, yoghurt, cheese, eggs, bread, cereals, nuts, seeds, pulses, dried fruit, root vegetables, ginger, garlic.

IRON is an essential component of haemoglobin, the red pigment in blood which transports oxygen through the body. Deficiency causes anemia. Iron is also important for the immune system and for proper brain function. Iron deficiency is the most prevalent nutritional problem worldwide, although it has been shown that vegetarians are no more likely to suffer from iron deficiency than non-vegetarians. Note: Tea can inhibit the absorption of iron; good intakes of vitamin C enhance the absorption of iron.
Sources include: baked beans, wholewheat bread, lentils and pulses, nuts, leafy green vegetables, eggs, pumpkin seeds, basil, cumin seeds, parsley, sesame seeds, dried fruits especially apricots, spinach, watercress, cocoa.

ZINC plays a wide-ranging role in enzyme systems. It is essential for the metabolism of DNA and growth. Sources include: buckwheat, aduki beans, lentils, garlic, egg yolk, nuts, sesame seeds and tahini paste, some cheeses, green vegetables, pumpkin seeds, wholegrain cereals, yeast, wholemeal bread.

POTASSIUM is important in maintaining the body's balance controlling the composition of blood and other body fluids. Sources include: cheese, yoghurt, citrus fruits, potatoes, beans, lentils, green vegetables, beetroot, chillies, garlic, nuts, seeds.

INDEX

aioli, sun-dried tomato, 168
Al Shami's broad beans, 93
almonds: chilled almond soup, 49
  toasted almond vinaigrette, 206
ange aux framboises, 215
apples: blackberry & apple tart, 209
apricots: apricot brulée, 212
  grilled Brie with apricots, 170
artichokes, 16
  tortellini 'Ivy', 132
asparagus, 13
  festival vol-au-vents, 183
  filo baskets with asparagus 'pesto
    Trapanese', 169
aubergines, 18
  aubergines & green beans in coconut
    milk, 104
  couscous with roasted aubergine, 182
  Italian aubergine & cheese bake, 101
  mini tacos with aubergine caviar, 86
  Persian aubergines, 107
  roasted aubergines & Gruyère, 42
  spaghetti alla Norma, 121
  spiced aubergines, 35
avocados: baby tomatoes guacamole, 36
  guacamole, 75

baked Alaska, 211
baking blind, 30
basil & garlic bread, 81
beans: bean burritos, 84
  spicy mixed beans, 138
beansprouts, 9
  spicy noodles with beansprouts, 128
béchamel sauce, 218
beetroot, 22
  fresh beetroot soup, 53
  with soured cream & garlic, 190
beurre rouge, 164
blackberry & apple tart, 209
bread, 70, 78-81
  basil & garlic bread, 81
  best cornbread, 80
  croûtons, 218
  garlic bruschetta, 78
  melting focaccia with Mozzarella, 70
  olive focaccia, 79
  plaited cob, 81
  sesame toasts, 78
  soda bread, 80

broad beans, Al Shami's, 93
broccoli, 18
  broccoli & Pecorino pasties, 154
  broccoli & potato frittata, 63
  creamy broccoli soup, 47
  lemon broccoli, 94
  rice noodles with, 150
  salad of tiny broccoli florets, 44
  spicy potatoes with broccoli, 113
bruschetta, garlic, 78
Brussels sprouts, purée of, 96
buckwheat, 18
buckwheat crêpes, 88
buckwheat pasta with beurre noisette &
  mushrooms, 123
buckwheat with roasted vegetables, 102
butter: beurre rouge, 164
  garlic, 218
butterfly pasta with squash, 127

cabbage, 22-3
  crispy 'seaweed', 72
  winter slaw, 198
Caesar salad, Grace Kelly's, 192
Californian quesadillas, 85
cannellini dip, creamy, 76
cannelloni, spinach & Ricotta, 122
caponata au gratin, 100
cappuccino meringue trifle, 211
carbohydrates, 219
carrots, 13
  carrot & lentil soup, 54
  spicy carrot & orange soup, 52
cauliflower: cauliflower & mushrooms in
  black bean sauce, 102
  mustard cauliflower flan, 156
  quick sauté of cauliflower & cashew
    nuts with spinach, 106
  spicy cauliflower blender soup, 57
  stir-fried cauliflower, 36
celeriac, 23
  celeriac & tomato salad, 39
  potato & celeriac purée, 119
celery, 23
  nutty celery soup, 57
cereals, 28
cheese, 66
  basil tagliatelle with quattro formaggio,
    135
  cheese flan 'Madame Recamier', 66

cheese sauce, 218
cheesy 'kookoo' with courgettes, 60
classic tarte au fromage, 185
creamy Mozzarella mushrooms, 43
Cretan tirisalata, 74
crisp-fried Mozzarella, 173
enchiladas with cheese & chilli, 91
fennel with blue cheese, 108
gougère with mushrooms, 61
grilled Brie with apricots, 170
melting croûtons, 35
melting focaccia, 70
nutty green salad, 164
Parisian penne, 127
roasted aubergines & Gruyère, 42
smoked cheese & garlic spread, 76
tiropitta with mint, 156
cheesecake, light orange, 210
chickpeas: hummus, 138
chicory, 9
  chicory & sweet pepper salad, 196
chilaquiles, 90
chilli beans with a cornbread crust, 142
chilli cold noodles, 133
chilli peppers, 9
chimichangas, spicy, 83
Chinese cabbage, 13
Chinese soup, 48
chocolate: walnut & white chocolate
    tart, 212
  white chocolate mousse, 210
coconut milk, 104
coffee: cappuccino meringue trifle, 211
corn fritters, 89
corn on the cob, 30
cornbread, best, 80
courgettes, 13-16
  filo wafers with, 38
  grated courgette fritters, 86
  sautéed grated courgettes, 172
  soft eggs with steamed courgettes, 64
  steamed courgettes, 42
  stuffed zucchini, 175
  summer courgette soup, 50
  tagliarini with garden herbs and, 126
couscous: couscous à la Marocaine, 148
  couscous with roasted aubergine, 182
cranberry & orange sauce, 173
crème fraîche sauce with dill, 176
crêpes, buckwheat, 88

cress, 9-12
Cretan tirisalata, 74
Cretan village salad, 194
croûtons, 218
cucumber, 16
   cucumber & mint salad, 192
   garlicky Greek tzadziki, 69
curried eggs, South Indian, 62
cutting vegetables, 31

dairy produce, 28
deep-frying, 30
desserts, 209-16
dhal, aromatic, 144
dipping sauces, 34
dragon sauce, 172
dressings, 202-7

eggs: broccoli & potato frittata, 63
   cheesy 'kookoo' with courgettes, 60
   classic Spanish omelette, 65
   eggs 'Foo Yong', 64
   leek & noodle timbale, 63
   oeufs St. Germain, 65
   poaching, 64
   potatoes with eggs & peppers, 113
   soft eggs with steamed courgettes, 64
   South Indian curried eggs, 62
   spicy scrambled eggs, 75
   whisking whites, 60
Emanuele's polenta, 139
enchiladas with cheese & chilli, 91
equipment, 29

fajitas, vegetable, 84
fats, 219
fennel, 18-19
   fennel & French bean salad, 40
   fennel with blue cheese, 108
   roasted fennel & grilled polenta, 178
fettuccine with pine-nuts, 134
filo baskets with asparagus, 169
filo leeks, 98
filo parcels, crispy, 174
filo pastry parcels, 184
filo wafers with courgettes, 38
flans and tarts: blackberry & apple tart, 209
   cheese flan 'Madame Recamier', 66
   classic tarte au fromage, 185
   fresh tomato & herb tarts, 176
   mustard cauliflower flan, 156
   onion tarte Tatin, 158
   walnut & white chocolate tart, 212

focaccia, olive, 79
French beans, 13
   French bean & tomato salad, 189
   French beans with walnut oil, 192
frittata, broccoli & potato, 63
fritters, 86, 89

garlic, 16
garlic butter, 218
garlic vinaigrette, 204
Gianfranco's pasta salad, 196
gougère with mushrooms, 61
Grace Kelly's Caesar salad, 192
grains, 19
Greek spinach filo triangles, 40-1
green beans, Oriental stir-fry of, 104
green herb mayonnaise, 207
green peppercorn mayonnaise, 207
guacamole, 75

herbs, 16-17
hummus, 138

ice cream: baked Alaska, 211
Italian aubergine & cheese bake, 101

Jerusalem artichokes, 23
   artichoke soup with hazelnuts, 165
   lightly curried artichoke soup, 50

kidney beans: bean burritos, 84
   chilli beans, 142
   red bean dip with cheese, 76

lambs' lettuce, 23
lasagne, mushroom & chèvre, 128
leeks, 23-6
   creamy gratin Dauphinois with, 103
   festival vol-au-vents, 183
   filo leeks, 98
   leek & noodle timbale, 63
   leeks with Roquefort dressing, 194
   pastel terrine, 180
   potato & leek crunch, 116
lemon: best lemon meringue pie, 216
   lemon snow, 216
   lemony brown rice, 144
lentils: aromatic dhal, 144
lime vinaigrette, 205
linguine with roasted peppers, 130

Malay-style salad, 188
mangetout, 17
   tagliatelle with, 124

Marlise's dressing, 204
mayonnaise, 206-7
meringues, 211
   baked Alaska, 211
   best lemon meringue pie, 216
Mexican tomato relish, 74
minerals, 220
miso, 27
mousse, white chocolate, 210
mushrooms, 12
   buckwheat crêpes with, 88
   buckwheat pasta with, 123
   cauliflower & mushrooms, 102
   Chinese soup, 48
   creamy Mozzarella mushrooms, 43
   crispy mushroom rolls 'Dragon Inn', 91
   festival vol-au-vents, 183
   fried mushrooms with garlic, 94
   gougère with mushrooms, 61
   grilled marinated shiitake, 163
   grilled polenta with cheese and, 140
   mushroom & chèvre lasagne, 128
   mushroom crostini, 179
   mushroom risotto, 147
   mushroom sandwiches, 75
   mushroom stroganoff, 101
   puff pastry plait, 158
   South Indian mushroom rice, 146
   spicy mushroom salad, 189
   spinach & oyster mushrooms, 44
   tasty mushroom burgers, 74
   warm shiitake mushroom salad, 193
mustard, 170
   mustard cauliflower flan, 156
   mustard vinaigrette, 204

noodles: chilli cold noodles, 133
   noodles with quick-steamed vegetables 'sweet & sour', 132
   rice noodles with broccoli, ginger, garlic & black bean sauce, 150
   spicy noodles with beansprouts, 128
   Thai rice noodles, 137
   Vietnamese rice noodles, 151
nuts, 28

oeufs St. Germain, 65
oils, 28, 199
okra, 19
olives: garlicky tapenade, 43
   olive focaccia, 79
omelette, classic Spanish, 65
onions, 26, 30-1
   crispy filo parcels, 174

onion tarte Tatin, 158
  soupe à l'oignon gratinée, 56
orange cheesecake, light, 210
Oriental dressings, 203
Oriental stir-fry of green beans &
  courgettes, 104

Parisian penne, 127
parsnips, 26
  parsnip gratin, 97
pasta, 121–35
  basil tagliatelle with quattro formaggio,
    135
  buckwheat pasta with beurre noisette &
    mushrooms, 123
  butterfly pasta with squash, 127
  fresh egg pasta with tomatoes, tarragon
    & crème fraîche, 123
  garlicky fettuccine, 134
  Gianfranco's pasta salad, 196
  linguine with roasted peppers &
    hazelnuts, 130
  mushroom & chèvre lasagne, 128
  Parisian penne, 127
  pasta ribbons with peperoncini, 124
  pasta salad with roasted squash, 133
  penne with spinach, petits pois &
    chèvre, 130
  spaghetti alla Norma, 121
  spinach & Ricotta cannelloni, 122
  tagliarini with baby courgettes, 126
  tagliatelle with mangetout, 124
  tortellini 'Ivy', 132
pastel terrine, 180
pasties: broccoli & Pecorino, 154
  spinach & blue cheese, 154
pastry: blender shortcrust, 218
  crisp oil, 218
  sweet crust, 218
patties, Thai vegetable, 34
pear, blackberry & walnut crisp, 214
peas, 17
  oeufs St. Germain, 65
  riso verde, 150
penne: Parisian penne, 127
  with spinach, petits pois & chèvre, 130
peppers, 17, 30
  grilled yellow pepper & Mozzarella
    salad, 33
  linguine with roasted peppers &
    hazelnuts, 130
  mushroom risotto with sweet red
    peppers, 147
  puff pastry plait, 158

red pepper & tomato soup, 56
red pepper dressing, 203
red pepper sauce, 182
  warm red pepper salad, 197
Persian aubergines, 107
Peruvian vegegrills, 76, 77
pesto, roasted vegetables with, 100
pies: autumn squash pie, 159
  puff pastry plait, 158
  tiropitta with mint, 156
pilaff with orange & raisins, 146
pizzas, 160–1
plaited cob, 81
polenta: Emanuele's polenta, 139
  grilled polenta with cheese, 140
  roasted fennel & grilled polenta, 178
potatoes, 17, 26–7
  creamy gratin Dauphinois with leeks,
    103
  crispy potato skins with salsa, 111
  new potatoes with capers, 118
  oil-roasted new potatoes, 118
  potato & celeriac purée, 119
  potato & leek crunch, 116
  potato & spinach ring, 119
  potato & watercress salad, 193
  potato salad with sun-dried tomatoes,
    116
  potatoes Hongroise, 112
  potatoes Lyonnaise, 112
  potatoes with eggs & peppers, 113
  rosti of potato, celeriac & carrot, 96
  spiced potatoes, cauliflower & okra,
    114
  spicy potatoes with broccoli, 113
  summer potato salad with dill, 114
  Tuscany potatoes, 118
protein, 139, 219
puff pastry pizzas, 160
puff pastry plait, 158
pulses, 27, 28
pumpkin: pumpkin soufflé, 59–60
  pumpkin soup with Gruyère, 52
  risotto with Pecorino, 145

quesadillas, Californian, 85

radishes, 12
raspberries: ange aux framboises, 215
  raspberry vinegar, 188
  raspberry vinegar mayonnaise, 207
ratatouille: savoury puff pastry 'Tatin', 70
relish, Mexican tomato, 74
rice, 19, 143, 144

lemony brown rice, 144
  riso verde, 150
  South Indian mushroom rice, 146
  spicy pilaff with orange & raisins, 146
  with yellow split peas & garlic, 147
risotto: mushroom with sweet red
    peppers, 147
  pumpkin or squash with Pecorino, 145
Roquefort vinaigrette, 205
rosti of potato, celeriac & carrot, 96
runner beans, 13

saffron, 61
saffron mayonnaise, 206
salad leaves, 17, 30
salads, 187–98
  beetroot with soured cream & garlic,
    190
  celeriac & tomato, 39
  chicory & sweet pepper, 196
  Cretan village, 194
  cucumber & mint, 192
  fennel & French bean, 40
  French bean & tomato, 189
  French beans with walnut oil, 192
  Gianfranco's pasta, 196
  Grace Kelly's Caesar, 192
  grilled yellow pepper & Mozzarella, 33
  leeks with Roquefort dressing, 194
  Malay-style, 188
  mixed leaf, 190
  mixed summer leaves, 187
  nutty green, 164
  pasta with roasted squash & mint, 133
  potato & watercress, 193
  potato with sun-dried tomatoes, 116
  red & yellow, 165
  salade gourmande, 168
  spicy mushroom, 189
  sprouted seed, 188
  summer potato with dill, 114
  tiny broccoli florets, 44
  warm red pepper, 197
  warm shiitake mushroom, 193
  warm spinach, 198
  winter slaw, 198
salsa, quick, 84
salsify 'beurre noisette', 166
sandwiches, mushroom, 75
satay sauce, 34
sauces: béchamel, 218
  cheese, 218
  cranberry & orange, 173
  crème fraîche with dill, 176

dipping, 34
dragon, 172
light tomato & basil, 174
light tomato & Pecorino, 179
red pepper, 182
satay, 34
tomato coulis, 185
savoury puff pastry 'Tatin', 70
'seaweed', crispy, 72
seeds, 28
sesame toasts, 78
shallots, 12
soda bread, 80
sorrel, 12
soufflé, pumpkin, 59-60
soups, 47-57, 165
soured cream & garlic dressing, 202
South Indian curried eggs, 62
South Indian mushroom rice, 146
soya bean products, 27
spaghetti alla Norma, 121
Spanish omelette, 65
spinach, 19
  Greek spinach filo triangles, 40-1
  penne with petits pois, chèvre &, 130
  potato & spinach ring, 119
  riso verde, 150
  spinach & blue cheese pasties, 154
  spinach & courgette soup, 48
  spinach & oyster mushrooms, 44
  spinach & Ricotta cannelloni, 122
  warm spinach salad, 198
split peas, rice with, 147
spring rolls, 153
sprouted seed salad, 188
squashes, 19-22
  autumn squash pie, 159
  butterfly pasta with, 127
  pasta salad with roasted squash, 133
  squash risotto with Pecorino, 145
  stuffed squash, 103
steaming, 30
stir-frying, 31
stock, vegetable, 218
strawberries: strawberry shortcake, 214
  vacherin aux fraises, 215
swedes, 27

sweet potatoes, spicy, 117
sweetcorn, 22
  corn fritters, 89
  pastel terrine, 180
  sweetcorn & pepper soup, 49
  warm baby corn 'beurre noisette', 166

tacos with aubergine caviar, 86
tagliarini with baby courgettes, 126
tagliatelle: basil tagliatelle with quattro
    formaggio, 135
  with mangetout & creamy saffron
    sauce, 124
tahina: hummus, 138
tamari, 27
tapenade, garlicky, 43
tarts see flans & tarts
techniques, 30-1
tempeh, 27
tempura of summer vegetables, 89
terrine, pastel, 180
Thai rice noodles, 137
Thai vegetable patties, 34
Thousand Island dressing, 202
tiropitta with mint, 156
tofu, 27
tomatoes, 17-18, 30
  baby tomatoes guacamole, 36
  fresh egg pasta with, 123
  fresh tomato & herb tarts, 176
  light tomato & basil sauce, 174
  light tomato & Pecorino sauce, 179
  Mexican tomato relish, 74
  pastel terrine, 180
  quick salsa, 84
  tomato coulis, 185
tortellini 'Ivy', 132
tortillas: bean burritos, 84
  Californian quesadillas, 85
  chilaquiles, 90
  enchiladas with cheese & chilli, 91
  spicy chimichangas, 83
  tortilla shells, 85
  vegetable fajitas, 84
trifle, cappuccino meringue, 211
turnips, 22
  turnips in cream with Parmesan, 97

Tuscany potatoes, 118
TVP, 27
tzadziki, garlicky Greek, 69

vacherin aux fraises, 215
vegegrills, Peruvian, 77
vegetables, 8-27
  caponata au gratin, 100
  couscous à la Marocaine, 148
  lemony spring vegetable soup, 53
  noodles with quick-steamed vegetables
    'sweet & sour', 132
  roasted vegetables with pesto, 100
  sautéed vegetables with melted cheese,
    107
  special vegetables satay, 106
  spring rolls, 153
  tempura of summer vegetables, 89
  vegetable fajitas, 84
  vegetable stir-fry, 108
  vegetable stock, 218
  Vietnamese rice noodles, 151
  winter vegetable soup, 54
vermicelli, crispy, 72
Vietnamese rice noodles, 151
vinaigrettes, 204-6
vinegars, 28, 199
  raspberry vinegar, 188
vitamins, 219-20
vol-au-vents, festival, 183

walnuts: spicy walnut mayonnaise, 207
  walnut & white chocolate tart, 212
  walnut vinaigrette, 205
watercress, 12
  stir-fried with croûtons, 96
winter slaw, 198
winter vegetable soup, 54

yellow bean sauce, spiced vegetables
  with, 39
yoghurt: dill yoghurt dressing, 202
  garlicky Greek tzadziki, 69
  orange & yoghurt dressing, 203

zucchini see courgettes

40-750-1